W9-DFQ-916

Book Design: Practical Graphics, Inc.

ISBN: 1-886745-06-4

Library of Congress: 95-71353

Publisher's Cataloging in Publication
(Prepared by Quality Books Inc.)

Rhoads, B. Eric.
  Blast from the past : a pictorial history of radio's first 75
years / by B. Eric Rhoads.
    p. cm.
    Includes index.
    Preassigned LCCN: 95-71353.
    ISBN: 1-886745-06-4.

   1. Radio broadcasting--United States--History--Pictorial works.
I. Title.

HE8698.R46 1996   791.44'09
                                   QBI95-20710

Printed in the United States of America

Streamline Publishing, Inc.
224 Datura Street, Suite 718
West Palm Beach, Florida 33401
(407) 655-8778
1-800-226-7857

A PICTORIAL HISTORY OF

RADIO'S
FIRST 75 YEARS

BY B. ERIC RHOADS

Dedication

In loving memory of Roxie and Brady Goad and Walter and Luella Rhoads, my grandparents, who left a legacy of love, and taught me of God's love through their example.

To Laurie, my wife, who brings me love and laughter.

To my family members who I love so much: My father Dean, mother Jeanne, brothers Dennis and John. Special family members Cara, Ryan, Molly, Frank, Martin and Morena.

Professionally, this book is dedicated to Charlie Willer, who introduced me to radio as a lifetime career, and to Dexter Andrews (Bill Anthony), who made sure I had a chance to make my career happen. To Jerry Clifton, Dwight Case, Rhody Bosley, Chris Rathaus and Kaye Levine, my mentors.

Special heartfelt thanks to Ron Kyle, who taught me the value of optimism.

Thanks to so many wonderful friends and business friends who have each made a difference and contribution in my life. Listing each of you would be impossible, but you know who you are.

Table Of Contents

Foreword

by Rush Limbaugh

There once was a "toy" called the Caravelle. It was made by a company called Remco. My parents got me one for Christmas when I was 10 or 11 years old, and I drove them batty with it. What it did was simple: broadcast a scratchy, mostly unintelligible signal on any AM frequency you chose for a range of 75 feet. With this toy, one could actually be a DJ — not pretend, mind you, but actually be on the air.

My parents, God love them, sat patiently by the radio and listened to me play music they did not like, listened to me mimic Harry Caray doing St. Louis Cardinals' baseball play-by-play and listened to me read news from the newspaper.

I would call friends in the neighborhood and ask them to turn their radios to 890 (I was bound and determined to be on the same frequency as WLS!) and see if they could hear me. They, of course, could not, which forced me to jury rig, with masking tape, a larger telescopic antenna than what was supplied with the machine. Alas, to no avail. This inability to be heard throughout the neighborhood frustrated me and lit the fires of motivation to be heard.

What is it about radio that so fascinates? For one thing, radio is intimate. The microphone is right there, just inches away, which means the audience is also just inches away. Think of that. This is why radio audiences form such deep bonds of loyalty with the programs they love.

Radio is real, which makes it spontaneous. There is very little about radio that is artificial. It is almost always live and of the moment, and so makes its impact immediate.

But perhaps the most important ingredient is imagination. You cannot listen to the radio without it. There are no pictures in the real sense, yet pictures there are, painted and drawn by the listener, as guided and prompted by the program. And herein lies the real secret of the impact and uniqueness of radio.

Listeners devote all their attention to one sense: sound. This is why there is no name for radio comparable to television's "Boob Tube." If you really listen to radio, you apply no other of the human senses to it. It is the concentrated application of just this one sense that arouses the imagination. And if a radio program or personality is exceptionally talented, what follows all this is inspiration.

Radio has inspired millions and millions of people in countless ways, but the most important is that radio unlocks the imagination, which unleashes the full range of human potential from within. Devoted radio listeners are thinkers, not robots. They are active, not lazy, and they are adventurous, for they never know what they are going to get.

I am honored to be on radio, to speak each day to the people who make this country work.

Foreword

by Paul Harvey

Should you visit my skyscraper offices, your attention will focus first on a large portrait on the reception room wall. It's a portrait of a young boy whose clothing dates itself to a generation past: the plus-fours are wretchedly wrinkled, the mis-shapen shoes are worn out; one is worn through.

But the boy, leaning forward on one elbow, is listening enrapt to a 1930s-vintage cathedral-shaped multi-dial radio.

The boy does not resemble any person in particular except to me. The artist is an Oklahoman, Jim Daly, whom I have never met, but with the painting he included this note: "There is no way for me to express the pleasure I received from listening to the old radio programs. In my mind those wonderful heroes were magnificent. No movie ... no television program ... not even real life, could have equalled what my imagination could conjure up. Amazingly, all those heroes looked a little bit like me."

Radio people, in their preoccupied haste, have been letting go of the might and majesty of the well-spoken word.

Van Gogh is pleasing to the eye; Shakespeare is fathomless.

Our industry's poets you can count on your thumbs: Charles Kuralt when he has time and Jack Whittaker when some classic sporting event deserves added dimensions.

Trust me to paint pictures on the mirror of your mind and I will let you feel such agony and ecstasy, such misery and such magnificence as you would never be able to feel by looking at it.

Let me paint you a picture of unrequited love in 17 words: "When the fire in me meets with the ice in you what could remain but damp ashes?"

Now tell me, with what picture in oil or on film could you duplicate that poignancy?

We court with the lights turned down to remain undistracted. We savor a fragrance, a kiss or a foot massage with our eyes closed.

Or comedy.

In my book For What It's Worth, I was able to match cartoon sketches with some stories; not with this one:

On page 135, you meet Martha and Chris Gertson of Gering, Nebraska. Every weekday afternoon at 2, Martha lowers the window shades, disconnects the telephone and turns on the TV — to watch the wrestling matches.

Martha admits that she loves to watch those big bruisers head-butt one another and body-slam one another. Then, when she gets sufficiently worked up, she throws a stepover toe-hold on her husband, Chris, and there on the floor in front of the TV set they wrestle until one is able to pin the other.

Don't tell Martha Gertson that wrestling matches on TV are staged. She says if there's anything on TV that's faked, it's soap operas.

She says the wrestling matches are for real, including hers with Chris. Which she usually wins.

Martha Gretson is 76. Husband Chris is 82.

The picture you are right now imagining is infinitely more entertaining than any cartoon of the same thing.

As a boy, I fell in love with words and ran away from home and joined the radio.

It was really something. Close your eyes and see ...

It still can be.

Acknowledgements

A project of this magnitude requires contributions from many people to see it through. I'd like to thank the many people who gave time, effort and information to create this historical document for radio.

Thanks to my wife, Laurie, who has seen little of me for six months, and who saw me disappear for three solid months following our wedding.

Many thanks to the team at *Radio Ink* who kept things running smoothly during my absence while completing the book: John Montani, Yvonne Harmon, Anne Snook, Tom Elmo, Linda DeMastry, Chuck Renwick, Helen Brown, Marianne Young, Shawn Deena, Joan Benca, Cecelia Brown and Ken Lee. Special thanks to Bruce Buchanan and Ed Boyd.

Many contributed by access to photo files or by sending photos and information: Tom Daren, Jim Duncan, Ben Freedman, Don Hagen, Peter Hammar, Connie Hansel, Bob Harlow, Bob Henabery, Lisa Hodor, Julie Hoover, Gina Jarrin, "Shotgun Tom" Kelly, Stu Laiche, John Long, Darryl

McCann, Jeff Mazzei, Chester McKown, Bill Meeks, Willard Scott, David Brenner, Tim Moore, Howard Risk, Dickie Rosenfeld, Dave Scholin, Erika Farber, Hurricane, Bob Shannon, Rick Shaw, Doug Tinney, Jim Turano, Barry Umanski, Jim West, Bob Wogan, Bob Doll, Gary Fries, Eddie Fritts, Charles Michaelson, Zenith Radio Corporation, Charlotte Ottley, Walt Sabo, Tom Shovan, Kent Burkhart, Charlie Furlong, Bruce Dumont, ABC Radio Networks, David Kantor, Marty Raab, Leslie Halprin, Westwood One, Rene Casis, Norm Patiz, Laurie Peters, Mary Kitano Diltz at KNX, George Nickolau, Jim Williams, Evelyn Cassidy, Associated Press, Ken Costa, Rush Limbaugh, Ed McLaughlin, Paul Harvey, Gary Fisher, Maurice Tunick, Sally Jessy Raphael, Tom Snyder, Casey Kasem, Bart McClendon, Norman Corwin, Paul Drew, Dick Downes, Garrison Keilor, Dwight Case, Jaye Case, Pacific Pioneers, Peggy Weber, Jeanne D. Brown, Gordon Mason, Bill Ward, Marty Halprin, Ron Wolf, USC Department of Special Collections, Mrs. Taub, Steve Raymer, Jim Wychore, Pavek Museum, Jay Hickerson, Chuck Scaden's Nostalgia Digest, John Terry and Antique Radio Classified, SPERDVAC, Dan Haefele, Gordon Hastings, Dick Clark, Nick Verbitski, Tom Rounds, Ron Jacobs, Sarah McCann, Chris Lytle, Skip Joekel, Mike McDaniel, Celia Rocks, Dr. Laura Schlessenger, Mike Henry, Mike Mashon, Broadcast Pioneers Library, Tom Connors, Art Schreiber, Fred Bergendorf, Joe Franklin, Barry Skidelski, Charles Zoeller at Associated Press, Jade Luthi, Old Time Radio Digest, Vicky Bowles, Clarke Blacker, Michael Keith, Kaye Levine, Clyde Hanale, George Ross, John Rook, Jane Sparaza, Ralph Guild and Jim Shulke.

Preface

I was born a "baby boomer" in the mid-50s, and as I was growing up, the radio industry was trying to catch its footing and re-establish itself as a viable medium. Television had killed the radio star. The golden era of radio had passed. Radio drama and the force of the big entertainment radio networks had died.

As I listened to the radio as a child, I had no experiences of sitting up late glued to *The Lone Ranger*, as boys my age had done a half generation before me. Instead, the radio influences in my life were disc jockeys. Although I was born a part of the television generation and watched the countless hours of *Leave It To Beaver* and *Bonanza* that my generation was supposed to rack up, I was fascinated by the radio at an early age.

At about seven or eight years old, I can remember imitating disc jockeys by talking into a hand-held strainer (the closest thing I could find to a microphone) and playing my mom's old "45s" on her RCA record player that I found in the attic.

Later, I graduated to reel-to-reel tape when my dad brought home a Wollensack tape recorder with seven-inch reels. He used to buy "albums" on tape, which was the latest craze in the "hi-fi" era. To this day, I still have the tapes I made playing deejay on the recorder with my brother Dennis and cousin Jim. Amazingly, we all later became radio deejays.

At that young age, I got the impression that the music I was hearing came live from the stations. I could imagine The Monkees live in the radio studio, and I was disappointed later to find out that they weren't live, but were on vinyl. Yet I was fascinated with the deejays I grew up listening to, local Fort Wayne, Indiana, deejays on WOWO and WLYV like Bob Dell, Jay Walker, Bob Severs, Bob Barnes, Chris O'Brien, Gary Lockwood, Bill Anthony and Guy Hill.

They had become a part of my life as a typical American kid, as I grew into my early teens. As I became more aware of radio, I tuned in to the big booming AMs that came in as well as local stations, and I listened to CKLW from Detroit. My favorite was ABC's WLS in Chicago. Larry Lujack, Fred Winston, Charlie Van Dyke, Lyle Dean, John Records Landecker, JJ Jefferies, Bill Bailey and Yvonne Daniels were the coolest people I "knew."

Then, one day, it happened. All my role playing of being a deejay came true when Charlie Willer, a kid my own age, invited me to watch him do a radio show at a local college station. We were both about 14. He was already a deejay, and I was just a kid who came home from school, ate bags of potato chips with my brothers and watched *Dark Shadows* on television. My life changed that day.

Radio got into my veins as a listener at an early age. It stayed as a profession throughout my career to date. There is something magical about radio — albeit difficult to define. People who get into the radio industry will often leave, only to return because they missed it so much. Many got into television and stayed because the financial rewards were so much higher than most could make in radio, yet they tell me that radio was where they would rather be.

Why? Radio is a more personable medium. People can relate to the people on the radio more than the ones on television. They can interact with them by telephone and actually feel they can get to know them. And radio allows creativity unsurpassed on television — because all the vision is in your head. To create the vision, the listener need not watch anything; he/she must only listen and imagine.

I've spent a career based on the premise that all you need to do is listen to see the vision. I've created the vision as an air personality, directed the vision as a programmer and sold the vision as a station owner. Later, as the publisher of a radio industry trade magazine, I hope I've helped others see the need for continuing the vision, and for keeping the power of radio alive in their hearts.

In most cases, radio is an moneymaking enterprise. Yet some of the most romantic stories are of the pirates who loved radio so much that they lived on-board ships for months and years on end, broadcasting from international waters so others could hear their vision for radio. Countless broadcast companies sprang up across America from young hobbyists who just couldn't get enough of the medium, so they built their own stations and exercised their passions for the airwaves. Many still exist today in this age of balance sheets and bottom line concerns; some barely survive, but hang on because they love being in the radio business.

The passion goes beyond the inside of the business. It is felt and lived by many listeners. Hundreds upon thousands have caught the radio bug and become addicted to listening. For many who are confined to their homes, a talk radio personality may be their only form of social friendship and human connection.

Radio has influenced all of our lives. Each of us has a special moment when listening to the radio changed our lives forever. One of mine was a few years back when young "baby Jessica" was rescued from a shaft deep beneath the earth.

While driving down the road, I listened as the announcer explained the progress and every detail of what was happening. I could hear the background of workers' voices — and then cheering as the child was pulled from the shaft alive and handed to her crying mother.

The announcer had tears in his voice; I had tears in my eyes. I did not know this child, her family or the dozens of people who put their own lives at risk to save her. But when I heard it on the radio, it became real, the emotions poured out and I was touched and felt I was a part of what had just occurred.

It's funny, but when I see the same kind of thing on the television, it doesn't seem as real. I often feel I've become numb to what I see on television — perhaps because we see so much in films, knowing it's not real. But when it's on the radio, it has an impact.

I have a passion for the radio business, and for the sounds I hear coming out of the speaker. I have become a collector of old radio sets; I love the radio dramas, comedies, newscasts, deejays — everything radio had to offer in the past and most of what it has to offer today. My passion for this thing we call radio is why you have this book in your hands today.

A combination of several events led to this book. I was contacted by a major publisher and we struck a tentative deal to publish this book. About the same time, I heard from Charlie Furlong, a friend and fellow radio buff. He informed me that 1995 would be the 75th anniversary of radio, and that to his knowledge nothing was planned. He suggested that as publisher of a trade publication, I might promote the event and create some attention for this momentous occasion.

Putting the two thoughts together — the idea of a book, and the occasion of the anniversary — it became obvious that one should be related to the other. The solution was obvious, and today you have a book in your hands commemorating this important anniversary.

Like any project, this one took more time than I ever imagined, cost more to produce than anticipated and was more difficult to do than I would have ever guessed.

I searched the country for photographs that have never before been published. Although there are many stock publicity shots you may have seen before, I've worked diligently to bring you mostly photos that should be new to you. I hope it will give you a continued (or new) passion for radio, and as much pleasure reading this book as I had writing it.

— *B. Eric Rhoads*

A Pictorial History Of

Radio's
First 75 Years

BY B. ERIC RHOADS

Pre-1920s

J ust who did invent radio and what was the first station? If you ask most people who invented radio, the name Marconi comes to mind. Usually, KDKA, Pittsburgh, is the response when you ask which was the first radio station. But are these really radio's firsts? In the interest of curiosity and good journalism, we set out to determine if these were, in fact, radio's firsts.

Of course, you can always find a way to rank firsts to make a point. Such is the case with the inventors of radio and the first radio stations. Was the inventor of radio the person who discovered that electromagnetic waves could be sent through the air, or the person who actually sent them? Was it the person who sent signals the farthest, or the one who sent the first signals with voice? Was the first station the first one to be licensed, or was it the first licensed experimental station? The answers aren't easy.

Wireless itself is a relatively broad term. Within the wireless category are many subcategories and industries, of which radio broadcasting is just

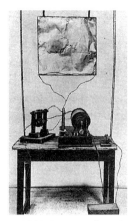

In 1895, Marconi achieved a transmission of almost two miles using an antenna and ground at both the transmitter and receiver.

Broadcast Pioneers Library

Piece of equipment used by Marconi to transmit between vessels anchored off the Italian coast, circa 1914.

Broadcast Pioneers Library

one, as are wireless telegraph, wireless ship-to-shore communication and so on.

To go back to the development of wireless, we must first track events leading up to the discovery of electricity. Although some documentation goes farther back, electricity as a science began in 1600 when Dr. William Gilbert, who was Queen Elizabeth's personal physician, invented the electroscope, which detected electromagnetic energy in the body. He coined the word electricity.

From that point forward, many people had their hand in the development of electricity: Sir Thomas Browne, Benjamin Franklin, Alessandro Volta and Georg Simon Ohm, among others. For brevity's sake, we'll look at wireless after electricity was invented.

Exploring Wireless

The real interest in wireless began with Samuel F. Morse's invention of the telegraph in 1837, which required wires (a very expensive proposition). In 1867, a Scottish mathematician, James Clerk Maxwell, conceived of the electromagnetic theory of light. This theory holds that light, electric waves and magnetic waves of

varying frequencies travel through the same medium: ether. Maxwell was never able to prove the theory.

In 1865, a Washington, D.C., dentist, Dr. Mahlon Loomis, explored wireless. He developed a method of transmitting and receiving messages using the Earth's atmosphere as a conductor.

Loomis sent up kites 18 miles apart from two West Virginia mountaintops. The kites were covered with a copper screen and were connected to the ground with copper wires. The wire from each kite string was connected to one side of a galvanometer; the other side was held by Loomis, who was ready to make a connection to a coil buried in the Earth.

The receiving station connection, between the meter and the coil buried in the Earth, was always closed, and whenever the circuit was closed at the transmitting end, the galvanometer at the receiving station actually dipped. Congress then awarded Loomis a $50,000 research grant.

In 1879, David Edward Hughes discovered that when a stick of wood covered with powdered copper was placed in an electrical circuit, the copper would adhere when a spark was made.

In 1885, Sir William H. Preece and A.W. Heaviside sent sig-

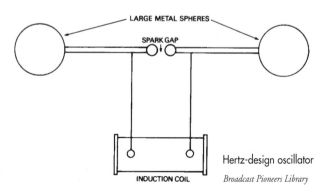

Hertz-design oscillator

Broadcast Pioneers Library

nals to one another at a distance of 1,000 yards with two parallel telegraph lines and an unwired telephone receiver in the middle. This was the discovery of induction, or crosstalk.

The real experiments leading to radio's discovery started with Heinrich Hertz in 1887. Some call him the father of radio because his experiments created interest by Marconi. Radio waves were commonly called Hertzian Waves in the early days.

Hertz studied Maxwell's theories and, in attempting to develop further data, actually set up the first spark transmitter and receiver. The transmitter consisted of a Leyden jar and a coil of wire, the ends of which were left open so that a small gap was formed. For the receiver, he used a similar coil at the opposite end of the room.

Nathan B. Stubblefield and son posing with his wireless telephone demonstrated on his farm in Murray, Kentucky, as early as 1892.

Broadcast Pioneers Library

When the jar was charged, sparks flew across the gap and were received on the other end. Hertz then measured the velocity of the waves and found they were the same as light, 186,000 miles per second.

It was in the year 1880 that Alexander Graham Bell patented the first wireless telephone device, called the Photophone. It used a voice signal to modulate a light beam, then used a photoelectric cell to convert the light to electricity, which could then power a conventional telephone. It was displayed at the World's Fair until 1893.

Later, a French electrician, E.F.P. Mercadier, created a version of Bell's invention and called it the Teleradiophone. This is the first known use of the word "radio" to describe wireless.

Bell also collaborated with John Trowbridge of Harvard through this period to build a wireless telephone using both the Earth and water as conductors. This technique, according to radio historian Dr. Bob Lochte of Murray State University, had been used successfully for many years for wireless telegraphy. Morse first employed it in 1842.

In 1882, Bell transmitted from a boat in the Potomac near Washington to other boats and to shore, but the results were unimpressive. Bell soon gave up work on wireless; however, Trowbridge continued to experiment with wireless until 1891.

In 1892, a French inventor, Edouard Branly, created a tube containing loose zinc and silver filings, with contact plugs on each end. The shavings would stick together after the first spark was received; a method of separating them for the next signal was necessary. Popov, a Russian, came up with the idea of using a vibrator and the hammer of an electric bell to strike the tube and cause the filings to separate.

Cambridge University professor James Clerk Maxwell published his theory of electromagnetism in 1873.

Broadcast Pioneers Library

Professor Amos Emerson Dolbear came up with a wireless telephone design by accident when he disconnected the telephone he had set up in his physics lab at Tufts College in Boston. To his surprise, he could hear sounds from across the room through the receiver. He then learned that the current in the coil at the transmitter was inducing a current in the passive coil at the receiver, and that his electromagnetic induction was completing the audio circuit.

He then perfected this wireless telephone so that he could reliably communicate from his lab to his home, a third of a mile away. To achieve this, he used aerial condensers elevated to the same height and attached to both the transmitter and the receiver.

Dolbear demonstrated this at scientific conferences throughout the world and patented it in 1886. Lee De Forest bought the patent and attempted to prove that Dolbear had invented radio a decade before Marconi because the device generated an RF signal and used crude antennas as a tuning mechanism. It lacked, however, any way to detect the RF (Radio Frequency), so any communication was solely the result of induction.

Building an induction wireless telegraph to communicate with moving trains occupied the attention of several people, including Thomas Edison, Lucius Phelps of Western Union and Granville Woods, a talented African-American inventor from Cincinnati. Both Edison and Phelps used telephone receivers as detectors, a common modification

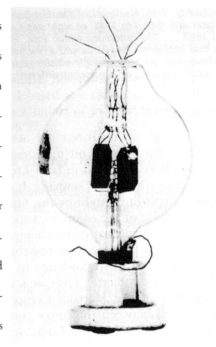

De Forest's audion tube.
Broadcast Pioneers Library

of telegraph systems of the era, but Woods devised a complete wireless telephone apparatus, which he patented in 1887.

In England, William Preece and Willoughby Smith pursued parallel experiments. Preece also designed and tested induction wireless telephones to communicate with coal mines and nearby islands.

Three patents in wireless telephone already existed by the time Marconi, Tesla and Stubblefield emerged on the scene with their forms of wireless.

Tesla, Marconi and Stubblefield

In 1893, a Serbian, Nikola Tesla, suggested a means of conduction using the Earth. He invented the Tesla coil, which created high-frequency oscillations.

In 1895, Marconi experimented with Hertzian waves and was able to send and receive messages over a mile and a quarter. He made great strides when he created

Stubblefield demonstrates a ship-to-shore broadcast on the Potomac on March 20, 1902.
Broadcast Pioneers Library

transmission between two ships 12 miles apart. He then solicited and secured investors for the Marconi Wireless Telegraph Company, the first to commercialize wireless. He was 23. By 1899, he had covered distances of 74 miles.

In 1899, he adopted Sir Oliver Lodge's principles of tuning circuits, perfecting them and obtaining a patent in 1900. In December 1901, when Marconi sent the first trans-Atlantic signal, inventor H. Otis Pond told Tesla: "Looks like Marconi got the jump on you." Tesla replied: "Marconi is a good fellow; let him continue. He is using 17 of my patents." Tesla's attitude toward Marconi later changed, after years of litigation between them. Tesla later referred to Marconi as "a donkey."

Tesla had come up with something different from and superior to Hertz's original ideas. He developed a series of high-frequency alternators producing frequencies up to 33,000 cycles per second (33,000 Hz). This, of course, was the forerunner to high-frequency alternators used for continuous wave radio communication.

Tesla went on to build the Tesla coil, an air-core transformer with primary and secondary coils tuned to resonate — a step-up transformer that converts low-voltage high current to high-voltage low current at high frequencies. It is used today in all radios and televisions.

Thomas Edison's impact on radio was great because of his invention of the phonograph. He also conducted significant work on wireless transmission but later ignored it for other projects. He is seen here at age 32 with Charles Batchelor and an early phonograph model. This rare April 1878 photo was taken in Washington by President Lincoln photographer Mathew Brady.

Associated Press

Nikola Tesla

Broadcast Pioneers Library

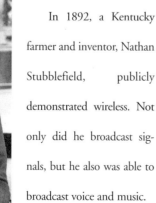

In 1892, a Kentucky farmer and inventor, Nathan Stubblefield, publicly demonstrated wireless. Not only did he broadcast signals, but he also was able to broadcast voice and music.

He demonstrated wireless again in 1898 to a documented (by *The St. Louis Dispatch*) distance of 500 yards. He demonstrated a ship-to-shore broadcast on the Potomac River in Washington, D.C., on March 20, 1902, and received patent number 887,357 for wireless telephone on May 12, 1908.

However, Stubblefield, it was said by *Scientific American* on May 24, 1902, had merely replicated Bell's 1882 experiment. The difference was that Stubblefield showed he could broadcast to multiple receivers simultaneously. Stubblefield was so afraid that

Radio inventor Guglielmo Marconi at his receiving set at St. John's, Newfoundland, on December 12, 1901.

Broadcast Pioneers Library/Havrilla Collection

someone would steal his invention, he sheltered it from everyone.

He had been offered $500,000 for his invention to The Wireless Telephone Company of America for 500,000 shares of worthless

David Sarnoff at a radio station atop the Wanamaker store in New York.

Broadcast Pioneers Library

stock and became forever fearful of being ripped-off.

Stubblefield envisioned the device in motorcars (as shown on his patent). Following another demonstration in Washington, his "secret box" with his apparatus inside was stolen (documented February 13, 1912), and he believed his invention was copied.

Nathan B. Stubblefield died of starvation and a pauper in Murray, Kentucky, after going into seclusion because of his failed attempts at acceptance. No evidence, however, lends credence to a claim of total originality in Stubblefield's idea, or that his inventions generated electromagnetic waves associated with an RF signal, or that there would be any way to vary the oscillations and tune the circuits if RF existed.

Tesla's wireless demonstration in St. Louis was an interesting event. He excited a 5-kilovolt transmitter and turned on a light across a stage, some 30 feet away. Although this apparatus was capable of sending and receiving RF, it's believed that it was more likely that this illumination was the result of atmospheric conduction, considering the power and distance involved.

Tesla patented his device in 1900, and convinced J.P. Morgan to put up $150,000 to build a transmitting tower at Wardenclyffe, on Long Island, in 1901.

The project ran short of money before the tower was completed, and Tesla was forced to ask Morgan for more money, admitting that his true goal was not communication but the wireless distribution of high-voltage, high-frequency electrical power. Morgan refused, and the land was sold to pay back the debts.

Iowa State's 9YI at the 1915 Iowa State Fair, giving public demonstrations.
Broadcast Pioneers Library

Fessenden, De Forest and Fleming

In 1900, Professor Reginald A. Fessenden realized that Marconi's work was limited to telegraphy and wanted to find a way to transmit and receive telephony (voice). He began experimenting with continuous wave transmissions, which led to the perfection of the arc transmitter.

High-frequency alternator used by Fessenden.

Broadcast Pioneers Library

A 1916 WHA Display at Agricultural Hall at the University of Wisconsin shows existing wireless stations and offers wireless receiving sets for sale at a cost of $35 to $200, a very steep price for the time.

Broadcast Pioneers Library

He also developed an alternator, similar to today's alternating current, with a higher frequency, and thus eliminated the spark gaps that wasted energy. His work was to become a major milestone in the development of radio.

Simultaneously, Lee De Forest built a wireless outfit, also less cumbersome than Marconi's. He used the electrolytic detector, as did Fessenden, which later created legal conflicts between the two. (De Forest spent years in litigation with many other inventors and was often accused of taking credit for the inventions of others.)

In 1904, J. Ambrose Fleming developed his two-element (diode) valve, the Fleming Valve, while working for Marconi. Although significant, the invention was short-lived due to De Forest's invention of a three-element (triode) valve, which later became the audion tube, said to be the most significant invention in radio.

Unfortunately, De Forest could not interest the public in buying stock in his company, and he was forced to sell the rights to the American Telephone and Telegraph Company for $500,000. The decision made by AT&T was thought to be foolish at the time, but later proved to be the investment that made the company.

On Christmas Eve in 1906, Fessenden delighted listeners up and down the East Coast by broadcasting voice and music from his transmitter at Brant Park, Massachusetts, using a high-frequency alternator based on Tesla's designs and principles. The program consisted of music from phonograph records, a violin solo and a speech by the inventor.

Fessenden's program did not prove to be a pioneering effort, however. For several years, radio remained a communications medium devoted to sending and receiving messages. It proved especially valuable to the armed forces during World War I. The broadcasting potential was not realized until after the war, although David Sarnoff in 1916 envisioned the possibility of a radio receiver in every home. (He later became head of the Radio Corporation of America and the National Broadcasting Company.)

In 1907, G.W. Pickard discovered that minerals made an excellent detector, which led to the invention of the crystal detector. It was an effective and inexpensive method, which made the availability of wireless receivers even more widespread.

The Radio Act of 1912

In 1910, the government required all ships to have a wireless telegraph. In 1912, the Titanic hit an iceberg and sent the first SOS signal, which was heard by a nearby ship that came to the rescue of many survivors. It was later learned that another ship was closer, which would have resulted in more lives being saved, but that ship only had one wireless operator on board who happened to be "off-watch" at the time the Titanic went down. That resulted in the Radio Act of 1912, requiring that two operators be employed on all ships with constant watch.

When the Titanic sank, a young wireless operator was stationed at the Wanamaker radio station in New York City to receive signals between the distressed ship and its rescuers, reports about the rescue work and a list of the survivors so that the anxious world could be advised. This kid stayed at the telegraph for 72 hours. His name — David Sarnoff. It was this event that made the public aware of the importance of the wireless.

Nikola Tesla gave the first demonstration of radio communication in 1893 in St. Louis. He fought a Supreme Court battle to be named the "Father of Radio." The court awarded him the title in 1943, after his death. He was an electrical genius who created the alternating current industry, and the multiple spark gap.

Radio Ink Collection

In 1913, Edwin H. Armstrong (who much later invented FM radio) created a way to increase the sensitivity of receivers. This regeneration system ended up in litigation with De Forest, who claimed he was the inventor. Ultimately, De Forest prevailed. De Forest also continued to perfect the audion tube he had sold to AT&T. It now had the ability to function as an oscillator (generator of high frequencies). This led to the oscillator circuit created by W.E. Hartley. The result was improved long-distance transmission of speech, the forerunner of radio broadcasting.

The First Stations

In 1916, an amateur operator and engineer for Westinghouse Electric began broadcasting pro-

The University of Wisconsin at Madison was instrumental in the development of radio. Their experimental station 9XM was sending Morse code weather forecasts in 1917. The station began voice tests in 1919 with occasional music programs. This aerial was mounted on Sterling Hall, resulting in broadcasts being heard as far away as Texas.

Broadcast Pioneers Library

grams from his garage on amateur station 8XK in Wilkinsburg, Pennsylvania. The broadcasts were enthusiastically received by other radio amateurs who liked hearing wireless music.

The broadcasts resulted in a newspaper article which generated such interest that Westinghouse decided to build a station for the purpose of broadcasting. The station — KDKA — was rushed to launch its first broadcast for the election returns of the Harding-Cox presidential race. It was the first programming to reach a sizable audience (perhaps 1,000 people — mainly ham and amateur radio operators).

The returns were read by Leo Rosenberg, who later claimed

One of the first voices heard on the first station — KDKA's Harold W. Arlin.

Broadcast Pioneers Library

Dr. Frank Conrad is a part of radio's romantic history. He re-licensed his home amateur radio station, 8XK, and began to transmit music and speech instead of dots and dashes. This station became KDKA, Pittsburgh. Conrad died shortly after this photo was taken in 1941.

Broadcast Pioneers Library

This beautiful batch of wires became the first official broadcast transmitter of KDKA, Pittsburgh, built by Dr. Frank Conrad in his garage as 8XK.

Broadcast Pioneers Library

to be the first professional radio announcer. KDKA also hired the first full-time announcer, Harold W. Arlin, who became the first sportscaster to do play-by-play football. The newspapers (2,000 across the country), having not yet realized that they were promoting a competitor, were so enamored with the medium that they printed daily broadcast schedules.

The first commercial was claimed to be sent out over WEAF in New York City in 1922; however, that is disputed because in KDKA's initial broadcasts announcers mentioned a record store in exchange for records to play on the air, as did KQW announcers in San Jose, California, much earlier. (It's interesting to note that Westinghouse, which owned KDKA, was founded by George

Westinghouse, the first owner of an electric company to employ the principles of alternating current. These principles were obtained through a relationship with Nikola Tesla, who held the patent and also had the patent on wireless transmission.)

But was KDKA the first station? Although its November 2, 1920, debut is considered the official start of radio broadcasting, others were doing the same prior to KDKA. Earlier that same year in Detroit, WWJ, using call letters 8MK, began regular broadcasts; they too gave election returns. And, much earlier, in 1912, Charles David Herrold began regular, continuous broadcasts of music and information in San Jose. The amateur station was well-known around the Bay area. It eventually became KQW and then KCBS.

Having the distinction of being the first live singer on radio, Vaughn de Leath appeared in 1916 on Lee De Forest's early radio telephone entertainment experiments. She was frequently heard on WJZ, Newark, and became one of the first radio stars. Her style became known as crooning.

Broadcast Pioneers Library

In 1913, the physics department at Iowa State University began wireless demonstrations and is documented by a newspaper article to have done one such demonstration at the Iowa State Fair in 1915. It became station 9YI and later WOI.

With groundwork dating back to 1904, the University of Wisconsin in Madison experimented with voice and music transmission in 1917. Their calls were 9XM, and later WHA.

Radio's Father

So who was the father of radio? We have credited Marconi traditionally; however, there is much doubt that he is the true father of radio. He was very industrious, highly inventive and had the strongest and most successful entrepreneurial spirit of any of radio's fathers. He made excellent com-

mercial applications for wireless telegraphy.

However, our exhaustive research points to the father of radio as Nikola Tesla, who had disclosed wireless and the technology at a lecture in 1893, preceding Marconi's wireless inventions and practical demonstrations. In fact, a Supreme Court case in 1943 ruled that Tesla was the father of radio. Marconi's first patent was issued in 1900 and Tesla's in 1898.

Evidence indicates, however, that Tesla's main objective was not communication but the distribution of electricity. Additionally, Oliver Lodge and John Stone were also involved in the Supreme Court case, and it was ruled that they, too, had been infringed upon by Marconi. So perhaps they should receive equal credit as the fathers of radio?

The court did rule that Marconi's original wireless patent

The home of Dr. Frank Conrad is also the home of radio, where Conrad's 8XK experiments and broadcasts took place.

Radio Ink Collection

The HORNE DAILY NEWS

 *de cologne—is very refreshing.
Toilet Goods Section.*

*Discount on Relief Lagraveo
Christmas Cards to order—Sta-
tionery Section, Main Floor.*

| Joseph Horne Co. | The Best Place to Shop, After All | Penn, Fifth and Stanwix | 8:30 A. M. to 5:30 P. M. Daily |

A B C D E F G
H
I
J
K
L
M

For One Week---Starting Tomorrow

13 Open Stock Patterns of Dinnerware---25% Off

We have two objects in view in this special discount. First, to give our many customers, who are now using these popular patterns, an opportunity to fill in needed pieces at a
reduced price; and, secondly, to introduce these patterns to others of our customers who
may be in the market for new chinaware at this season.

The discount is a most substantial one, and represents even a greater saving than is indicated, because the regular prices here quoted are generally under prevailing prices for
these fine qualities.

The selection offers two grades of American porcelain dinnerware, six of English porcelain and five of chinaware—a Theodore Haviland, a Limoges, a Syracuse and two Nippons.
The patterns are suggested in the accompanying sketch, with their regular and special prices
indicated below.

**The prices quoted below are for complete sets of
100 pieces. Smaller sets and single pieces may be
had during this sale at the same reductions.**

A—100 pieces English Por-
celain, regularly $123.50.
25% off, $84.12.

B—100 pieces English Por-
celain, regularly $123.50.
25% off, $92.63.

C—100 pieces English Por-
celain, regularly $96.75.
25% off, $72.57.

D—100 pieces English Por-
celain, regularly $113.00.
25% off, $84.75.

E—100 pieces Nippon
China, regularly $92.00.
25% off, $69.00.

F—100 pieces American
Porcelain, regularly $30.30.
25% off, $22.92.

G—100 pieces English Por-
celain, regularly $47.85.
25% off, $35.80.

H—100 pieces American
Porcelain, regularly $23.15.
25% off, $24.86.

I—100 pieces English Por-
celain, regularly $49.25.
25% off, $37.02.

J—100 pieces Theodore
Haviland China, regularly
$253.50—25% off, $190.13.

K—100 pieces Limoges
China, regularly $266.75—
25% off, $200.07.

L—100 pieces Syracuse
China, regularly $95.65.
25% off, $71.74.

M—100 pieces Nippon
China, regularly $69.40.
25% off, $52.00.

—"Floor of Ideas," Third, East

Large, Direct Importations of Swiss Curtains for Fall

Our Curtain Buyer, on his recent trip abroad, selected a
considerable quantity of fine Lace Curtains and Lace Paneling in Switzerland. They are distinguished by the pains-
taking workmanship—much of it handwork—that distin-
guishes the peoples who make an art of lacework, and the
prices are based on the much-lower Swiss wage rates.

Lace Curtains embroidered on nets that can be relied
upon for service; sill or full lengths; in ivory, champagne
and beige shades; with scroll, border and novelty designs—
in plain-centered styles, Duchesse Curtains, and also patterns with detached figures in the centers. Priced—Sill-
Length, $12.50 to $30.00 pair; Full Length, $18.50 to $40.00
pair.

The Paneling comes in strips that may be cut to fit any
sized window, and enables you to treat all your windows,
whether big or little, in one curtain design. Priced, $3.00
to $4.50 strip.

—Fourth Floor

Madeira Embroidered Pillow Slips

Slips for Slumber Pillows, of fine white batiste with deli-
cate hand-embroidery in many different dainty designs—
$2.00 to $4.25 each.

Stamped Pillow Cases of a good grade of muslin, in an
assortment of patterns, and with scalloped edges; specially
priced, $2.35 pair.

—Art Needlework Section, Fourth Floor

The Kiddie-Koop

is widely recognized as the ideal crib for babies, from infancy through to the fourth year. In fact, it combines a
Bassinette, Crib, and Play-Pen in one, and yet cost no more
than a good crib, alone. It may be used outdoors as well
as in the house, for it can be wheeled through doorways
easily, and is screened to protect Baby from insects and
animals.

Our present stocks of Kiddie-Koops were ordered before
the recent increase in wholesale cost, so we are selling under
prevailing prices at

$23.00 and $25.00
(Mattresses included)

Kiddie-Koops will be trimmed as Bassinettes, according
to mother's desires; at a reasonable extra charge.
The Infants' Shop also carries the necessary bedding,
including:
Sheets at $1.00 upward. Pillow Cases, 50c upward.
Blankets at $1.50 to $16.50.
Silk Comforts, hand-embroidered—$8.00 to $16.50.

—Third Floor

Folding Chairs
---40c Each
—A small lot to close at this
reduced price. Folding Tables,
25% off.

—Basement

Air Concert "Picked Up" By Radio Here

Victrola music, played into
the air over a wireless telephone, was "picked up" by
listeners on the wireless receiving station which was
recently installed here for
patrons interested in wireless
experiments. The concert was
heard Thursday night about
10 o'clock, and continued 20
minutes. Two orchestra numbers, a soprano solo—which
rang particularly high and
clear through the air—and a
juvenile "talking piece" con-
stituted the program.

The music was from a Vic-
trola pulled up close to the
transmitter of a wireless telephone in the home of Frank
Conrad, Penn and Peebles
avenues, Wilkinsburg. Mr.
Conrad is a wireless enthusiast and "puts on" the wireless
concerts periodically for the
entertainment of the many
people in this district who
have wireless sets.

Amateur Wireless Sets,
made by the maker of the
Set which is in operation in
our store, are on sale here
$10.00 up.

"You did a big thing, when you gave women

Air Concert "Picked Up" By Radio Here

Victrola music, played into
the air over a wireless telephone, was "picked up" by
listeners on the wireless receiving station which was
recently installed here for
patrons interested in wireless
experiments. The concert was
heard Thursday night about
10 o'clock, and continued 20
minutes. Two orchestra numbers, a soprano solo—which
rang particularly high and
clear through the air—and a
juvenile "talking piece" con-
stituted the program.

The music was from a Vic-
trola pulled up close to the
transmitter of a wireless telephone in the home of Frank
Conrad, Penn and Peebles
avenues, Wilkinsburg. Mr.
Conrad is a wireless enthusiast and "puts on" the wireless
concerts periodically for the
entertainment of the many
people in this district who
have wireless sets.

Amateur Wireless Sets,
made by the maker of the
Set which is in operation in
our store, are on sale here
$10.00 up.

—West Basement

The Boys' Haberdashery

—is one side of the many-sided Store
for Boys here.

It borders the Suit and Coat Sections, which is a large point of convenience.

The stocks of Boys' Furnishings in
this Haberdashery comprise all the
Fall "incidentals" of boys' dress—
new Shirts and Blouses, Neckwear,
Pajamas, Night Shirts, Bathrobes, Belts, Silk
Scarfs, Sweaters, Sweater Sets and many others.
The qualities are of the same high standard as in all
the other sections of the Store for Boys, and prices
moderate.

Hats and Shoes are nearby.

—Second Floor

noon. And there is a surprising showing of stout
women's models, in sizes up to 46.

The Dress illustrated at the left is one of them, copied
after a $125.00 model. It comes in Meteor Satin, navy, black

This department store news ad may be one of the most important events in radio history. The offer of wireless sets was so well-noticed that Westinghouse executives were motivated to get involved, resulting in KDKA going on the air.

Broadcast Pioneers Library

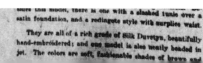

29

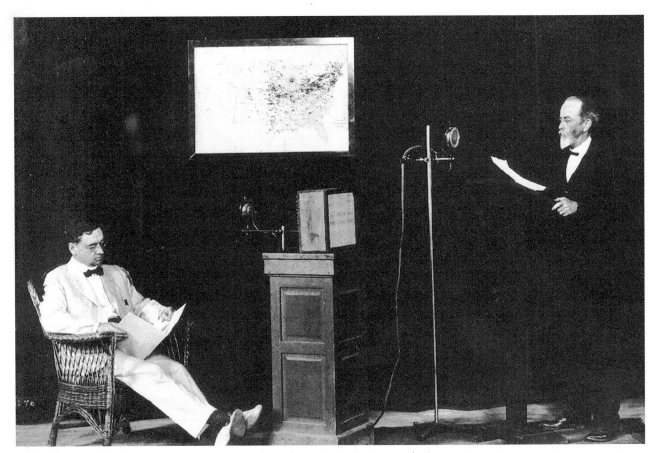

Earle M. Terry and Professor W.H. Lighty (standing), former director of extension teaching and first program director of WHA, Madison, Wisconsin, were radio pioneers.

Broadcast Pioneers Library

stood intact, but invaded claims made in a subsequent patent. This means that Marconi invented a wireless device and improved it by appropriating the work of others.

But what about Nathan Stubblefield, who had demonstrated wireless back in 1892? If you travel to Murray, Kentucky, you'll find a plaque there honoring native son Stubblefield and inscribed with the words: "Murray, Kentucky — Birthplace of Radio."

Could it be that a forward-thinking, albeit eccentric, farmer from Kentucky outwitted the intellects of Tesla, Marconi, Edison (who once worked on wireless experiments and also won a suit against Marconi for patent infringement) and others?

You will recall that after he was very protective of his proprietary knowledge, Stubblefield's apparatus was stolen following a demonstration in Washington, D.C. Could it have resurfaced as someone else's invention? Documents prove his early demonstrations of an actual working wireless system to have occurred one year before Tesla's lectures about radio, which were prior to his working experiments.

No one will ever know for sure. Perhaps Stubblefield was nothing more than an eager inventor who was able to expand upon the ideas of others.

Invention is a curious thing. Simultaneous events lead to simultaneous ideas.

Lee De Forest, inventor of the audion tube, the most important discovery toward hearing the human voice on the radio. De Forest's tenacity enabled radio to occur.

Broadcast Pioneers Library

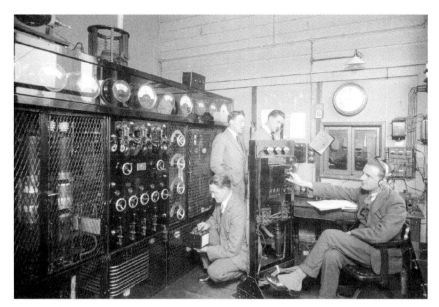

The Manchester, England, debut of the BBC in 1923.

Broadcast Pioneers Library

The Supreme Court ruled that Tesla is the father of radio — and Marconi is not. The question remains whether the honor should really go to Stubblefield, Bell, Dolbear, Phelps, Woods, Trowbridge or Edison. ◼

David Sarnoff first got attention as a young telegraph operator for the Marconi company when he received distress signals from the sinking Titanic on April 12, 1912. For 72 hours he provided lists of survivors to newspapers. He later became head of the Radio Corporation of America, which built radio receivers. To sell receivers, he believed America needed compelling programming, and so he created the Red and the Blue Networks. The Red became NBC and the Blue was sold to Edward J. Nobel, the maker of Lifesavers, and became ABC.

Broadcast Pioneers Library

An experimental antenna was carried aboard this KDKA dirigible. Winds snapped the tether of the blimp and station personnel had to shoot it down.

Radio Ink Collection

Charles D. "Doc" Herrold

Radio Ink Collection

The cover sheet of a song published in 1877, The Wondrous Telephone. The illustration shows examples of how the telephone might be used. These drawings are some of the first that show uses of radio as we know it.

Radio Ink Collection

1920s

P rior to 1920, entertainment in America came in the form of the written word or the theater. Thanks to inventor Thomas Edison, some had phonographs, but money was tight and phonographs were expensive, as were phonograph records.

Occasionally, a select group of people found their way into theaters featuring traveling vaudeville acts, while others wandered into concert halls and speakeasies to hear music. Those in search of drama meandered to the theater to see their favorite Shakespearean play performed.

Meanwhile, the common man made his way to the motion pictures, another Edison entertainment contribution. There were no radios, no televisions, no video games, no cassette or CD players and no computers. Yet generations have grown up knowing no different, having difficulty imagining life without the unappreciated entertainment vehicles we commonly refer to as the media.

Before radio was invented, it was hard to imagine. The idea of send-

Announcing the results of the Harding-Cox presidential election, KDKA created the first official broadcast on November 2, 1920.

Broadcast Pioneers Library

ing something through the air was considered an impossibility, just as the concept of sending people through the air in a *Star Trek*-like manner seems farfetched today.

But the 1920s changed all that. For years, amateurs had been dotting and dashing the ether with wireless telegraphy. Then, suddenly, it was put to a halt by the U.S. government, which wanted total control of the airwaves during World War I. Wireless experiments were not allowed, and progress in the area of casting telegraph signals without wires was left to the Navy and ships at sea. In fact, the government swallowed up all the technical details it could control, including ownership of patents, to keep wireless out of the hands of the enemy.

It wasn't long after the first World War that the ban on wireless activities was lifted, in late 1919, and experimentation once again became prevalent. That flurry of activity led to the desire to broadcast voice, an accomplishment developed by Mr. De Forest's Audion tube.

In early 1920, experiments were occurring at *The Detroit News*' 8MK. In Hollywood, California, Fred Christian operated 6ADZ. In Charlotte, North Carolina, a former GE employee built 4XD. Several stations were licensed as experimental wireless radio telephone outlets, but it was not until an experiment by Westinghouse Electric Company employee Dr. Frank Conrad got everyone's attention that broadcasting, as we know it, officially began.

Conrad ran experimental station 8XK out of his home work-shop, casting his message to other amateurs. To allow himself to leave his transmitter site so he could test reception throughout different parts of Pittsburgh, Conrad figured out how to play his Edison phonograph into the wireless station. The phonograph records were provided by The Hamilton Music Store in Wilkinsburg in return for mentions on his broadcasts. These wireless communications began gaining in popularity with a couple dozen wireless enthusiasts in the Pittsburgh area. The word spread rapidly, and people wanted to purchase kits to build their own wireless receivers so they too could listen in on the experimentation of Conrad and others. One enthusiast was a bright retailer at Hornes Department Store, which ran a story in their *Pittsburgh Sun* newspaper advertisements telling of the experiments and advising that the store carried these wireless receivers for $10. The store sold out.

When Westinghouse Electric executive Harry P. Davis heard

A farmhouse near Hastings, Nebraska, in which a receiving set was located to jack-up low-wave transmission from KDKA in Pittsburgh.
Broadcast Pioneers Library

of the success, he became interested in this wireless apparatus and began discussing the possibilities with Conrad.

In the past, experimental broadcasts were only heard by people who were technically inclined, with the ability to build their own apparatus. The department store sale of pre-built units made Davis take notice of the commercial possibilities in the sale of the sets.

The next day, Davis invited Conrad to bring his experiments to the Westinghouse plant, where continuous service could be achieved, and with higher power. Davis saw the possibility of selling receivers as limitless, and felt the effort would be a good public relations move for Westinghouse.

Looking for a dramatic launch of the service, Davis asked Conrad if he could be set up in time for the rapidly approaching presidential election between rivals Warren G. Harding and James M. Cox. On October 16, the Department of Commerce received their application for a special broadcasting

T.H. Baily (left) , KDKA literary critic, and T.F. Harnack, announcer on KDKA, in 1924.

Broadcast Pioneers Library

service. On October 27, the Department of Commerce assigned call letters KDKA, which were commercial shore station call letters. They were given a permit to broadcast on 360 meters, which was free of interference and away from the traditional experimental stations.

At 8 p.m. on November 2, 1920, a tiny wooden shack on the roof of the six-story Westinghouse Electric building would give birth to an industry called broadcasting with the first non-experimental, and first scheduled, public wireless service. And although there were only a few hundred receivers able to hear the first official licensed broadcast, word spread as quickly as a lit match on a field of dry weeds. Radio rapidly engulfed the world.

Interestingly, similar activities also occurred in Detroit at *The Detroit News'* experimental station 8MK; however; rival newspapers refused to pick up the news of its broadcast. Since Westinghouse was not in the newspaper business, it received enormous amounts of publicity. That was followed by a massive

This early photos shows a broadcast over KZN radio in Salt Lake City on May 6, 1922, featuring Mormon Church president Heber J. Grant at the microphone. The call letters were changed in 1925 when the station became KSL.

Radio Ink Collection

advertising and publicity blitz to sell Westinghouse receivers.

In his book *A Tower In Babel*, author Eric Barnouw states that the effect of the KDKA continuous broadcasts was to bring radio into the home. Prior to this, wireless experimenters suffered through the cold in their garages and worksheds to listen to the wireless. Conrad's regular broadcasts brought interest from the whole family and those who were not technically inclined.

Referred to as the Wireless Music Box, wireless telephone and radio telephone, the new invention began a national fad. The vision of executives at Westinghouse Electric fueled this undefined medium, leading to the emergence of regular programs.

It was the presence of programming that further inspired interest among American consumers, leading to the sale of

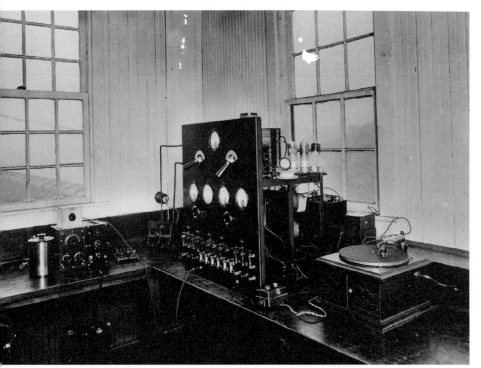

The first KDKA control room in east Pittsburgh in 1920, the first year of operation.

Broadcast Pioneers Library/ Westinghouse Photo

thousands of ready-made radio sets by 1921. This, too, was the vision of Westinghouse Electric, which saw the production of wireless receivers as a new business opportunity.

As unsophisticated as it was, radio was here to stay. People would listen long hours and into the late night in hopes of hearing distant stations. They wore pre-set volume headphones and listened to very tinny, garbled, often hard-to-understand signals. Crackle and pop were the lay of the land.

Following KDKA's license, many other entrepreneurial companies felt compelled to enter the wireless marketplace. Within two years from KDKA's humble beginning, radio stations were pumping out wattage in Detroit, Philadelphia, Omaha, Los Angeles, New York and many other cities. Many electric companies like General Electric followed suit

Now beyond the initial experimentation stages of transmission, the KDKA transmitter room increases in size and equipment (January 1921).

Broadcast Pioneers Library

When KDKA first began broadcasting on a regular basis from the Westinghouse Electric Company building, there was no space for a studio. This tent was erected on the roof of the building to serve as a temporary headquarters.

Broadcast Pioneers Library

and moved into ownership, as did department stores, car dealers and just about any other type of business.

Of course, Westinghouse also wanted to expand its radio empire, establishing WJZ in Newark, New Jersey, KYW in Chicago, Illinois, and WBZ in Springfield, Massachusetts. One of the biggest business groups to own radio stations were newspapers such as *The Detroit News*, *The Los Angeles Examiner* and *The Kansas City Star*.

When 1922 ended, there were nearly 70 newspapers that owned radio stations, more than 550 licensed radio stations in total and more than 1.5 million radio receivers — and radio was barely two years old!

With 550 stations on the air, utter chaos erupted. As this newborn industry was trying to discover itself, regulatory problems became exaggerated. Especially in light of the overlap of stations on the same frequency of 360 meters, many had to shut down so distant stations could be heard on what were

RADIO BROADCASTING NEWS

Vol. 3   FEBRUARY 24, 1923   No.

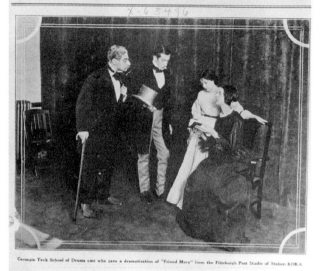

Carnegie Tech School of Drama cast who gave a dramatization of "Friend Mary" from the Pittsburgh Post Studio of Station KDKA

Carnegie Tech School of Drama class provided early radio dramas on KDKA, as shown in this February 24, 1923, issue of *Radio Broadcasting News*.

Broadcast Pioneers Library

termed "silent nights."

Chicago stations shut down on Monday nights, Dallas on Wednesday, Kansas City on Saturday and so on. The practice was observed until 1927. And if emergency ship-to-shore distress signals were heard, stations had to shut down altogether on a moment's notice so the distress signal could get through.

Stations had to work out their own conflicts without government intervention. For instance, in 1922, Bamberger Department Store's WOR came on the air. It worked out a schedule with WJZ wherein the stations would alternate daytime hours and evening hours every other day. Listeners were the most confused, not knowing when their station would be on the air. Although stations were often cooperative, they frequently were uncooperative, jamming the broadcast of a rival station if they disagreed with what it was airing.

Much of the chaos, however, was in the programming offered by the stations. The choices were very limited, and entertainment ranged from an occasional dry lecture on vegetable gardening to the playing of limited musical recordings.

Radio broadcasts were crude, and radio programmers were blindly finding their way, learning as they experimented. And not only was the programming crude, but the environment for radio entertainers was usually cramped, hot and uncomfortable.

KDKA announcer Harold Arlin told author J. Fred MacDonald in his book *Don't Touch That Dial* that a locomotive once passed the studio, filling the room with smoke and covering with soot the elegantly dressed, world-renowned soprano who was singing on the station. The studio shook and the noise from the train was heard on the air, completely drowning her out. Arlin also recalled humorous stories of bugs flying into people's mouths while they were speaking or singing, making them gasp for air.

KDKA's first studios were on the roof of the Westinghouse Electric plant because the acoustics were much better than the reverberation that occurred in a hall. Weather permitting, the outdoor location worked well. When the weather didn't cooperate, they moved under a tarp. After the tarp blew down, KDKA moved into a small, unoccupied office in the building. To overcome the acoustical problems previously encountered, an indoor tent was constructed.

With the beginning of radio came the beginning of many forms of radio entertainment and information gathering. From day one, KDKA continued to offer programs, even if for an hour or two, every day.

Five days following the first KDKA broadcast, Texas A&M's experimental station aired the first college football game. Sports was to become a major part of radio broadcasting

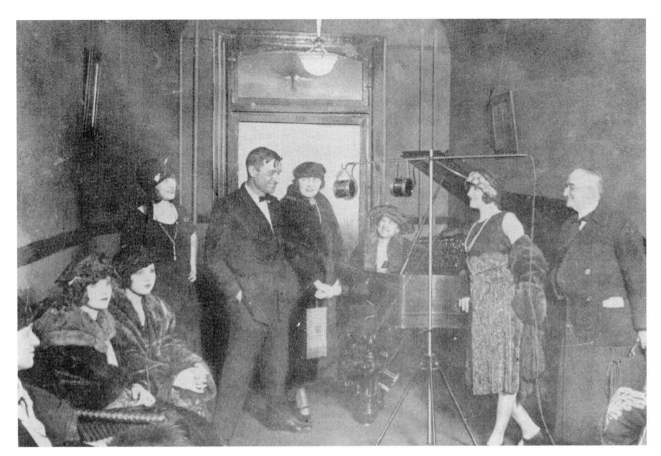

Will Rogers visits KDKA in 1922.

Broadcast Pioneers Library

in early, and later, years. In fact, many sports like baseball, boxing and football were not popular prior to their broadcasts on radio. The first "running description" of the World Series was aired on WJZ in 1921.

Early sports announcers like Ted Husing and Graham McNamee gained celebrity often bigger than the players themselves. Sporting events became one of the most important programming elements on radio and have remained important to this day.

In January 1921, KDKA set up a broadcast from The Calvary Episcopal Church for the first religious broadcast, and possibly the first remote broadcast. Engineers wore choir robes to keep from distracting the congregation.

Close on the heels of that first came the first debate, aired on WHJ in Washington, D.C.; the first theatrical broadcast, on WJZ in Newark in 1922, and the first radio drama, on WGY, Schenectady, New York, in 1922.

Dilworth's Little German Band with Schnitzel the dog. Directed by Gus Smaltz on KDKA in the late '20s.

Broadcast Pioneers Library

Imagine, if you will, a dramatic production without anything but voice — no sound effects or music. Yet that was how early radio dramas were conducted. The theater of the mind was eventually added when the use of sound effects came shortly after the WGY broadcast.

Radio and music have always had the perfect marriage, which began when the first phonograph record was played on the air. But playing phonographs on the air was considered an insult to the listeners. After all, radio was something special and phonograph records, although costly, were available to the public elsewhere. Records were to be replaced by live performers, mostly opera singers and classical pianists initially. In 1921, KYW was formed in Chicago for the express purpose of airing opera.

Although a glut of new radio stations arose, there was a drought in effective programming until AT&T came on the

T.J. Vastine conducted radio's first band concert in 1921 over KDKA. Musicians were Westinghouse employees.

Broadcast Pioneers Library

Leo Rosenburg, the first voice on KDKA, reporting the Harding-Cox election returns.

Broadcast Pioneers Library/Westinghouse Photo

Acoustics became important in early broadcasts, forcing stations to drape their studios, like this early KDKA studio in Pittsburgh.

Broadcast Pioneers Library

scene. American Telephone and Telegraph saw a bright future for radio, especially because it was considered a form of telephone, an industry AT&T dominated.

According to an article from *The Wall Street Journal* on August 25, 1920, AT&T entered a joint venture with General Electric, Westinghouse, several others and The Radio Corporation of America to further develop the medium by sharing patents and previously proprietary information.

An article in *Technical News Bulletin* from The Bureau of Standards in Washington saw the possibilities for this wireless telephone, then called the portaphone:

"The portaphone opens up many new possibilities. For instance, at 8:30 o'clock each evening a central station might send out dance music from its transmitting apparatus and those who cared to dance could set up their portaphones on a table, turn on

the current and have music furnished sufficiently loud to fill a room. Or in the morning a summary of the day's news might be sent out to be received by portaphone and digested by a family at breakfast, in which all could participate whether paterfamilias had the paper or not."

Programming was considered an extension of the theater. A KDKA broadcast once contained these words: "Fellow patrons of KDKA: Now that we are assembled again in KDKA's unlimited theater, where the rear seats are hundreds of miles from the stage and where the audience, all occupying private boxes, can come late or leave early without embarrassing the speaker or annoying the rest of the audience ..."

But it was AT&T's entry that was to change programming forever with the invention of "toll broadcasting." The idea came when KDKA requested phone lines from a church to the radio

KDKA was responsible for many radio firsts, including the first church broadcasts. Broadcasting live from the pulpit at the Shadyside Presbyterian Church in Pittsburgh is William Jennings Bryan.

Broadcast Pioneers Library

Farm reports changed farming by giving crop reports, market rates for produce and weather reports to aid farmers. The first farm reports came from KDKA, Pittsburgh.

Broadcast Pioneers Library

station for a remote broadcast in Pittsburgh. From that seed of a thought came a plan to create a network of stations via toll telephone lines, generating income from the use of the lines.

To begin the process, they erected WBAY in 1922 atop the AT&T building at 24 Walker Street in Manhattan and began to broadcast, only to find out that their engineering didn't work and the station could barely be heard because of absorption from the metal in the building.

They moved to the Western Electric building at 463 West Street and became WEAF (and years later WRCA, WNBC and WFAN). A studio was built at 195 Broadway in the AT&T headquarters and started to provide programming

The real impact of WEAF began on August 28, 1922, when it aired the first commercial at 5:15 in the afternoon for The

Queensboro Corporation to sell tenant-owned apartment houses at Jackson Heights, New York. The commercials ran until September 21, and thousands of dollars in sales were reported. The Tidewater Oil Company and The American Express Company also began making announcements.

These commercials caused a national flurry of press asking if a public medium like radio should be used for commercial gain. But that didn't stop WEAF, which continued to innovate commercial programming and a means of tracking the results so more commercials could be sold.

WEAF broke new ground by creating the first variety programming when it brought local vaudeville acts in to do music and comedy. Billy Jones and Ernest Hare became known as The Happiness Boys when the Happiness Candy Company became the first company in history to sponsor a program.

This concept changed radio forever, becoming one of the most popular ways of selling products without blatant commercials. At the time, "direct" advertising was not allowed and was considered offensive to listeners on WEAF, so sponsorship was the only alternative.

Famous acts followed, like The Cliquot Club Eskimos (gin-

No one really knew what a radio studio should look like, since there were none. So KDKA put this one together in the K building of the Westinghouse plant's ninth floor.

Broadcast Pioneers Library

One of the reasons Westinghouse became so committed to broadcasting was the possibility of selling radio sets. The Aeriols Jr. set was developed by Westinghouse as a portable receiver.

Broadcast Pioneers Library

The station began employing announcers like Graham McNamee who, as a result of WEAF's broadcasts, became the world's most popular announcer. His broadcasts of the World Series and numerous prizefights, made possible by AT&T telephone lines, made him a local celebrity.

He became a national celebrity when WEAF began forming networks and offering broadcasts of sporting events to other radio stations across the country. In 1925, he received 50,000 letters following the World Series.

The first "chain" began in 1923 between WEAF and WMAF in Round Hills, Massachusetts. Later, a chain of four stations evolved, including WEAF,

ger ale), The Ipana (toothpaste) Troubadours, The Gold Dust Twins (Gold Dust cleaning powder), The Silvertown Cord Orchestra (Silvertown Cord Auto tire manufacturer) and its star, The Silver Masked Tenor, The Lucky Strike (cigarettes) Orchestra, The Interwoven (socks) Pair, The Best Foods Boys, The Taystee Loafers (Taystee bread), The Astor Coffee Dance Orchestra and The A&P Gypsies (groceries).

The Eveready Hour was the first program to become known totally by the sponsor name without mention of the entertainers like Will Rogers. In fact, Eveready insisted WEAF link up with WJAR and eventually other stations to increase its advertising reach, thus forming the first entertainment network.

It was the income generated by WEAF's advertising that allowed the station to build elaborate studios to attract entertainers and all forms of talent to the station. In spite of its financial success, the station refused to pay talent for their appearances in unsponsored time slots.

The light pole also served to support the KDKA microphone at the first church broadcast ever made.

Broadcast Pioneers Library

General Electric's WGY Schenectady, KDKA Pittsburgh and KYW in Chicago. This nationwide broadcast was a breakthrough in broadcasting and became a huge source of income for AT&T.

Another huge income source was AT&T's partnership in The Radio Corporation of America. RCA and its partners, General Electric and Westinghouse, were accused of monopolizing the transmission and reception of broadcast equipment.

Of 600 stations on the air, only 35 used Western Electric transmitters; the others used RCA. Additionally, RCA vacuum tubes were required in most transmitters, including those made by Western Electric. To top it off, most radio receivers manufactured in America required RCA parts or tubes to operate. Additionally, stations not participating in the AT&T network were unable to get AT&T lines for network broadcasts of their own, having to rely on inferior Western Union

A KDKA remote on board a train, designed to prove that the signal could still be sent despite the speed of the moving train.

Broadcast Pioneers Library

A KDKA mobile transmitter truck outside the Pittsburgh chamber of commerce in 1924.

Broadcast Pioneers Library

Announcer Rex Willets with engineer Frank Pierce at the WOC, Davenport, Iowa, control room. WOC was the smallest station in the 13-station chain of the first radio network of AT&T stations.

Broadcast Pioneers Library

The WJZ, Newark, studios and performers.

Broadcast Pioneers Library

If you weren't listening to the radio, you might miss something. As a result, people came up with their own portable wireless sets, including wireless backpacks.

Hearst Newspaper Collection; Special Collections; University of Southern California Library

and postal telegraph lines.

Monopoly arguments continued until AT&T agreed to get out of the RCA deal, and out of the radio business altogether. In January 1926, the RCA Board of Directors approved a new company and the purchase of WEAF from AT&T for an overvalued $2.5 million, although it would continue to lease land lines to the new corporation. By August, the deal was done, and on September 9, 1926, a new company, The National Broadcasting Company (NBC), was incorporated.

NBC was instantly wealthy. More than five million homes had radios, and stations across America were craving good programming. For the first time in history, one voice was positioned to speak to the entire country simultaneously.

At 8:05 p.m. from the Waldorf-Astoria, the first official NBC broadcast took place with an audience of 12 million people. The room was filled with celebrities who listened as Walter Damrosch conducted the New York Symphony, as Mary Garden sang from Chicago, as Will Rogers told jokes from Kansas City and others performed from different cities in the link. The comedy team of Weber and Fields entertained on the program, which ran well past midnight. This enormously expensive event kicked off national radio programming and generated publicity that sent millions more out to buy radios.

Soon after the NBC premiere, two networks originated. The Blue Network was a feed from WJZ, and the Red Network from WEAF. Sponsors climbed on board as fast as they could be signed. Everyone wanted to be a part of radio.

In January 1927, NBC spent $400,000 on new air-conditioned studios at 711 Fifth Avenue. Radio stocks were soaring on Wall Street, with NBC at the lead. By 1927, NBC had 600 sponsors and programming that ranged from entertainment to religion, from farm reports to lectures to educational programming for children.

All the while NBC's activities were taking place, local programs were attracting attention. In markets like Chicago, San Francisco, Detroit and Los Angeles, local programming became part of the network.

Starting at a little New Orleans station as *Sam and Henry*, Freeman Gosden and Charles Correll created black-faced characters on WEBH and later Chicago's WGN. When they later moved to WMAQ and the Red network, they were not allowed to take the names Sam and Henry with them, so they recreated the characters under the names *Amos and Andy*. It became the most popular radio program of all time, with 40 million listeners.

The network business was not to go unchallenged. In 1927, a 26-year-old William Paley placed a $50-a-week advertising schedule on WCAU in Philadelphia for his father's cigar company. As a result of *The La Palina Hour*, sales doubled. Seeing the value of the medium, Paley purchased a chain of failing radio stations in 1928 to become the Columbia Broadcasting System (CBS).

Within two years, he had amassed 70 stations and profited $2.35 million. The dominant NBC was no longer a monopoly.

In order to beat NBC, which charged affiliates for programming, Paley offered it for free. Suddenly, stations that could hardly afford to provide local programming could air CBS programs all day long, picking and choosing what they needed. In return, Paley could sell national sponsorships and secure certain guaranteed slots for

This cornerstone is mounted to the Shadyside Presbyterian Church in Pittsburgh commemorating KDKA broadcasts to the arctic regions in 1922 and the first church broadcasts to the arctic, received by Admiral Byrd in 1929.

Broadcast Pioneers Library

Gentlemen pose with remote equipment for KDKA outside Syria club or hotel.

Broadcast Pioneers Library

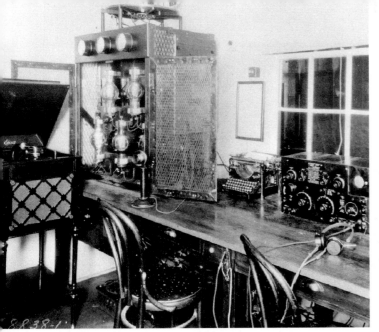

The first WJZ, Newark, control room, complete with victrola.
Broadcast Pioneers Library

The first WJZ, Newark, transmitter in 1921 was 500 watts.
Broadcast Pioneers Library

those sponsors. Local New York personalities like Jessica Dragonette, Billy Jones and Ernie Hare, and Major Bowes became national stars.

During the late 1920s, serialized programming was introduced to the American public. Programs like *The Rise of the Goldbergs* aired on NBC. Variety programming thrived when Rudy Vallee was introduced with *The Fleischmann Hour* in 1929. His show introduced more stars than any other, and featured regulars like Fanny Brice, Eddie Cantor, Ed Wynn and Olson and Johnson.

The 1920s were probably the most important decade in American radio broadcasting, as the industry was born from the garages of experimental stations to give birth to radio networks and sponsored programming.

Radio was hot. Americans had a passion about radio that was to last for decades. They couldn't buy enough radio sets and they couldn't hear enough radio. This fresh, new, experimental medium went from inception to become a way of life in fewer than 10 short years.

The KDKA Little Symphony Orchestra with Victor Saudek, conductor (1922).
Broadcast Pioneers Library

The 1923 staff of WJZ at Aeolion Hall, 33 W. 42nd Street in New York.
Broadcast Pioneers Library

Powel Crosley was one of the most important entrepreneurs in radio. When he discovered the high cost of purchasing a radio set for his son to build, he found a way to do his own cheaper. He then began selling them. In order to sell sets, he created a radio station in Cincinnati that became known as WLW. To sell more sets, Crosley was one of the first to create entertainment programming on the radio. He was also the first to build a 500,000-watt radio station, which was later downgraded due to new FCC rules.

Radio Ink Collection

KDKA wasn't the only station on the air in Pittsburgh; long-forgotten were KQV's experimental operations the same year. This shows the KQV "air studio" on an old telegraph table.

KQV Collection

The first WJZ, Newark, broadcast in October 1921, featuring The Shannon Quartet. Previous to this broadcast, only records and piano rolls had been used on the air.

Broadcast Pioneers Library

The original transmitter at WFAA in Dallas, one of the pioneers in broadcasting.

Broadcast Pioneers Library

The WEAF experimental tower farm in Deal Beach. The facility was owned by the Bell System and was used for pioneering ship-to-shore experiments in 1920.

Broadcast Pioneers Library

The very cramped WBZ studio in Springfield, Massachusetts, on September 10, 1921.

Broadcast Pioneers Library

Announcer Kolin Hager (right) and assistant announcer Robert Weidaw present a performance from a local harpist on General Electric's WGY in 1923.

Broadcast Pioneers Library

The WEAF, New York, studio at 24 Walker Street. AT&T-owned WEAF started as WBAY, later became WRCA and then WNBC.

Broadcast Pioneers Library

Very early KGO, San Francisco, curtained studio.

Broadcast Pioneers Library

Like Westinghouse, General Electric was a broadcasting pioneer. Shown here is the first WGY, Schenectady, control room.

Broadcast Pioneers Library

A singing group broadcasting live on WGY, Schenectady. At left is James Wallington, who went on to become an NBC announcer. Because of broadcast signals all being on the same frequencies in the very early days, it would not be unusual for an announcer to say: "We now pause for a distress signal from a ship."

Broadcast Pioneers Library

Taking the prize for the most unique studio design in the infant days of radio is WOC, Davenport, which decorated with taxidermy and rustic wood. To broadcast records, a microphone was placed in front of the speaker horn (circa 1923).

Broadcast Pioneers Library

WOC's first manager, Stanley W. Barnet, known as Announcer B.W.S.

Broadcast Pioneers Library

Ruth St. Denis and Ted Shawn, known as The Denishawn Dancers, on radio for the first time (circa 1923).

Broadcast Pioneers Library

Jessica Dragonette had a 12-year run with *Cities Service Concert.*

Broadcast Pioneers Library

Shortwave and longwave receiving sets at the Westinghouse Telegraph transmitter control at WBZ in Springfield, Massachusetts.

Broadcast Pioneers Library

A performer we know only as Ralph by his signature on WRNY in August 1925.

Broadcast Pioneers Library

The smallest WOC, Davenport, studio, decorated with a rustic interior.

Broadcast Pioneers Library

The main studio of WRNY, a converted hotel room at the Hotel Roosevelt on the 19th floor (circa 1925).

Broadcast Pioneers Library

The WHA transmitter at The University of Wisconsin began regular radio-telephone voice broadcasts in January 1921.

Broadcast Pioneers Library

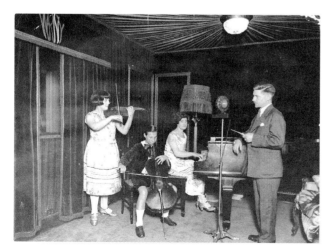

The Volga makes its first appearance in America on WRNY as Paul Dumont announces the event (circa 1925).

Broadcast Pioneers Library

Station WOC in Davenport, Iowa, is said to be the first independent station to use paid professional musicians for regular broadcasts (circa 1923).

Broadcast Pioneers Library

The WSAI, Cincinnati, concert studio. At the time it was thought that the more elaborate the studios, the higher the likelihood famous concert and opera stars would visit to do a broadcast.

Broadcast Pioneers Library

Pictured is the De Forest OT-10 transmitter in an improvised phone room on the second floor of *The Detroit News* building in 1920. From left: Frank Edwards and Clyde E. Darr of WWJ. The station was one of the first to innovate by regularly playing the phonograph on the air.

Broadcast Pioneers Library

Listeners would never have known the difference if fitness instructor Spike Shannon hadn't been doing the exercises before the microphone on KDKA, Pittsburgh.

Broadcast Pioneers Library

Ethel Barrymore broadcasting from WJZ in 1923 on *Laughing Lady*: (l-r) Alice Johns, Katherine Emmet, Violet Kemble Cooper and Barrymore.

Broadcast Pioneers Library

The 'Mr. & Mrs.' in Action was first heard on WEEI in the early '20s. E. Lewis Dunham and Gertrude Lamothe were original cast and are inside the ovals. The show was originally based on a comic strip and eventually ran nationally with a different cast on CBS in 1929.

Broadcast Pioneers Library

Herbert Hoover speaks on WCAU, Philadelphia.

Broadcast Pioneers Library

Milton J. Cross broadcasting from WJZ Detroit's early studio.

Broadcast Pioneers Library

A special commemorative microphone used on KDKA by President Herbert Hoover in 1921.

Broadcast Pioneers Library

Marjorie Drew of Boston station WEEI, one of the few women announcers at the time.

Broadcast Pioneers Library

During experiments at WJZ, Detroit, Thomas "Tommy" Cowan was told to go up to the roof and talk, making him the first announcer on WJZ. For the station's opening, he personally borrowed a phonograph from Thomas Edison, his former employer. He also did the first play-by-play sportscast ever on the radio, on October 5, 1921.

Broadcast Pioneers Library

Clarence Eddy, concert organist, seen broadcasting for the first time from the pipe organ studio in the home of Dr. B.J. Palmer, owner of WOC, Davenport, Iowa.

Broadcast Pioneers Library

Milton J. Cross was one of the first performers to sing on WJZ in 1921. He was later hired as announcer because of his skills as a tenor, which allowed him the opportunity to fill two roles. At the time, announcers only identified themselves with the initial of their last name, preceded by A for announcer and N for network. Cross used AJN since another announcer had the C in his name.

Broadcast Pioneers Library

The FLIT Soldiers, a band formed by Harry Reser prior to his famous Cliquot Club Eskimos.

Broadcast Pioneers Library

Henry Field of KFNF, Shenandoah, Iowa, one of many broadcasters who received local broadcasting licenses.

Broadcast Pioneers Library

In an effort to secure the advertising of the sparkling ginger ale that had a parka-hooded Eskimo on its label, WEAF executive George Podeyn suggested the company sponsor a band, call it The Cliquot Club Eskimos and make them wear parkas like the label of the bottle. It resulted in huge sales for Cliquot Club ginger ale.

Broadcast Pioneers Library

The greatest baseball player of all time and the first sportscaster: Babe Ruth with Graham McNamee. McNamee started with WEAF in New York and because of his voice and sports background was hired as announcer. He also announced the first World Series from New York's Polo Grounds.

Broadcast Pioneers Library

Baseball legend Babe Ruth made his first radio appearance on WWJ on January 31, 1922, while in Detroit for a vaudeville engagement at the Temple Theater.

Broadcast Pioneers Library

One of the pioneering women on the air, Marie Neff, started on NBC Chicago in 1927 and was NBC's Chicago women's editor from 1928 to 1932.

Broadcast Pioneer s Library

Pete Bontsema and his Hotel Tuller Orchestra. Pete is the second from right (1923).

Broadcast Pioneers Library

Starting out as The Jap O Lac Twins, they later became known as Al & Pete (Al Cameron and Peter Bontsema).

Broadcast Pioneers Library

A story told by author Eric Barnouw says a former employee went to Thomas Edison (left) to borrow a phonograph for a broadcast. Edison later asked that WJZ stop using it, saying: "If the phonograph sounded like that in every room, nobody would ever buy it." When the phonograph was returned, Edison sketched a circuit and gave it to the lad. Back at the station, engineers studied it, resulting in a circuit breakthrough for radio.

Broadcast Pioneers Library

The devices used in the early days of radio broadcasting to create sound effects were very basic. Some blew horns, another rolled a ball against a pair of tenpins, shown here with artist Ernest Hare. Still, the public took odd background noises as part of the program and enjoyed them thoroughly.

Associated Press

An early NBC microphone.

Associated Press

One of the first well-known radio singers on the West Coast, Peggy Champan was heard from NBC San Francisco in 1928.

Pacific Pioneers Library

Matt Gravenhors was one of the early NBC Orchestra directors.

Pacific Pioneers Library

The Merry Milkmen, heard on Boston's WEEI in the early '20s.

Broadcast Pioneers Library

A portrait of the young entrepreneur and founder of The Columbia Broadcasting System (CBS). William S. Paley discovered the power of radio when purchasing time on WCAU, Philadelphia, in 1927 for his father's cigar company. With a loan from his dad, he purchased United Independent Radio Stations, a chain of 16 failing radio stations. It was reborn as The Columbia Broadcasting System.

Broadcast Pioneers Library

The KGO players sang regularly on KGO, San Francisco.

Pacific Pioneers Library

Vaudeville team Burns and Foran on WEEI, broadcasting their dance routine.

Broadcast Pioneers Library

Joe White, The Silver Masked Tenor, and WEAF announcer Phillips Carlin with the Goodrich Silvertown Orchestra. Carlin was also studio director at WEAF, New York.

Broadcast Pioneers Library

The Gold Spot Pals, an early NBC radio equivalent to *The Little Rascals*, starred Graham McNamee and was sponsored by Graton & Knight Leather.

Broadcast Pioneers Library

NBC Red's Dork Quartet: Harry Stanton, Ben Klassen, Everett Foster and Myron Neisley.

Pacific Pioneers Library

In the early '20s a trend developed to name acts and programs after sponsors. The Cliquot Club Eskimos were named for Cliquot Club Ginger Ale. Director Harry Reser, banjo in hand, required the band to perform in their winter parkas — even on hot summer days.

Broadcast Pioneers Library

For some unknown reason, Hawaiian music was considered THE thing to play in the early days of radio. Something about the vibrating tones of steel guitars came across well on the air. Shown are Al Davis and the WKAV, Laconia, New Hampshire, Hawaiian Boys: (standing l-r) Charles Shastany, Anncr; Clint Elkins and Walter Varrel. (sitting) Ed Coulburn, William Blake, Al Davis and Jim Penmore.

Broadcast Pioneers Library

Whitings Grade A Entertainers at WEEI, Boston.

Broadcast Pioneers Library

Comedy teams, a lot of patter and moth-eaten jokes, and music that shattered the airwaves helped fill up hours of programming in the early days of radio. Then came a surge in novelties, and the radio listeners got an earful of the bizarre. A ladies band was considered an unusual feature, and the Melody Belles here blared and thumped away, to the amusement of listeners.

Associated Press

Entertainers in the early days of radio felt a need to entertain in costume, even though there was often no live audience. Sponsored by Neapolitan Ice Cream on WEEI, this 1925 photo shows the Neapolitan dutch girls.

Broadcast Pioneers Library

Freeman Gosden (Amos, left) and Charles Correll (Andy, right) pictured during their early years in broadcasting on Chicago's WGN as Sam and Henry. They changed their names a year later when the show was picked up by the red network and became a national hit. Theirs was the first nightly program to be continually broadcast (circa 1928).

Associated Press

Referring to themselves as "dispensers of information" were KMTR Hollywood's 8 Ball, played by Vol James, and Charlie Lung, played by B.C. Davey. During this early period, blackfaced whites and pretend Orientals gained popularity across America, reinforcing negative stereotypes.

Pacific Pioneers Library

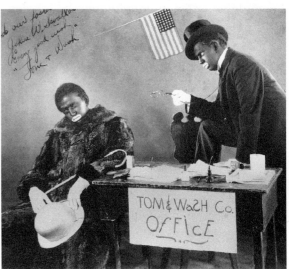

Early minstrel act Tom and Wash. Tom was Tom Breneman, who later went on to national fame with *Breakfast at Sardi's*.

Pacific Pioneers Library

A pioneer in radio entertainment, NBC San Francisco's Dapper Max Dolin.

Pacific Pioneers Library

Tom Breneman of Tom and Wash became most well-known for his program *Breakfast at Sardi's*, which was eventually renamed *Breakfast in Hollywood*. Breneman's show ran nationally from 1941 until 1948, when he died suddenly at age 47.

Pacific Pioneers Library

WTAT, Boston, uses a converted firetruck for its live broadcast onboard a ship.

Broadcast Pioneers Library

KOA Rocky Mountain Broadcasting Station
GENERAL ELECTRIC COMPANY

OPENING PROGRAM
MONDAY EVENING, DECEMBER 15, 1924
EIGHT O'CLOCK
(323 Meters)

PART I.

1. Band Selection, "Star Spangled Banner" - - - - Key
   PUBLIC SERVICE COMPANY OF COLORADO SAXAPHONE BAND
   Guy B. Hopkins, Director

2. Invocation
   CHAPLAIN ERNEST W. WOOD
   Fort Logan, U. S. Army

3. Instrumental Selection, "Kamennoi Ostrow—Op. 10" - - Rubinstein
   KOA ORCHESTRA

4. Address, "Education and the Modern Revolution"
   GEORGE NORLIN
   President of the University of Colorado

5. Violin Solo—Finale to Concerto in E Minor - - - - Mendelssohn
   HENRY TRUSTMAN GINSBURG
   MEYER CASTLE
   Accompanist

6. Address, "The Rocky Mountain Broadcasting Station"
   MARTIN P. RICE
   Manager of Broadcasting, General Electric Company

7. Band—Selections from the Opera "Faust" - - - - Gounod
   DENVER PUBLIC SERVICE SAXAPHONE BAND

8. Address
   HON. BENJAMIN F. STAPLETON
   Mayor of Denver

9. Instrumental Section—Reverie - - - - - - Vieuxtemps
   KOA ORCHESTRA

10. Address
    I. I. BOAK
    Denver Chamber of Commerce

11. Band Selection—"Entrance of the Gladiators" - - - - Sucike
    SAXAPHONE BAND

12. Address—"Electricity in the Development of the Rocky Mountain Region"
    ROBERT MILLER
    Acting District Manager, General Electric Company

13. Violin Solos—(a) Rondino on a theme - - - - - Beethoven
    (b) Waltz in A Major - - - - - Brahms
    HENRY TRUSTMAN GINSBURG

PART II.

Song Cycle—"In a Persian Garden" - - - - - - Liza Lehman
(Words Selected From the Rubaiyat of Omar Khayyam)
VIVIENNE PERRIN STEPHENS - - - Soprano
FLORENCE LAMONT HINMAN - - - Contralto
ROBERT H. EDWARDS - - - - Tenor
L. R. HINMAN - - - - - Baritone
R. H. MINTENER - - - - - Piano

A program for KOA Denver's opening program in December 1924.

Broadcast Pioneers Library

WLW, Cincinnati, became one of the innovators in radio due to the entrepreneurial spirit of owner Powel Crosley Jr., who built the station to sell radios. Crosley built the first and only 500,000-watt station in the United States, which operated with experimental authority. He is seen here (front, left) at a 1929 transmitter dedication.

Broadcast Pioneers Library

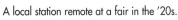

A local station remote at a fair in the '20s.

Broadcast Pioneers Library

KDKA programming entertains train passengers in 1925 as receiver sets were mounted in train cars.

Broadcast Pioneer Library

The wonder of radio was shown to Arctic Eskimo tribes on a 1925 expedition. Zenith Radio's founder, E.F. McDonald (standing right), listens as the Eskimos sing to audiences around the world on a special shortwave broadcast.

Radio Ink Collection

He may look like any ordinary door-to-door salesman, but this man, Admiral Donald B. MacMillan, is carrying the world's first portable radio (1924).

Radio Ink Collection

High buildings were used for tower sites in the early days of radio. This tower sits-atop Gimbels Brothers department store in 1924. Gimbels was also the first sponsor of entertainment programs to ever use radio. It was so forward-thinking that it built a studio on its top floor to feed WEAF in New York in 1923.

Associated Press

When the Zenith Electronics Corporation got into the business of owning radio stations, it added a unique twist — it made them mobile like Zenith radios. Chicago's WJAZ base studios were built in 1922 and the mobile unit in 1925.

Radio Ink Collection

One of radio's pioneer comedy teams, Al & Pete (Al Cameron and Peter Bontsema).

Broadcast Pioneers Library

An early ad for Zenith, which, interestingly, uses the same slogan today.

Radio Ink Collection

Vaudeville personalities Billy Jones & Ernest Hare were regularly featured on WEAF, New York, in 1923 and simply introduced as The Pioneer Comedian Team of Radio. Since direct advertising was not allowed at the time, an indirect approach was required, thus *The Happiness Boys*, a program sponsored by The Happiness Candy Stores. The boys were the first program on radio to take on the name of their sponsor.

Broadcast Pioneers Library

John Florence Sullivan, who later changed his name, took his vaudeville act on the road, where he met and fell in love with a chorus girl in 1922 and married her in 1928. The two, Fred Allen and Portland Hoffa, shared their careers the rest of their lives, becoming top stars on radio's *The Fred Allen Show.*

Broadcast Pioneers Library

Prior to his illustrious radio career, Jack Benny (right) had teamed up with pianist Lyman Woods doing vaudeville on the Orpheum circuit.

Broadcast Pioneer Library

Many radio performers started out as vaudevillians, including comedian Jack Benny (right) in 1925. Actor William Frawley is the man in the center; the man on the left is unidentified.

Associated Press

Sponsored by The Great Atlantic & Pacific Tea Company in 1923 on WEAF was *The A&P Gypsies*. Ed Thorgerson was the announcer for this early radio program. Ed was also one of the early sportscasters.

Broadcast Pioneers Library

Pioneer broadcaster Gilson Willets of WOC, who conceived *The Woman's Hour*, in December 1924.

Broadcast Pioneers Library

WEEI's Lewis Whitcomb interviews a guest in 1924.

Broadcast Pioneers Library

The Voice of Firestone, Franklyn Baur.

Broadcast Pioneers Library

Salvy Cavicchio, one of the early musical performers, originating from WEEI in 1925.

Broadcast Pioneers Library

Starting as *The Perfect Fool* on WJZ, Newark, in 1922, Ed Wynn later became *The Fire Chief* on NBC. Coming from the theater, Wynn was more of a visual comic than a radio comic, yet he pioneered comedy programming on radio. His program had huge ratings and he made an unprecedented $5,000 a week during the Depression. He also started his own radio network, which closed after less than a year of failure.

Broadcast Pioneers Library

New York Symphony conductor Walter Damrosch, seen here with General Electric's Martin P. Rice, was NBC's first musical conductor. He was ridiculed in the musical community for lowering himself to participate in radio broadcasts; however, he believed the medium would educate millions of youngsters in symphonic music, resulting in his creation of *The NBC Music Appreciation Hour.*

Broadcast Pioneers Library

Starting out as an announcer with Graham McNamee on WEAF, New York, in November 1923, Phillips Carlin was later to become an NBC executive and chief of sustaining shows.

Broadcast Pioneers Library

Radio detective Segmind Spaub on NBC.

Pacific Pioneers Library

Metropolitan Opera singer Anna Case, shown with NBC announcer Phillips Carlin, was the first singer to conduct a national broadcast on a link between KYW, Chicago; KDKA, Pittsburgh; WGY, Schenectady, and WEAF, New York. The broadcast originated from Carnegie Hall on June 7, 1923.

Broadcast Pioneers Library

Breaking ground in a new profession, that of announcer, was Carleton Dickerman, who pioneered the profession in 1926 on Boston's WEEI.

Broadcast Pioneers Library

C.B. Collins, known in the early days as *The Radio Janitor* at WEEI, Boston, one of the first stations in the Red Network.

Broadcast Pioneers Library

Boston's WEEI took an important place in radio history as one of the first stations in America. It launched many dramatic and comedy shows including *The Radio Janitor*, played by C.B. Collins.

Broadcast Pioneers Library

Dave Rubinoff directed the NBC Orchestra in its makeshift studios, the RKO soundstage and rehearsal hall, when the network first moved to Hollywood in 1929.

Pacific Pioneers Library

Marian Driscoll and Jim Jordan met and married in Peoria, Illinois, and went on to a lifetime of radio. After hearing a bad act on the radio in 1924, the Jordans wandered into their local station telling the management that they could do a better job than what they had just heard. They were hired on the spot. Playing many radio roles, they ended up with their own show, *Fibber McGee and Molly*, on NBC's Blue Network in 1935; it lasted until 1957.

Pacific Pioneers Library

Orchestra leader Glennhall Taylor and the first NBC dance orchestra in San Francisco in 1926.

Pacific Pioneers Library

When NBC first moved to Hollywood in 1929, it used the RKO soundstage for broadcasts while its studio was being built. Audiences look on during a broadcast of Rudy Vallee's *Fleischmann Hour*.

Pacific Pioneers Library

Gene Autry's *Melody Ranch* ran for 16 years on CBS, from 1940 to 1956. Starting in Tulsa in 1929 at KVOO radio, Autry eventually landed on the WLS *Barn Dance*, catapulting him to national fame as a cowboy singer.

Broadcast Pioneers Library

The Rhythm Boys sang with the Paul Whiteman band in the late 1920s on *The Old Gold-Paul Whiteman Hour*. The singing group spawned the career of crooner Bing Crosby. The original members were Crosby, Al Rinker and Harry Barris.

Associated Press

Columbia Broadcasting's WABC transmitter was on Columbia Island, a manmade concrete island in the middle of Long Island Sound. In order to get to the transmitter, the network employed the WABC Ferry.

Broadcast Pioneers Library

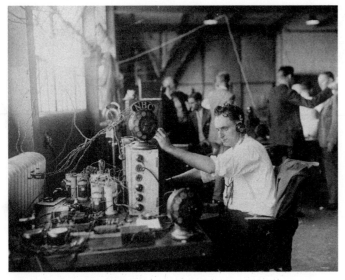

An NBC engineer concentrates on preparation for a broadcast.

Broadcast Pioneers Library

Columbia Island, manmade by Columbia for the transmission tower of WABC.

Broadcast Pioneers Library

TO MY DEAR FRIEND EDYTHE FROM Baby Rose Marie.

One of radio's first child stars, Baby Rose Marie, first sang at age three on NBC in 1926. She eventually was given her own 15-minute Sunday morning show on NBC's Blue Network in 1932. As she became more popular, the show gained more frequency, staying on the air through 1938. As an adult, she played Sally Rogers on TV's *The Dick Van Dyke Show.*

Broadcast Pioneers Library

On October 24, 1929, Marconi inaugurated wireless service between Spain and America. Seen here are Spain's King Alfonzo, General de Rivera, Marconi and his wife.

Associated Press

An NBC display at a Financial Advertisers Association Convention in Atlanta in 1929. The Crash occurred during the convention.

Broadcast Pioneers Library

Many radio stations would broadcast from high atop a hotel to draw in-person audiences and cover some of their expenses by selling admission. Broadcasting from atop the Hotel MacAlpin in New York are: (l-r) WMCA's A.C. Alexander, Jeff Sparks, Harry Mack and Del Ellwood.

Broadcast Pioneers Library

In the late 1920s, a remote broadcast was no easy feat, requiring loads of equipment and a couple of operators.

Broadcast Pioneers Library

Natty Max Dolin conducting the NBC Firestone Group in 1929 from the San Francisco studios.

Pacific Pioneers Library

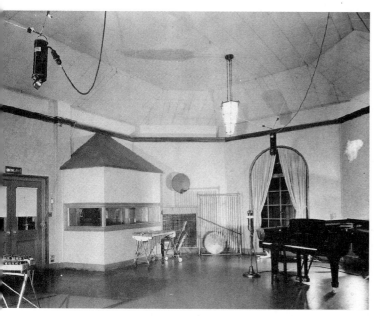

WABC Studios in New York (circa 1929). WABC was the flagship owned-and-operated radio station for CBS. The call letters were later changed to WCBS.

Broadcast Pioneers Library

Orchestra in close quarters to be heard by recording horn used before electrical microphones.

Radio Ink Collection

These lovely ladies posed by the latest in high-tech equipment at a radio show in 1927. This Zenith radio sold for about $800, very pricey for its day, yet every home wanted one. The radio was not only a form of entertainment but also a major piece of furniture — and usually the central focus of a room.

Radio Ink Collection

Without radios to listen to, broadcasting had little purpose. Hundreds of manufacturers saw opportunities to sell millions of radio sets. In 1926, Zenith created the first commercially produced set to operate on AC (alternating current), freeing consumers of cumbersome batteries.

Radio Ink Collection

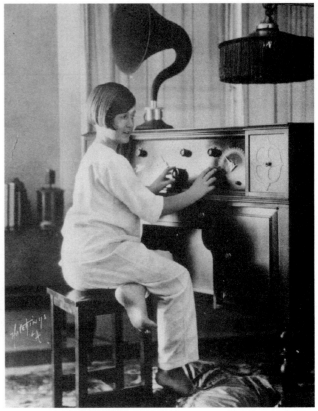

Perhaps the original giant boom-box, pulled by oxen at WLW studios.

Radio Ink Collection

"Was this the lady I seen (sic) you with last night?" With jokes like this, Weber and Fields established lasting fame in the vaudeville world. They performed on NBC's opening network show in 1926.

Associated Press

These newfangled devices called microphones were intimidating to even the most seasoned performers like Alice Brady. In order to eliminate the intimidation of the microphone, stations created lampshades to disguise them. Surely performers were fooled when told to speak into the lampshade (1926).

Broadcast Pioneers Library

WGY, Schenectady, in 1926 performing *Rip Van Winkle*. In this production, there were more sound effects people than actors.

Broadcast Pioneers Library

Singer Sally Rand and banjo player board a KFBI aircraft with the first portable remote equipment to broadcast from the air en route to San Francisco in 1927.

Pacific Pioneers Library

Updated WLW boom-box driven by flappers.

Radio Ink Collection

Opera singer Ruth Peter stands before a decorative microphone for a 1926 broadcast.

Broadcast Pioneers Library

A youthful Jack Benny.

Hearst Newspaper Collection; Special Collections; University of Southern California Library

Considered a superstar, Jessica Dragonette sang beautiful operatic arias on NBC's *Cities Service Concert* from 1927 to 1937, making guest appearances on other programs like *Show Boat* in 1932.

Broadcast Pioneers Library/Havrilla Collection

1930s

The Great Depression began with the stock market crash of 1929, which set the tone for the early '30s. America was without jobs and money. All unnecessary spending in the average household came to a halt — except radio.

Radio was booming in spite of the Depression. Perhaps it was because people could get their entertainment for free without purchasing tickets to the theater for a motion picture or a play. Perhaps the curiosity about radio and the momentum was so strong, nothing could kill it. If there was one purchase to be made, it was a radio set, something every home felt it had to have.

Yet, in 1931, listener boredom set in. America's top program, *Amos and Andy*, had seen its high water mark, and it began to lose listeners. Listener losses soon translated into revenue losses, which had to cease.

This sudden drop forced the networks to invent a new type of programming — the dramatic series. NBC looked to literature and film for

Married on January 7, 1926, vaudeville act George Burns and Gracie Allen were on vacation in England when asked to do a couple of days onstage and ended up doing their routine on the BBC (British Broadcasting Corporation), their first radio appearance. They returned to America and debuted on *The Eddie Cantor Show* and then on Rudy Vallee's *Fleischmann Hour*. Soon thereafter, CBS snatched them up for their own show.

Broadcast Pioneers Library

established characters, launching programs like *The Adventures of Sherlock Holmes* and *Rin-Tin-Tin Thrillers*. New forms of a dramatic series were created, incorporating romance, comedy, and mystery. This spawned programs like *The Eno Crime Clues, The Shadow, The First Nighter Program, With Canada's Mounted* and numerous others.

In spite of these efforts, radio listening declined. The only programs that seemed to survive were those featuring big-name established talent from the stage and the movies. *The Rudy Vallee Show* was one of the few that maintained huge success, built on the strength of its celebrity guests and Vallee himself.

The signal was clear. In order to keep the interest of advertisers, network executives had to get bigger talent in order to maintain listener interest in radio, so that's just what they did. Stars like

Live radio music with groups organized expressly for broadcasting on WWJ.
Broadcast Pioneers Library

Eddie Cantor and Ed Wynn were given their own programs. Radio saw a huge surge in popularity, with acts like George Burns and Gracie Allen, George Jessel, Fred Allen and Portland Hoffa, The Marx Brothers, Jack Benny, Mary Livingston, Eddie "Rochester" Anderson, Mel Blanc, Joe "Wanna Buy A Duck" Penner, Stoopnagle and Budd, and Jack Pearl.

Vaudevillians were given programs of their own, many of whom were great on stage but didn't seem likely to work on radio because of their visual acts. Yet radio grew with visual acts such as tap dancers, ventriloquists and even dog acts. Radio comedy soared in the '30s. In spite of its decline, *Amos and Andy* was so strong it became an industry unto itself, with candy bars, toys, comic books and phonograph records. They proved that comedy on the radio was appealing and set the stage for more comedy acts to fill the airwaves with laughter.

Leading the way was comedian Eddie Cantor, who held more than 50 percent of the listening audience. Comedy skits became the best way to keep the programs

Wendell Hall, known as the Red-headed Music Maker, broadcasts in the '30s from the announcing booth, with engineer Herb Tank at the controls.

Broadcast Pioneers Library

The WJW, Detroit, players are said to have introduced the concept of original dramas with use of sound effects. Pictured is the WWJ sound effects squad.

Broadcast Pioneers Library

interesting from week to week.

There were also those like Will Rogers and James Thurber who used humor in their philosophy and political commentary. Rogers especially liked to target President Roosevelt, "The Houdini of Hyde Park," and his New Deal for America. Along with the surge in comedy talent came

Pioneer sportscaster E.L. Tyson at WWJ, Detroit, with Edwin Boyes at the controls (1931).

Broadcast Pioneers Library

a vast array of talented singers like Al Jolson, Ruth Etting, Gertrude Niesen and Bing Crosby.

The craze for amateur programming began in 1934 with the introduction of *Major Bowes' Original Amateur Hour*. Talent scouts roamed America looking for the next big stars to come on the show to win prizes, and possibly fame. The show received 10,000 talent applications per week. It became one of the top shows but spawned very few national successes. One of those discovered was Frank Sinatra, who appeared with the Hoboken Four.

Before long the concept was airing on all the networks in one form or another and remained popular until about 1937, when quiz shows began to gain huge popularity. They included *Professor Quiz, Kay Kyser's Kollege of Musical Knowledge, Beat the Band, Spelling Bee, Cab Calloway's Quizzical, It Pays To Be Ignorant, Ben Bernie's Musical Quiz* and *Can You Top This? Pot o' Gold* became one of the highest-rated quiz shows because of its huge cash prizes.

The '30s began a new age for radio, which now offered a huge variety of programs ranging from quiz shows and news programs to soap operas, melodramas, Westerns and detective shows. Radio became the great escape from the problems of the Depression.

The demand for radio programming was high. Some of the hottest shows were the dramatic programs like *True Romances* and *Redbook True Story*. Additionally, the romantic comedies like *The First Nighter Program, Real Folks, Grand Central Station* and *Curtain Time* became popular.

But Hollywood still held the biggest fascination with

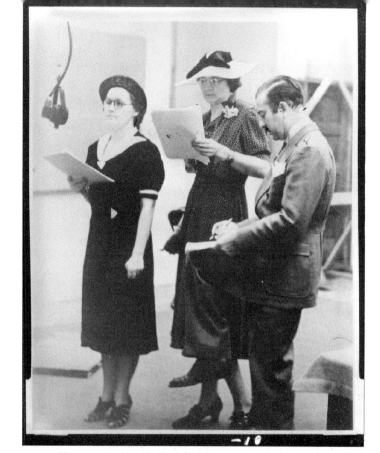

A rare *Fibber McGee and Molly* shot from the early days of the program.
CBS

Amos 'n' Andy.
Broadcast Pioneers Library

WGNY BREAKFAST CLUB OFFICIALS

Local programming tried its best to keep up with the networks. Pictured is a local morning show, *The WGNY Breakfast Club*, starring The Swamie, The President and Chatterbox.

Broadcast Pioneers Library

Starting as a regular on *Show Boat*, young, good-looking tenor Lanny Ross was elevated to a major star in less than a year. He also played on *The Packard Hour* and was a major vocalist on *Your Hit Parade* (1932).

Broadcast Pioneers Library

One of the first studios for The Columbia Broadcasting System.

Broadcast Pioneers Library

An early photo showing an all-female band on NBC.

Broadcast Pioneers Library

the public, and the big-name talent brought the biggest audiences. Shows like *Hollywood Hotel, Talkie Picture Time* and *D.W. Griffith's Hollywood* were huge. Each incorporated major talent or gossip about Hollywood's biggest stars. Hedda Hopper, Louella Parsons, Jimmy Fidler and Walter Winchell satisfied an appetite for information and gossip about Hollywood.

Perhaps the biggest and best-known program to incorporate Hollywood's biggest stars was *Lux Radio Theatre*. The program re-enacted dramatic scripts using Hollywood's top names, like Cary Grant, Clark Gable, Humphrey Bogart, James Cagney, Jimmy Stewart, Katharine Hepburn, Helen Hayes, Myrna Loy, Claudette Colbert and hundreds of others. The show was directed by legendary film director Cecil B. DeMille.

After the success of *Lux Radio Theatre*, copycat programs like *Warner Academy Theater, Cavalcade of America, Silver Theatre* and *The Screen Guild Theatre* emerged. None was as successful as the originator of the concept.

Silent film star Irene Rich's career began to fade when sound came into vogue, so she attempted a career in, of all things, radio. Starring in *The Irene Rich Dramas*, she started on the NBC Blue network in 1933 and kept the show on for 10 successful years with sidekick Gale Gordon.

Broadcast Pioneers Library

Serious drama also emerged in the '30s, with Shakespearean plays, Tolstoy and other literary works adapted for radio. This attracted a breed of high-brow theater actors and actresses who were often considered above doing films or radio. A breakthrough came in the mid-'20s when Ethyl Barrymore, one of the top stage actresses, took the forbidden step into a radio studio. This allowed stage players to consider radio acceptable, although most still shied away from the garish world of Hollywood films.

In 1936, *The Columbia Workshop* emerged as another important vehicle for serious works. CBS brought acclaimed writers like Dorothy Parker, Archibald MacLeish, James Thurber and others

Warren Sweeny became a prominent CBS announcer with long-running programs like *The FBI in Peace and War, Let's Pretend* and *Pet Milk's Saturday Night Serenade*. Sweeny is seen here as a local announcer on WJSV.

Broadcast Pioneers Library

Known as The Old Maestro, Ben Bernie had an interesting command of the English language that made his on-air patter appealing to radio listeners for years. Starting in 1923, he landed at WJZ, New York, in 1930 and on NBC by 1932. His career blossomed through the early '40s, when it all ended with a sudden illness which resulted in his early death.

Broadcast Pioneers Library

Early in 1933, the airwaves were filled with the combination of piano and organ music provided by this little known duet of Billie and Irene. Their program was simply called *Piano and Organ*.

Broadcast Pioneers Library

into radio, creating many radio classics.

One of the most memorable moments of *The Columbia Workshop* years was a young poet by the name of Norman Corwin. His captivating writing style exposed radio audiences to the classic arts of poetry and literature. He created many memorable radio plays, such as *The Plot To Overthrow Christmas* and *The Pursuit of Happiness*. Corwin emerged as the greatest radio director and writer of all time.

Perhaps the pinnacle of radio drama was the Halloween broad-

Radio was all the rage in the early '30s. People were looking for new ways to carry their radio set with them, in spite of all the wires needed. These flappers wore garter radios and hid the required wires and equipment under their coats.

cast of Orson Welles' *The War of the Worlds* on October 30, 1938, on *Mercury Theater*. His enactment of the H.G. Wells play sent fear through households across America, causing panic and hysteria. Even though disclaimers aired at the start and end of the program, people reacted to the supposed invasion. For months following the broadcast, Welles was chastised by the press for the re-creation.

The event took a third-rate program into the top ratings slot and elevated the young Welles to major star status. It also demonstrated the power of radio. After all, *Mercury Theater* was not a highly rated program, yet with the listeners it had, the broadcast caused a severe panic.

With the huge number of stations on the air in the '30s, many were left with programming voids if unable to affiliate with NBC's Red or Blue Networks (there was also an Orange and a White network from NBC), or with CBS.

This left openings for new entries, and in 1934 The Mutual Broadcasting Network was formed by pooling several large stations like WGN, Chicago; WXYZ, Detroit; WOR, New York, and WLW, Cincinnati, as sources for programming, along with the Don Lee Network on the West Coast. By 1938, Mutual already had secured 110 affiliates.

Even comedian Ed Wynn thought he could get into the act.

The Songbird of the South, Kate Smith, became a phenomenon in radio. She was so prominent that she and Jack Benny had the only non-cancelable contracts in radio, only breakable by war. Her rendition of Irving Berlin's *God Bless America* became so popular that there was a movement to make it the National Anthem.

Broadcast Pioneers Library

He founded his own network — Amalgamated Broadcast System — acquired 100 affiliates and was bankrupt nine months later.

In the meantime, CBS and NBC had become giants and names like NBC's David Sarnoff and CBS' William Paley were gold on Wall Street. NBC began building Radio City in the heart of New York and Hollywood, with new studios in Chicago, Cleveland, Detroit and several cities. CBS, too, broke ground for new facilities like Columbia Square in Hollywood, a massive facility to house West Coast network programming.

Control of programming content did not rest with the networks as much as the public believed. In reality, it was the advertisers pulling the strings. At least 33 percent of all radio programs were produced by advertising agencies, and talent contracts were

Vera Van, CBS house singer.

Broadcast Pioneers Library

often with the agencies themselves and not the networks.

Rudy Vallee, for instance, was an employee of J. Walter Thompson, the agency for Standard Brands. In fact, unemployed actors applied at the agencies, as did producers with new program concepts. Clearly, the sponsors had the power, ranging from script approval to guest stars and success or failure of a program, no matter how much the networks liked or disliked it.

In fact, radio premiums were invented to track listening. If a program or star could generate a lot of mail requesting the free premium, the program was considered highly rated.

Audience ratings first came on the scene in 1930, when WLW, Cincinnati, owner Powel Crosley created the C.A.B. (Cooperative Analysis of Broadcasting). The station telephoned listeners in 30 cities, asking them to name programs heard that day. Interestingly, the same simple ratings procedure is still used today.

The "Hoopers" created by C.E. Hooper became the standard starting in 1935 and maintained dominance until A.C. Nielsen bought the company out in 1949.

Actress Agnes Moorehead was the first lady among character actresses of the airwaves and one of the busiest radio actresses. She was a part of NBC Blue Network's first soap opera, *Betty and Bob*. Her other radio credits include *CBS Radio Mystery Theatre*, *Helen Hayes Theatre*, *The March of Time*, *Mercury Theatre of the Air*, *The Shadow*, *Suspense*, *Terry and the Pirates* and *This Is My Best*.   *Broadcast Pioneers Library*

Ratings afforded agencies information beyond asking listeners to mail in requests for premiums. They became the sole criteria by which programs were judged. Even the most popular programs were canceled if the ratings showed their popularity diminishing. About the only programs not sponsored and ratings-sensitive were educational programs, news programs and *The Columbia Workshop*.

For years, program commercialization was looked upon by some as downright inappropriate for the radio. At one time, the president created a commission to study the effects of commercials, and the effect of radio in general on the listening public. What they

The Boswell sisters were the first popular sisters trio on the radio, inspiring acts like The Andrews Sisters and The Pickens Sisters.

Broadcast Pioneers Library

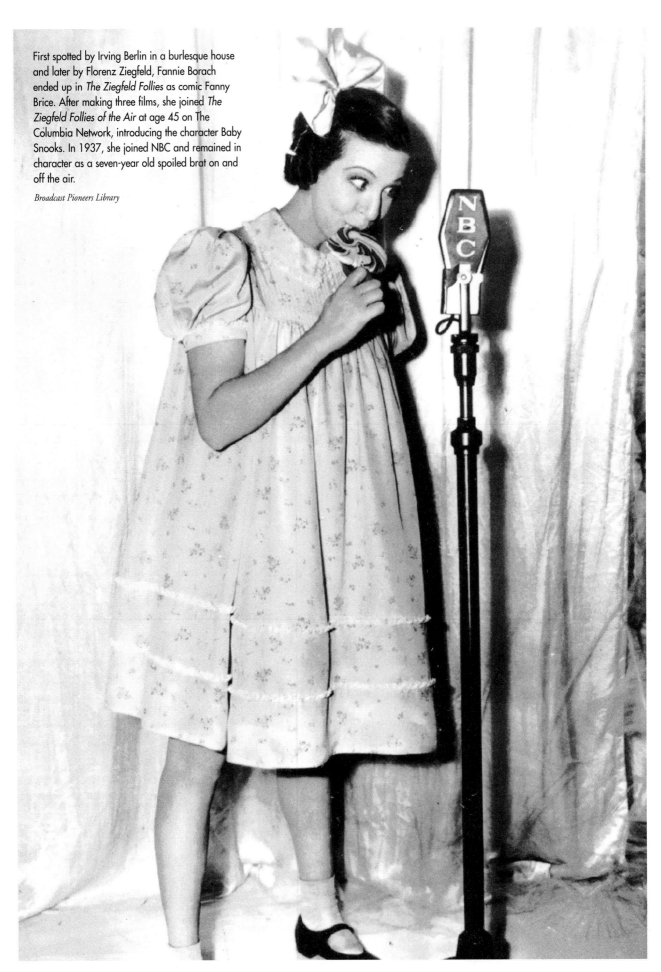

First spotted by Irving Berlin in a burlesque house and later by Florenz Ziegfeld, Fannie Borach ended up in *The Ziegfeld Follies* as comic Fanny Brice. After making three films, she joined *The Ziegfeld Follies of the Air* at age 45 on The Columbia Network, introducing the character Baby Snooks. In 1937, she joined NBC and remained in character as a seven-year old spoiled brat on and off the air.

Broadcast Pioneers Library

made its own stars who did not come from Broadway, Hollywood or vaudeville.

People like Kate Smith ("the Songbird of the South"), Fannie Brice and Arthur Godfrey were household names whose careers were made from radio.

Radio also elevated the spirits of America with music, and the end of the decade brought with it a new way of hearing music: the record. *Make Believe Ballroom,* invented in Los Angeles by Al Jarvis and perfected in New York by Martin Block, brought a way to hear variety without having the artists make live appearances. These programs gained vast popularity, and Jarvis and Block were immortalized as the first disc jockeys.

But music wasn't only coming from discs. A new form of music called "swing" had emerged as a nation jitterbugged across the dance floors of ballroom broadcasts. Bands like Tommy Dorsey, Duke Ellington, Benny Goodman and Glen Miller popularized programs like *Your Hit Parade.* These programs featured the biggest singing sensations, like Doris Day, Rosemary Clooney, Mel Torme, Bing

Lowell Thomas' broadcasts became so important that NBC placed two microphones before him to assure the broadcast went on if one mic failed (July 1934).

Broadcast Pioneers Library

found was an increase in interest in sports, enrollment in colleges with active sports teams with radio broadcasts and increased interest in the climates of California and Florida.

Most importantly, it was found that radio had improved communication to the American people, and had developed a national community of sorts. Most recognized was that radio listening had become the second-highest activity, second only to sleeping.

Toward the decade's end, radio no longer relied on bringing big stars to the radio dial to create radio listening; radio had

For decades every New Year's Eve, Guy Lombardo and his band would play *Auld Lang Syne,* so much so that it has remained the official rendition decades later. Guy Lombardo was one of the early orchestra directors on radio, first signed by CBS for *The Guy Lombardo Show.*

Broadcast Pioneers Library

Jimmy Durante, known for his trademark nose, started performing as a piano player in a bar where Eddie Cantor was waiting tables. Both ended up working together years later on *The Eddie Cantor Show.*

Broadcast Pioneers Library

Comedian Phil Baker entered radio as *The Armour Jester* in 1933 but eventually landed his own *The Phil Baker Show* on CBS in 1935. Seen here with actress Peggy Cartwright, Baker was also Quizmaster on *Take It Or Leave It*.

Broadcast Pioneers Library

Crosby and Frank Sinatra, playing the hits of the week.

For the first time in history, radio was having an enormous impact on record sales as teens and young adults flocked to record stores for the latest recordings.

Radio brought attention to Washington, and in return Washington realized the value of radio in the '30s. Franklin D. Roosevelt was said to have been elected because of his great radio speaking voice, while his opponent had a horrible radio presence.

FDR was *the* radio president. His was the first inauguration ever heard on radio. He understood the power of the medium, and he knew how to work it to his advantage, gaining support for his "New Deal." Roosevelt was the first president to regularly use radio when he introduced his *Fireside Chats*, each of which began with

the words: "My dear friends …"

The '30s also saw the beginning of the serious broadcast journalist, as newsmen Lowell Thomas, H.V. Kaltenborn, Gabriel Heatter and Graham McNamee described such events as the Hindenburg disaster, the abdication of Edward VIII, the kidnapping of Charles Lindbergh Jr., the election and re-election of FDR and the start of World War II. For the first time in history, people were able to hear a war unfold before their eyes as foreign correspondents gave detailed accounts of every move.

As the '30s were ending and the country was coming out of the throes of the Depression, radio was an important part of life. Radio had become the main form of entertainment in America, and other media were reacting.

Movie theaters had to schedule movies at different times so they would not start until the top radio shows were over; otherwise, they had empty theaters.

Newspapers, many of which also owned radio stations, were doing their best to bring the medium to its knees. They were in a difficult position, because they could bring readership to their papers by printing radio listening guides, yet

A WOWO/WGL sportscaster does play-by-play of a local high school basketball game.

Broadcast Pioneers Library

they were loosing advertising dollars to radio. The newspaper publishers association met for the express purpose of developing a strategy to lessen radio's competitive threat to the loss of advertising dollars, a banner they have carried with them to the present day.

In a short 20 years, radio became the most powerful advertis-

When you own the station, you can speak when you want. Here Heber J. Grant, president of the Mormon Church, delivers a radio address over Mormon-owned KSL. On the right is Richard L. Evans, who did *The Spoken Word* for the weekly CBS Mormon Tabernacle Choir broadcasts for 40 years (circa 1930).

Bonneville Collection

ing and selling vehicle in the world. The radio was the most important piece of furniture in the home, and for some the most expensive. Big, high-quality radio sets became a status symbol, some costing more than automobiles.

The social structure of America had changed as radio brought families around the radio for their news, music, comedy, drama and their children's education. Radio had become a lifestyle. 📻

Many stations in the 1930s had bands of their own. This is the KSL, Salt Lake City, band (circa 1938).

Bonneville Collection

WESTINGHOUSE NEWSPAPER ADVERTISEMENTS ATTRACTING ATTENTION IN NUMEROUS CITIES

Westinghouse merchandise will sell in proportion to its exposure to the public. Newspaper advertising offers an opportunity to get this exposure at very low cost per reader.

Newspaper mats have been distributed and are now available at all houses. Get your dealers to use the newspapers.

Detroit Times

38003   Friday, November 2, 1934

"When You Dial Europe What Will You Get?"

A Word to the Wise by S. E. LIND

We know of no greater thrill that men await modern man than to cut through the ether and actually listen to foreign broadcasts in native settings. But the quality and type of reception you get depends on careful selection, proper installation and service. I know that the new Westinghouse world-wide radio is an engineering triumph, and is ready to perform magic, but even the genuine skill of the manufacturer is not enough to overcome poor installation. Let S. E. Lind's experts advise you and take charge of your problem, and Mr. Lind will give you a written guarantee of satisfactory foreign reception. Lind's service means so much to thousands of Detroiters, they wouldn't think of buying a radio from any one else.

Let Lind's Experts Demonstrate the New

WESTINGHOUSE

The famous Westinghouse engineers have packed this handsome radio with dozens of advanced new features. Combined with Lind installation, this set will give you foreign and local reception such as has never been possible before . . . at only $69.50. This and all other Westinghouse models await your inspection at any of Lind's Stores.

Get Europe With This Beautiful Long and Short-Wave Radio

AT ONLY

$69⁵⁰

Liberal Trade-In for Your Old Radio

● **TERMS ARRANGED**

For You to Pay as Little as **$1⁰⁰** a week

Lind's

9221 Grand River at Joy Road
13905 E. Jefferson at Lakeview
6325 Fenkell at Livernois
ALL STORES OPEN EVENINGS

RADIOS   REFRIGERATORS   WASHERS   ELECTRICAL APPLIANCES   GAS STOVES

Protect Your Radio Profits
WITH
Westinghouse

Cash in on the Growing Popularity of the New All-Wave Features
PRICED TO SPEED SALES

Whether you sell the Console All-Wave, the table All-Wave, or one of the smaller dual-wave or standard reception sets, you'll find there's a profit in it for you. Favorable retail prices on the full Westinghouse line are set to bring them wide popularity—and yet will make a sure profit for the dealer. Selective distribution and a controlled production schedule assure the continuance of an established price structure. Add to these reasons the tremendous public preference for Westinghouse products, and your answer should be to "Tune in with Westinghouse."

Write for complete information

WESTINGHOUSE *the Pioneer in* **RADIO**

Distributed by
IRON CITY ELECTRIC CO.
575 Sixth Ave., Pittsburgh, Pa.   AT. 9100

Westinghouse WR24

STOP!
AND INVESTIGATE
Before you Buy any Radio..

Hear the Amazing New Westinghouse

MODEL WR-29

FINER WORLD WIDE RECEPTION!

With the newest innovations in radio engineering and design! 6 tubes that equal 9-tube performance. 7 tuned circuits. Airplane dial, 540 to 1600 kilocycles on standard broadcasts—5600 to 18,500 on Short Wave. Beautifully matched Walnut Veneer Console.

| NEW SELECTIVITY | SMARTER DESIGNS |

Here's the World's Greatest News in
WORLD WIDE RADIO RECEPTION

69⁵⁰
COMPLETE WITH RADIOTRONS

Tune in where you will—London, Madrid, Honolulu, South America—Westinghouse, the pioneer in radio, brings the world right into your living room! Radio's most amazing radio—the marvel of all who hear it — power, range, tone, and beauty, together in the highest perfected form FOR THE FIRST TIME!

Be Sure to see it in the store of your nearest Westinghouse Dealer. Hear it. Operate any Westinghouse Radio yourself. You will be convinced that it is the best radio "purchase" that you can make, backed by a company the world respects.

Price Range From $19.95 to $1

WR 22 Dual Wave "Mighty Midget" Standard and Short Wave Reception.
31⁹⁵
Complete With Radiotrons

Proof from PHILADELPHIA RECORD, A Fighting Newspaper for Fighting Advertisers

Westinghouse
ELECTRIC SUPPLY COMPANY
Distributors
11TH AND RACE STREETS :: PHILADELPHIA
BALTIMORE   WASHINGTON   RICHMOND   READING
ALLENTOWN   YORK   WILMINGTON
EVERY HOUSE NEEDS WESTINGHOUSE

These 1934 Westinghouse advertising slicks were provided to dealers for use in local newspapers. Interesting how the first radio company used newspapers to promote the sale of radios.

Radio Ink Collection

Humorist Will Rogers pioneered radio entertainment. He first appeared on WEAF New York's *Eveready Hour* in 1923, had his own program, *The Gulf Show*, on NBC's Blue Network in April 1930 and was part of *The Ziegfeld Follies of the Air* in 1932. He was known for taking stabs at Congress, politicians and the president, but he did it in a gentlemanly, poking-fun way. Rogers was killed August 15,1935, with Wiley Post when their private aircraft crashed in Alaska.

Broadcast Pioneers Library

The original Radio City speaker's studio at NBC in 1933.

Broadcast Pioneers Library

The 1931 Chicago studios of NBC.

Broadcast Pioneers Library

NBC and RCA's World's Fair building in Chicago (1933-34).

Broadcast Pioneers Library

The sleek, streamlined lobby of NBC's fresh new Hollywood and Vine studios.

Broadcast Pioneers Library

A rare 1932 photo of Jim and Marian Jordan, who first played *Smackout,* a grocer who was "smack out" of groceries. This show's name was changed to *Fibber McGee and Molly* in 1935 when it went national.

Broadcast Pioneers Library

Once newspapers realized the impact of radio, they refused to allow newscasters to read from the newspapers. Many networks began gathering their own news. As a result, Lowell Thomas became extremely successful because of his clout and influence on the air, scooping both the other networks and the newspapers.

Associated Press

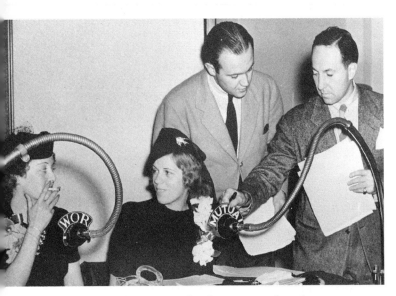

The Mutual Broadcasting Network and WOR New York's Radre Harris interviews actress Bette Davis (left). Dick Willard and Jeff Sparks assist.

Broadcast Pioneers Library

The Pertussin Playboys, one of the early acts heard singing on The Columbia Broadcasting Network (December 22, 1930).

Broadcast Pioneers Library

Peggy Lou Snyder played her first stage role in her actress-mother's arms, and spent her whole life on the stage. Traveling with the Orpheum vaudeville circuit as Harriet Hilliard, she met bandleader Ozzie Nelson, joined his band as a girl singer, married him on October 8, 1935, and eventually began *The Adventures of Ozzie and Harriet.*

Broadcast Pioneers Library

Telling stories of life in Grinders Switch, Tennessee, comedienne Minnie Pearl (Sarah Ophelia Colley Cannon) became an institution on *The Grand Ole Opry,* which ran on NBC and originated from WSM, Nashville. "Hoowww-dee, I'm just glad to be here" was her trademark opening. The program may be the second-longest continuously running radio show (after The Metropolitan Opera broadcasts) starting on November 28, 1925, and still on to this day.

Broadcast Pioneers Library

The Pickens Sisters: Jane, Helen and Patty, a popular NBC act in the mid-'30s, set the stage for the popularity of singing sister acts like The Andrews Sisters, The King Sisters and others. Sister Jane went on to appear as a solo vocalist on many programs (circa 1935).

Broadcast Pioneers Library

On October 8, 1933, *The Joe Penner Show* debuted on CBS after Penner was a huge success on *The Rudy Vallee Show*. The zany comedian became known for his phrase "Wanna buy a duck?" which had audiences in stitches every time he slipped it in. When he left the Vallee show, he earned $500 a week. With his own show, his salary went to $7,500 a week, one of the highest salaries in radio.

Broadcast Pioneers Library

Jack Benny (left) is seen at the mic during a party held by NBC to honor his success. Judging by the looks of the faces of Niles Trommel, his wife and Frank Freeman, Benny's words must have caught their attention.

Pacific Pioneers Library

In Our Opinion, broadcast every Sunday on WJR, Detroit, was a cracker barrel discussion from the General Store at Greenfield Village. Pictured: Judge Dewitt Merrian, George Cuishing, William Coughlin, Michael Butler, Eddie Guest and Lawrence Smith.

Broadcast Pioneers Library

America's Town Meeting of the Air broadcast from New York's Town Hall on ABC to discuss the topic: How we can get and keep good teachers in our schools. Shown are Rose Russell of the teachers' union, moderator George V. Denny Jr. and The Quiz Kids: Jack Rooney, Lonnie Lunde, Joel Kupperman and Naomi Cooks. The show aired at 9:30 p.m. on Thursdays, starting in 1935.

Associated Press

Bing Crosby and friends: (l-r) Carrol Pearson, Buddy Twiss, Bing and Swallow (1935).

Pacific Pioneers Library

Young and dapper, Robert Young had a phenomenal career in radio, with roles in the top programs like *Lux Radio Theatre*, *Suspense*, *Hollywood Startime*, *Good News of 1938* and several Norman Corwin features, which were considered the best radio had to offer. Young became best known for his role on *Father Knows Best*, which started in August 1949 and ran on radio through 1954. To his right are Sam Hayes and "Swallow."

Pacific Pioneers Library

WBZ, Boston, sets up an emergency broadcast station at the Portsmouth Navy Yard during a submarine tragedy. WBZ's F.M. Sloan stands to the left.

Broadcast Pioneers Library

Carved from a piece of pine wood by a carpenter named Theodore Mac for 35 bucks, Charlie McCarthy was eventually insured for $10,000 by partner Edgar Bergen, a pre-med student at Northwestern University who used ventriloquism to work his way through college. The team was first heard on the radio in 1936 and later became radio's No. 1 act.

Pacific Pioneers Library

Kaltenmeyer's Kindergarten ran on the NBC Blue Network from 1932 to 1940. It starred Jim and Marian Jordan, who later gained fame as *Fibber McGee and Molly*. (l-r): Bruce Kamman as Professor August Kaltenmeyer D.U.N. (Doctor of Utter Nonsense), Thor Ericson as Yohnny Yohnson, Marian Jordan as Gertie Glump, Merrill Fugit as Percy Van Schuyler, Jim Jordan as Mickey Donovan and Johnny Wolf as Izzy Finkelstein.

Broadcast Pioneers Library

A CBS group shot that includes Ann Miller, Nan Grey, John Boles and Red Barry.

CBS

Chester Lauck and Norris Goff showed up at an audition to do their blackface act, but when they arrived they found a room full of Amos and Andy wannabes, so they quickly shed their makeup and invented a skit as two hillbillies. They got the job and were on the air at KTHS in Hot Springs, Arkansas, only to take their show, *Lum and Abner*, national by 1931.

Broadcast Pioneers Library

Singing his heart out on CBS' *Roadways to Romance* is Mark Wavnon, with conductor Jerry Cooper.

Broadcast Pioneers Library

Lowell Thomas started his career in 1930 as a substitute for Floyd Gibbons, becoming one of America's most respected newscasters. Thomas, known for his travel adventures, founded the *Tall Tale Club*, a feature of his nightly program.

Associated Press

George M. Cohan (center) heard on WWJ, Detroit, in 1936 when interviewed by WWJ pioneer George Stark (left).

Broadcast Pioneers Library

WENR, Chicago, became a pivotal station for NBC because of the talent pool available in Chicago to build the network resources. As a result, Chicago became a major center for network broadcast origination. Seen here is the cast of one of the weekly playlets on the station.

Broadcast Pioneers Library

Americans were fascinated with broadcasting. WHAM, Rochester, takes advantage of the curiosity by conducting news broadcasts from the display window of a local department store.

Broadcast Pioneers Library

Franklin Roosevelt preferred to stand while doing broadcasts. Because he was stricken with polio, he had this special broadcast stand constructed.

Broadcast Pioneers Library

Premiering on CBS in 1931, *Myrt and Marge* was one of the first serial programs. This promotion piece shows the original cast.

Broadcast Pioneers Library

Fred Waring and his Pennsylvanians on The Old Gold Hour. Waring maintained a successful 20-year radio career, partly because of the size of his orchestra and its phenomenal sound. Although it was the most expensive orchestra on the radio, it was considered the best and was always on one of the major networks.

Broadcast Pioneers Library

Originating from KOA, Denver, *Light of the West* presented a dramatization of Western history (1935).

Broadcast Pioneers Library

Radio served its purpose well during an infantile paralysis epidemic that required kids to stay away from school for long periods. These Chicago youngsters got their lessons at home listening to the radio.

Broadcast Pioneers Library

Although radio bands were common, having female band leaders was not. Pictured is the Nellie Revell Band, which made numerous radio appearances.

Broadcast Pioneers Library

Thousands of country music artists made the trip to Nashville hoping to be discovered and put on *The Grand Ole Opry*. Roy Acuff and The Smoky Mountain Boys were rejected three years in a row before becoming a part of the show. Acuff became *The Opry*'s biggest star (1938).

Broadcast Pioneers Library

NBC broadcasts directly from scene of an Evansville, Indiana, flood in 1937.

Broadcast Pioneers Library

Hordes of people stand in line to get into the Peru Theater in Chicago to see WLS radio stars Al and Pete and Bill Childs (January 19, 1932).

Broadcast Pioneers Library

People pack the Rio Theater in Chicago to see WLS radio stars Gene Autry, Mac and Bob, The Prairie Ramblers, The Stranger Patsy and Montana Girls of the Golden West.

Broadcast Pioneers Library

Edward Reese played Dean on
CBS' *Eno Crime Clues*, a 15-minute
thriller in 1932.

Broadcast Pioneers Library

The Southern Harmony Four originating in 1937 from the NBC San Francisco studios: (l-r) Saunders King,
Eugene Anderson, Alvin Nurse and William Barber.

Pacific Pioneers Library

Dave Garroway worked with KDKA Pittsburgh from
1938 to 1940. He is seen here interviewing a river-
boat captain.

Broadcast Pioneers Library

The KDKA Band in the late '30s in the KDKA showcase studios.

Broadcast Pioneers Library

KDKA's transmitter in Saxonburg, Pennsylvania, in 1936.

Broadcast Pioneers Library

In 1935, Jimmy Durante scored his first regular part on *Jumbo*, an NBC show about the circus. Prior to performing in radio, Durante was the owner of Club Durant with Eddie Cantor, until prohibition agents closed it down. Much later, he was paired on *The Camel Show* with Garry Moore, whom he had never met before. Their on-air chemistry was so powerful that they ended up with their own show.

Broadcast Pioneers Library

Disguised as renditions of opening nights of Broadway plays, *First Nighter* actually originated from WMAQ in Chicago, although NBC said it was coming from The Little Theatre Off Times Square. Charles P. Hughes was the first host of the program, which began during the Depression in 1930.

Broadcast Pioneers Library

The growth of Marconi's wireless business depended on frequent travel between North America and England. This frequent cruising led to a later passion for yachting.

Hearst Newspaper Collection; Special Collections; University of Southern California Library

George Burns (left) wore a serious expression as he emerged from federal court in New York City after pleading guilty to a charge of smuggling. He was accused of receiving articles from N. Chaperau, previously indicted on smuggling charges (December 12, 1938).

Associated Press

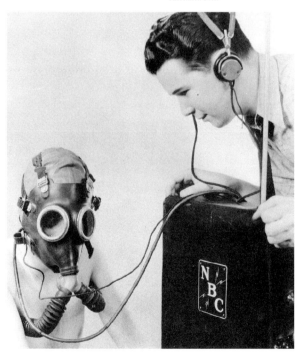

One of the most popular programs, which started on WEAF, New York, in 1923, was *The Eveready Hour* and a feature called Galapagos, which told the story of explorer William Beebe's trip to the Galapagos Islands. An engineer is preparing an underwater microphone apparatus for another Beebe Expedition to run on NBC in 1934.

Broadcast Pioneers Library

A KSL, Salt Lake City, remote broadcasting and amplification truck.

Broadcast Pioneers Library

They may look like devices from a submarine, but these are some very unusual early microphones Jerry Hoffman and Delores Del Rio are singing into. In the background, Harry Jackson conducts his orchestra with Russ Columbo looking on.

Pacific Pioneers Library

Sen. Guglielmo Marconi inaugurated a series of American short-wave broadcasts to the United States from Rome radio stations on October 29, 1934. He also gave an auricular demonstration of his latest invention, designed to guide ships safely into harbor through fog.

Associated Press

Sen. Guglielmo Marconi at the installation of the radio at the Vatican.

Associated Press

On the occasion of the 10th anniversary of the Fascist March on Rome, which was celebrated in Rome on October 16, 1932, Sen. Marconi broadcast to the nation from the Academy D'Italia. On the left, the famous Pietro Mascagni, who conducted the music in connection with the broadcast.

Associated Press

NBC is there for the maiden voyage of the amazing Hindenburg on May 25, 1936. She was the world's first trans-Atlantic commercial airliner, was 804 feet long, had a maximum diameter of 135 feet and was kept aloft by 7,000,000 cubic feet of hydrogen. Four 1,050-hp Daimler-Benz diesel engines provided a top speed of 82 mph.

Broadcast Pioneers Library

"Oh, the humanity" was the emotional cry heard around the world as NBC newsman Herbert Morrison described the Hindenburg exploding as it landed in Lakehurst, New Jersey, on May 6, 1937, almost a year after its maiden voyage. As the dirigible went down, millions listened to the blow-by-blow account of one of the most memorable events in radio news.

Broadcast Pioneers Library

Following the crash of the Hindenburg, the scope of the wreckage is described by NBC.

Broadcast Pioneers Library

A rehearsal for the cast of *The Goldbergs*, a program focused around the life of Jewish immigrant Molly Goldberg, her husband, Jake, and their kids. The show started in 1929 and aired, on and off, through 1945.

Broadcast Pioneers Library

Actress Dorothy Gish helps WWJ, Detroit, celebrate its 16th birthday in 1936. She is seen sitting at the original transmitter.

Broadcast Pioneers Library

Dale Evans was a regular on *The Jack Carson Show* as a singer. She is seen here with an interested visitor, Charlie McCarthy. Evans eventually married Roy Rogers.

Pacific Pioneers Library

Originating from WMAQ, Chicago, the dramatic series *The Story of Mary Marlin* first starred Joan Blaine (seated) in 1934.

Broadcast Pioneers Library

Tom Mix and The Ranch Boys: Shorty Carso, Curley Bradley, Jack Ross, Gene Arnold and Larry Larson. The Tom Mix Ralston Straightshooters started in 1933 from NBC in Chicago.

Broadcast Pioneers Library

Presidential candidate Wendell Wilkie with CBS director of talk Helen Sioussat.

Broadcast Pioneers Library

Making music on board a fast-moving train during a KOA, Denver, broadcast. And the point would be — ?

Broadcast Pioneers Library

The Revelers Quartet was one of the first singing groups heard on the networks, starting on *The Eveready Hour* on WEAF, the first toll station and first network link. Throughout the years, they were heard on programs like *The Cities Service Concert* on NBC, *The Harvest of Stars* and *The Gulf Show* on the Blue Network.

Broadcast Pioneers Library

The Last of the Red Hot Mamas, Sophie Tucker, sang on *Good News of 1938*, which was hyped as one of the biggest radio shows ever produced. Unfortunately, even with its star power, the program never lived up to the hype. Tucker also graced programs like *The Radio Hall of Fame* and *Your All-Time Hit Parade* on NBC in 1943.

Broadcast Pioneers Library

Massive studios that would house entire orchestras were common at radio stations across America. KSL, Salt Lake City, was no exception (circa 1938).

Bonneville Collection

When conductor Phil Spitalny started a search to put together an all-girl orchestra, people thought he had gone off the deep end at a time when a woman's place was in the home. He persisted with auditions in cities across America. Once the orchestra was together, he had difficulty soliciting sponsor interest because they assumed an all-girl orchestra would be substandard. Starting on CBS on January 3, 1935, *The Hour of Charm* was a huge success, and sponsors were no longer a problem.

Broadcast Pioneers Library

Broadcasting live from the Missouri State Legislature is a young Paul Harvey (1937).

ABC

Known to millions as Vic Cook on *Vic and Sade*, Arthur Van Harvey was first heard on NBC's Blue Network in 1932. He originated from Chicago.

Broadcast Pioneers Library

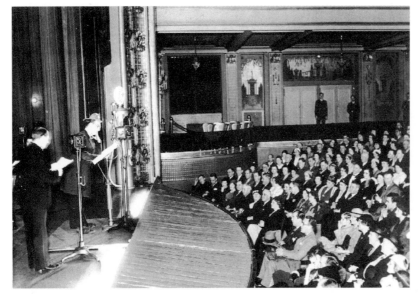

Ed Wynn as *The Fire Chief* with Graham McNamee in the 1930s, before NBC moved out of its Times Square Studio in New York.

Broadcast Pioneers Library

One of the great early announcers of radio, Norman Brokenshire was the original announcer for *The Theatre Guild on the Air* (1932 photo).

Broadcast Pioneers Library

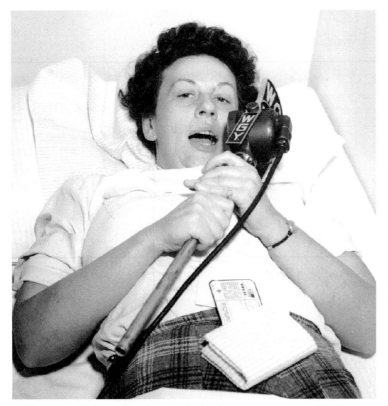

Local radio stations have always been involved in their communities. Here WGY's Martha Brooks was one of the first blood donors at the opening of the Schenectady Blood Donor Center, from which a special broadcast was made.

Broadcast Pioneers Library

A regular on *The Eddie Cantor Show* in the 1930s, comedian George Jessel played the male defender role in a group discussion about women's issues in *Leave It to the Girls*, a 1945 Mutual program. Jessel was also a singer.

Broadcast Pioneers Library

Trained as a singer for the concert stage in England, Leslie Townes Hope changed his name to Bob after ridicule from classmates when his family moved to the U.S. in 1907. His first stage name was Packy East, and his stage was the boxing ring, where he became a Golden Gloves finalist. After a stint in vaudeville as a blackface minstrel tap dancer, Hope began doing standup comedy and rose to the top of the vaudeville circuit. His radio debut came January 4, 1935, in *The Intimate Revue* on NBC's Blue Network.

Broadcast Pioneers Library

One of the regulars on NBC's *Lum and Abner* in the mid-'30s, Andy Devine went on to numerous radio parts, especially Westerns, including a role on *Wild Bill Hickock* in 1951.

Broadcast Pioneers Library

William Bucky Harris (left) of the Washington Senators with William E. Coyle of WMAL, Washington.

Broadcast Pioneers Library

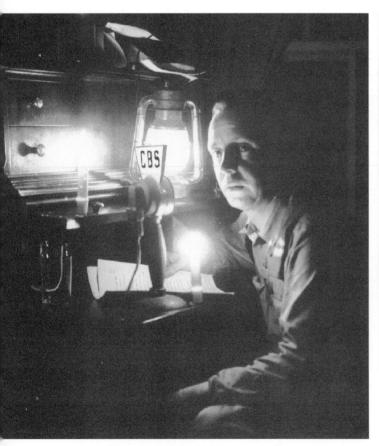

Broadcasting by the light of a lantern, CBS radio announcer John Daly brings news of a Texas hurricane to a nationwide audience.

Broadcast Pioneers Library

Ukulele player and singer Phil Cook became known as The Quaker Oats Man (his sponsor) on *The Phil Cook Show* on the Blue Network in the 1930s.

Broadcast Pioneers Library

WXYZ Detroit's Eddie Chase.

Broadcast Pioneers Library

Paul Carson was the organist on *One Man's Family* from April 1932 until May 1951, almost 20 years. The organ was an integral part of building drama and transitions in soap operas.

Broadcast Pioneers Library

Featured as a regular on *The Rudy Vallee Show*, Irving Caesar sang songs about safety, gaining national popularity and becoming the brunt of many a joke.

Broadcast Pioneers Library

Orchestra leader Shep Fields was heard coast-to-coast with his *Rippling Rhythm Music* originating from Chicago's WGN. He also directed the orchestra on *The Woodbury Soap Hour* for Bob Hope in the 1930s.

Broadcast Pioneers Library

Designed as a warm-up show leading into *The Grand Ole Opry*, hillbilly Judy Canova (Julia Etta) actually had higher ratings. Like many stars, Canova was discovered by Rudy Vallee and had her own show on CBS by 1943. In 1944, she moved to NBC, and *The Judy Canova Show* ran through 1953.

Broadcast Pioneers Library

NBC Orchestra leader Rudy Neumar (circa 1930).

Broadcast Pioneers Library

With a career launched on *The Ed Sullivan Show* and *Ziegfeld Follies of the Air*, Jack Pearl ended up with his own show, sponsored by Lucky Strike. Pearl was popularized by his dialect comedy, pretending to be Baron Munchausen, a German baron. His program was in the Top 10 for two years, starting in 1933. It then slipped and he spent until 1948 trying to return to the success he once had.

Broadcast Pioneers Library

Soap opera writer Irma Phillips pioneered the use of an organ to flow from scene to scene, and also created the cliffhanger. She wrote and created *The Guiding Light*, *Today's Children*, *Woman in White*, *The Brighter Day*, *Lonely Women*, *Masquerade*, *The Right to Happiness* and *Road of Life*.

Broadcast Pioneers Library

Eleanor Powell was frequently heard on the radio in the '30s.

Broadcast Pioneers Library

The remote control originated as a chairside unit in Philco's model LX. The signal was said to "spear across the room" (March 1,1933).

Associated Press

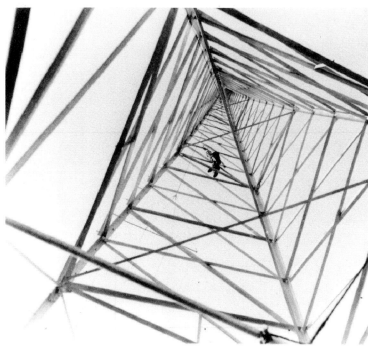

Free-standing towers were popping up across America. An engineer from KHJ, Los Angeles, climbs inside the station's new tower (circa 1930).

Hearst Newspaper Collection; Special Collections; University of Southern California Library

Actresses Aileen Pringle, Marion Davies and Benita Hume appear on a *Lux Radio Theatre* program in the summer of 1935, a year after the dramatic show's inauguration on the air.

Associated Press

Clark Gable and Claudette Colbert appear before the microphone in a *Lux Radio Theatre* show, *It Happened One Night*, in March 1939.

Associated Press

George Burns once said that he could give Gracie a straight line and she could ad lib for hours without him saying another word.

Pacific Pioneers Library

War of the Worlds director Orson Welles is bombarded by reporters' questions about his broadcast, which caused panic throughout America (October 31, 1938).

Associated Press

Seen here appearing on NBC's *The Magic Key*, singer Ruth Etting was also on NBC Red Network's *Music That Satisfies* in 1932, and was a pioneer singer on radio.

Pacific Pioneers Library

After two years on the air, Hollywood gossip reporter Jimmy Fidler was given his own show in 1934 on the NBC Blue Network. Many considered him the most feared man in Hollywood because of his blatantly opinionated reviews of films and shows. This overt frankness created problems for his own program, putting him at constant odds with network heads. During his reign he worked for NBC, ABC, CBS and Mutual. He is seen here with Dorothy Lee.

Pacific Pioneers Library

Playing roles on radio was an active part of Loretta Young's career, starting on CBS' *Silver Theatre* in 1937. She appeared on many theatrical radio productions through the late '40s.

Pacific Pioneers Library

Radio star Edgar Bergen wearing his toupee.

Pacific Pioneers Library

Caught outside the NBC studio door, Rudy Vallee (left) and John U. Reber.

Pacific Pioneers Library

After a tough try at making it in vaudeville, Red Skelton appeared on *The Rudy Vallee Show* in August 1937. In 1941, NBC gave Red his own show, and within two years he had the second-highest-rated show in America. He went on to become one of the biggest radio and television stars of all time.

Pacific Pioneers Library

New York Post columnist Franklin Pierce Adams on NBC's *Information Please*, the intellectual quiz show that ran on Tuesday nights on the Blue Network in 1938.

Broadcast Pioneers Library

A national NBC broadcast from Garden of the Gods, in Colorado Springs, on Easter Sunday, 1939.

Broadcast Pioneers Library

Crowds gather on December 15, 1934, at the new downtown studios for the flipping of the switch on KOA's new 50,000-watt transmitter.

Broadcast Pioneers Library

The 1936 dedication of Will Rogers' Memorial Shrine to the Sun at Cheyenne Mountain, near Colorado Springs, broadcast live on KOA, Denver.

Broadcast Pioneers Library

September 3, 1939, an NBC Red Network radio lounge outside a special radio auditorium constructed at the San Francisco Fair.

Broadcast Pioneers Library

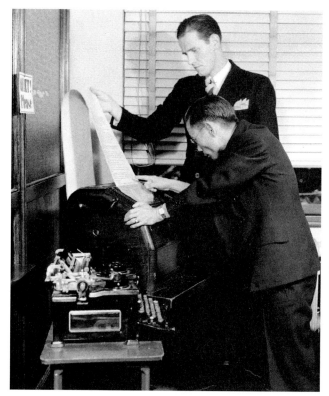

As the opening goes — With his faithful valet Kato (Raymond Hayashi), Britt Reid (Al Hodge), daring young publisher, matches wits with the underworld, risking his life that criminals and racketeers within the law may feel its weight by the sting of *The Green Hornet*!

Broadcast Pioneers Library

The Green Hornet (played by Al Hodge) catches a bad guy. The mystery-adventure show originated on WXYZ in Detroit from George W. Trendle, the same man who originated *The Lone Ranger*. The show ran from 1936 to 1952.

Broadcast Pioneers Library

Lenore Case (Lee Allman) and lazy reporter Michael Axford (Jim Irwin) of *The Green Hornet*.

Broadcast Pioneers Library

Britt Reid's secretary, Lenore Case, played by Lee Allman on *The Green Hornet*.

Broadcast Pioneers Library

Carlton E. Morse created the program *One Man's Family*, wrote most of the scripts and directed most episodes. It debuted on three NBC West Coast stations on April 29, 1932, at 9 p.m. Pacific time and went nationwide on May 17, 1933. It had the distinction of being the first serial to originate from San Francisco. There were 3,256 episodes in total, running through May 8, 1959, making it the longest-running radio serial.

Pacific Pioneers Library

Al Pearce as Elmer Blurp and Arlene Harris, the human chatterbox, on *Al Pearce and His Gang.*

Pacific Pioneers Library

Two of radio's biggest singing sensations, Bing Crosby and Frank Sinatra. Because of his jazz-like crooning style, Crosby was often referred to as a softer Sinatra.

Associated Press

Discovered as a member of The Hoboken Four, Frank Sinatra's radio debut came on Major Edward Bowes' *Original Amateur Hour* as a winning contestant in 1937. Sinatra mania began as the new superstar sang with the Harry James and Tommy Dorsey orchestras. Eventually, *The Frank Sinatra Show* made its debut on CBS on January 5, 1944. He was radio's hottest entertainer.

Associated Press

Marconi taking a stroll in the park.

Associated Press

Morton Downey was so popular he received 90,000 letters a week. He first sang on the radio in England at the BBC and landed *The Camel Quarter Hour* in 1931. Although known as The Irish Troubadour, Downey was born and lived in Wallingford, Connecticut.

Pacific Pioneers Library

One of radio's most-recognized voices, Ted Husing announced for many radio programs, including *Burns and Allen*, *The March of Time*, *Saturday Night Swing Club* and *The True Story Hour With Mary and Bob*. He is known by many as the greatest sportscaster of all time.

CBS

One of the first network singing stars, Singin' Sam The Barbasol man, played by Harry Frankel, had his first network program on CBS in 1930. He was known for singing: "Barbasol. Barbasol. No Brush, no Lather, no-rub in. Wet your razor, then begin." (1937).

Pacific Pioneers Library

Preparing for a full-length stage play on the radio are Ethel Barrymore and Walter Hampden (right), starring in *The Servant in the House* on WWJ, Detroit, in 1936. Wynn Wright (left) was the director.

Broadcast Pioneers Library

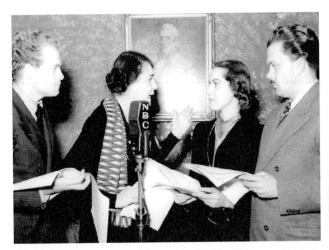

The True Story Hour recreated drama from *True Story Magazine* in 1937. Shown: (l-r) Van Heflin, Mrs. Wm. Faversham, Violet Gatley and Eric Rolf.

Broadcast Pioneers Library

Nigel Bruce was Dr. Watson and Basil Rathbone played the role of Sherlock Holmes on the NBC Blue Network in October 1939. During the show's 25 years, nine other sets of actors played Holmes and Watson.

Broadcast Pioneers Library

Inspired by New York crimebuster (and eventual presidential candidate) Thomas Dewey, *Mr. District Attorney* aired on the NBC Red Network in 1939 for 15 minutes each weeknight.

Broadcast Pioneers Library

Log Cabin was heard on NBC in 1938 and starred: (l-r) Warren Hull, Virginia Verrill, Jack Haley and Wendy Barrie.

Broadcast Pioneers Library

A June 15, 1936, *Lux Radio Theatre* broadcast of burlesque featuring Ruby Keeler and Al Jolson.

Broadcast Pioneers Library

Perhaps the most legendary of all radio dramas, *The Lone Ranger* captivated the hearts of every kid in America between 1930 and 1955. During the show's 25 years, The Lone Ranger was played by five different actors. Pictured is Earl Grasser, later killed in an auto accident.

Broadcast Pioneers Library

NBC comedian Frank Fay in 1936.

Broadcast Pioneers Library

NBC rapidly outgrew this studio because of the number of programs originating from Hollywood.

Hearst Newspaper Collection; Special Collections; University of Southern California Library

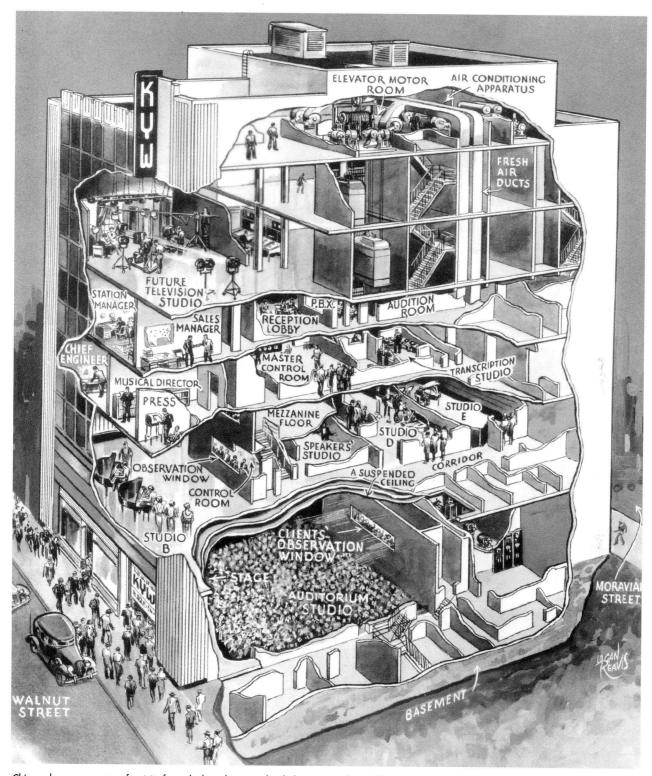

Labels within illustration:

KYW

ELEVATOR MOTOR ROOM
AIR CONDITIONING APPARATUS
FRESH AIR DUCTS
FUTURE TELEVISION STUDIO
STATION MANAGER
SALES MANAGER
P.B.X.
RECEPTION LOBBY
AUDITION ROOM
CHIEF ENGINEER
MUSICAL DIRECTOR
PRESS
MASTER CONTROL ROOM
TRANSCRIPTION STUDIO
STUDIO E
MEZZANINE FLOOR
SPEAKERS' STUDIO
STUDIO D
CORRIDOR
OBSERVATION WINDOW
A SUSPENDED CEILING
CONTROL ROOM
STUDIO B
CLIENTS' OBSERVATION WINDOW
STAGE
AUDITORIUM STUDIO
KYW
BASEMENT
WALNUT STREET
MORAVIAN STREET
LOGAN REAVIS

Chicago became a center of activity for radio broadcasts, and with that came a demand for more studio space. This drawing shows the proposed KYW/NBC Red Network studios on Walnut Street in 1938.

Broadcast Pioneers Library

Radio was booming and the networks were making more money than ever imagined, resulting in palaces for network operations. This was the new NBC facility in Hollywood.

Hearst Newspaper Collection; Special Collections; University of Southern California Library

J.R. Popele, WOR's chief engineer, showing Alfred J. McCosker, then-president of WOR, the new dynamic mic, the latest in microphones in 1935. Displayed is an evolution of WOR microphones: (l-r) Telephone transmitter with megaphone (1922), Double Carbon Button (1923-1928), Improved Double Carbon and mounting (1928-1933), Condenser Mic with amp (1928-1933), Lapel mic (1932) and the dynamic (1933-1935).

Broadcast Pioneers Library

WGAR, Cleveland, welcomes its new competitor, WJW, with a WGAR remote the night before WJW's debut: William O'Neil (left) of WJW shakes hands with John Patt of WGAR.

Broadcast Pioneers Library

If you want to know what's going on in Washington, this promotional photo speaks volumes about the value of radio.

Broadcast Pioneers Library

This promotional radio photo shows the excitement and variety offered by radio.

Broadcast Pioneers Library

A dapper young CBS newsman Robert Trout describes the 1937 Park Avenue Easter Parade using a trick broadcasting cane.

Broadcast Pioneers Library

Lecturer H.V. Kaltenborn came to WEAF, New York, as a lecturer on current events and became one of the most important commentators in history. His criticism of government was felt in Washington and often began the process that led to change.

Broadcast Pioneers Library

Vincent Price and Marta Abba celebrate Shakespeare's birthday over CBS.

Broadcast Pioneers Library

This promo piece from a radio manufacturer demonstrates what radio can bring to your home.

Broadcast Pioneers Library

THE NATIONAL BROADCASTING COMPANY

Presents

ARTURO TOSCANINI

Conducting the

NBC SYMPHONY ORCHESTRA

SATURDAY, NOVEMBER 25, 1939
10:00 to 11:30 P.M., EST.
In NBC Studio 8-H, Radio City

All-Beethoven Program

Overture, "Leonore," No. 1, Opus 138

* * *

Symphony No. 8, in F Major, Opus 93

I. Allegro vivace e con brio
II. Allegretto scherzando
III. Tempo di Menuetto
IV. Allegro vivace

Intermission

Two Movements from String Quartet in F Major, Opus 135

(a) Lento assai, cantante e tranquillo
(b) Vivace

* * *

Two Excerpts from the Ballet, "Die Geschöpfe des Prometheus" ("The Creatures of Prometheus"), Opus 43

(a) Adagio
(b) Allegretto

* * *

Overture, "Leonore," No. 2, Opus 72

The program for an NBC Symphony broadcast from November 25, 1939.

Radio Ink Collection

FDR speaking into a WQAM, Miami, mic just seconds before an assassination attempt by Guiseppe Zangara in Bayfront Park, Miami. FDR survived, but his friend Mayor Cermack of Chicago was killed (February 15, 1933).

Broadcast Pioneers Library

The 1932 Columbia election coverage team.

Broadcast Pioneers Library

CBS election coverage at WABC. A Morse code operator at the extreme right gathers bulletins from around the nation.

Broadcast Pioneers Library

A radio set design for upcoming NBC election coverage, including studios for the Red and Blue Networks of NBC.

Broadcast Pioneers Library

First Lady Eleanor Roosevelt was no stranger to radio — that is, after hiring a coach (Alan Funt of *Candid Camera* fame) to help her become more comfortable. She frequently did sponsored commentaries on NBC, CBS and ABC, with fees going to charity. She had her own show, *It's A Woman's World*, on CBS in 1935, and did a show with daughter Anna Boettiger in 1948 and '49 called *Eleanor and Anna Roosevelt* (1937 photo).

Broadcast Pioneers Library

Stations went all-out to showcase their call letters to live audiences. KSL, Salt Lake City, had its call letters on bandstands in 1938.

Bonneville Collection

Film star W.C. Fields on WABC's *Columbia Radio Theatre*, which aired Mondays at 9 p.m. in 1938. Fields was often heard doing sketches on programs like *Your Hit Parade* and *The Edgar Bergen and Charlie McCarthy Show*.

Broadcast Pioneers Library

A WWI intelligence officer, Major Edward Bowes was a partner in the Capital Theater in New York, which began featuring live radio broadcasts of *Roxy and His Gang*. With the sudden departure of Roxy from the theater, Bowes started his own program, which eventually became *The Original Amateur Hour*. Each show opened with: "Around and around she goes and where she stops nobody knows." The show went national in 1935 on NBC. The program is best-known for discovering Frank Sinatra.

Broadcast Pioneers Library

Radio writer-director Orson Welles relaxes in his $600-a-month Brentwood home with a script. The 24-year-old director shocked the entertainment industry with his on-air exploits and roles (December 1939).

Associated Press

The front entrance of The Grant Building, home of the new KDKA studios.

Broadcast Pioneers Library

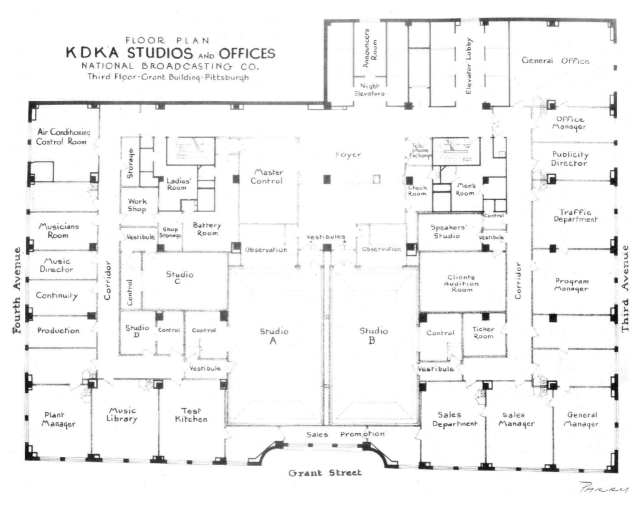

FLOOR PLAN
KDKA STUDIOS AND OFFICES
NATIONAL BROADCASTING CO.
Third Floor-Grant Building-Pittsburgh

The floor plan for new studios and offices at KDKA on the Grant Building's third floor.

Broadcast Pioneers Library

KDKA was proud of its heritage as a radio innovator and built state-of-the-art facilities, as reflected by this Master Control room.

Broadcast Pioneers Library

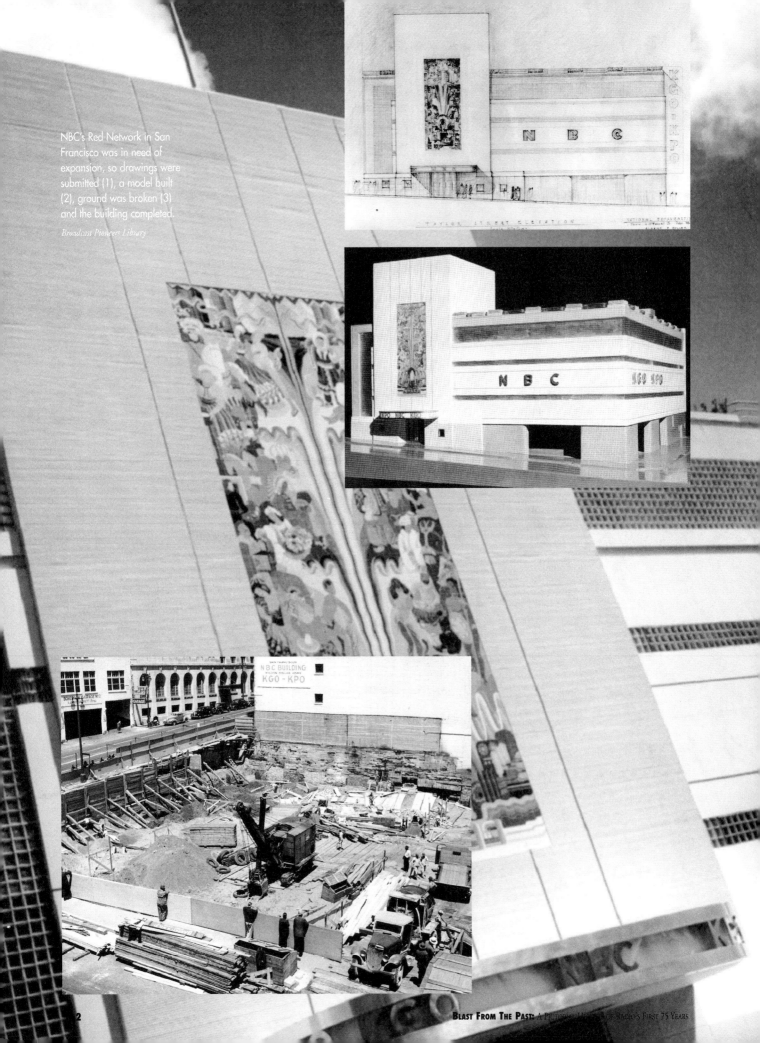

NBC's Red Network in San Francisco was in need of expansion, so drawings were submitted (1), a model built (2), ground was broken (3) and the building completed.

Broadcast Pioneers Library

Comedian Don Stuart on NBC, San Francisco.

Pacific Pioneers Library

After a failed year-long late show stint at NBC, Kate Smith landed on CBS on May 11, 1931, and stayed for close to 20 years. She started in theater but got out after she could no longer escape a rash of insensitive fat jokes. Initially scheduled against *Amos 'n' Andy*, America's highest-rated show, Smith had an impressive showing. She became a radio giant (excuse the pun).

Broadcast Pioneers Library

Little Miss Bab-O was played by child star Mary Small. The 15-minute music program aired on NBC Blue in 1934.

Broadcast Pioneers Library

America loved Kate Smith and her downhome Southern style. Not only could she capture America's heart in song, she also had a program called *Kate Smith Speaks* in which she conversed from her Park Avenue apartment.

Broadcast Pioneers Library

The Southernaires on NBC: soloist Lowell Peters, baritone Jay Stone Toney, bass William Edmondson, tenor Homer Smith and Clarence Jones.

Broadcast Pioneers Library

The Sinclair Minstrels, starring Mac McCloud, Joe Parsons, Bill Childs and Gene Arnold, the Interlocutor, ran on Monday nights in 1934 as *The Sinclair Minstrel Show*.

Broadcast Pioneers Library

Bill Stern got his first national break with sportstalk in *The Bill Stern Sports Review* on the NBC Blue Network in 1937. Stern developed a lively, entertaining style with his Colgate Sports newsreel, starting in 1939 and running until 1956.

Broadcast Pioneers Library

The Whitthall Anglo Persians on NBC for Whitthall Rug Co. of Worcester, Massachusetts. Their magic carpet never really took off.

Broadcast Pioneers Library

At age 11, Winifred Wolfe joined *One Man's Family* as Teddy and stayed with the show until her marriage in 1945 (photo 1937).

Broadcast Pioneers Library

The Vass family trio on NBC (1934).

Broadcast Pioneers

Ronald Reagan was one of the great radio orators. He started on WOC, Davenport, and WHO, Des Moines, as an announcer, then later became an actor. His speaking abilities got him elected head of the actors' union, then governor of California and finally president of the United States. In his first movie role he played a radio announcer.

Radio Ink Collection

Radio philosopher Tony Wons started his career at WLS, Chicago, in the 1920s. CBS then signed him for *Tony Wons' Scrapbook* from 1930 to 1934, when he moved to NBC's Blue Network. His poetry, humor and philosophy were also featured on *The Hallmark Show* in 1940 and '41. He once played Rip Van Winkle on WLS, acting out all the roles.

Broadcast Pioneers Library

Known as a jazz crooner on many musical programs, Mel Torme also played Joe Corntassel on *Little Orphan Annie*.

Broadcast Pioneers Library

Giving the OK signal, Jack Benny was probably feeling pretty good about the $2 million CBS gave him to jump ship at NBC in 1949. His show stayed on until 1955, with reruns till 1958.

Broadcast Pioneers Library

Because it was based in Hollywood and employed high-profile directors, *The Lux Radio Theatre* attracted Hollywood's finest to radio acting. Actor Humphrey Bogart made frequent radio appearances.

Broadcast Pioneers Library

Virginia Verrill was a cast member in radio's *Show Boat*, a variety show that ran on NBC in 1932.

Broadcast Pioneers Library

The *Jack Haley Show* ran on NBC in 1937 and CBS in '38 and '39. Haley is best remembered for his role as the Scarecrow in *The Wizard of Oz.*

Broadcast Pioneers Library

Morton Downey in 1931 on *The Camel Quarter Hour.*

Broadcast Pioneers Library

Actor Walter Pidgeon during a guest performance for Columbia's *Lux Radio Theatre.*

Broadcast Pioneers Library

Hollywood's top gossip, Hedda Hopper, was well-known for her hats, which could be described on her program but never seen. *The Hedda Hopper Show* was sponsored by Sunkist on CBS, starting in 1938.

Broadcast Pioneers Library

NBC's *Evelyn and Her Magic Violin* (a rare Bergonzi) on General Electric's *Hour of Charm* featured Phil Spitalny and his all-girl orchestra in 1938.

Broadcast Pioneers Library

Ray Lee Jackson

7668-16

The Nunn Bush Singers conduct a musical broadcast (circa 1930).

Broadcast Pioneers Library

WGY Schenectady's Stars of Tomorrow featured a clown and a local talent search.

Broadcast Pioneers Library

This young beauty, Sadie Marks, worked at The May Company in the hosiery department in 1926, when she met Jack Benny. They married a year later. She joined his program and became known as Mary Livingston. When Benny died in 1974, his will stated that a florist was to deliver roses to her every day for the rest of her life as a reminder of his love for her.

Broadcast Pioneers Library

1940s

Radio was well-established by 1940. The '40s were the last big hurrah for what was considered radio's Golden Era. As the decade dawned, a world war was being fought in Europe, and America was being dragged into it. As a result, the '40s are often referred to as The War Years in radio. Tremendous efforts went into the war effort, and radio led that charge with bond drives, entertainers enlisting or being drafted, and with special programs for the soldiers.

Programs like *Music for Millions*, *Treasury Star Parade* and *Millions for Defense* were scattered across the radio dial. For the first time in history, all the networks cooperated in an effort to produce star-filled programs that were sent via shortwave to "our boys overseas."

Radio was used to rally Americans behind the war effort for everything from collecting scrap metal to car pooling to selling war bonds and stamps. Program content often included war-related items from the start of the war through its end in 1945.

Born John Florence Sullivan in 1894, Fred Allen became one of the biggest radio stars of all time after starving in vaudeville. While in New York, he met and married Portland Hoffa, who became his sidekick on his CBS debut, on October 23, 1932, in the *Linit Bath Club Revue*.

Associated Press

Programs like *This Is War*, *An American in England* and *We Hold These Truths* were classics produced by Norman Corwin, whose prose evoked emotions throughout the country. Corwin, like others, went to the war zones and traveled the globe writing broadcasts about his experiences and recording the people and sounds he encountered.

Radio brought World War II into the living rooms for the first time. Every bomb, every march, every speech, every crisis,

Jack Benny admires a watch Phil Harris received as a going-away present, of course commenting that he'd never owned one because watches were so expensive. Benny's running gag was his miserly attitude.

Pacific Pioneers Library

every beat of the war was available on the radio.

Some historians believe radio is the reason America entered the war. Accounts by in-the-trenches newsmen like Edward R. Murrow, Eric Sevareid, William Shirer and Robert Trout made listeners aware of the atrocities going on in Europe, bringing those events into the lives of people who had never before experienced the sounds of war.

These correspondents risked their lives to bring the reality of war to the American public, which in turn put pressure on politicians to take action. Yet the networks and correspondents walked a thin line, trying to maintain objectivity prior to America's declaration of war.

According to author/historian J. Fred MacDonald, network policies prohibited any program from taking sides. Programs were not allowed to exhibit "sabotage, subversion or

spying in the United States." Instead, the networks devoted their efforts to waving the flag and building the patriotic spirit in America, to contrast with the fascist activities they were not to mention.

Unlike today, programming was audited to eliminate any hint of political prejudice. But one day changed everything in the United States and eliminated the policy of not taking sides.

On December 7, 1941, Pearl Harbor was attacked by the Japanese. It came to be characterized by President Roosevelt as "A Day That Will Live In Infamy." Within two days, Germany and Italy had declared war against America.

Programming began reflecting America's position immediately. Children's programming was filled with moral lessons about the war, and about things they could do to help. Kids were encouraged by their heroes to save electricity, gas, water, clothes and toys.

Heroes like Dick Tracy, Superman, The Green Hornet, Tom Mix and Jack Armstrong focused on the war effort with stories of spies, saboteurs and dissidents. Shows like *Hop Harrigan* and *Don Winslow of the Navy* were staged in the battlefields of the war.

Jack Benny entertains troops in 1943.

Pacific Pioneers Library

Like many entertainers who wanted to do their part in the war effort, Rudy Vallee was sworn into the service in WWII.

Pacific Pioneers Library

Jack Haley, Shirley Mitchell, Joan Davis and Verna Felton give Rudy Vallee (center) a sendoff as he heads off to the service in WWII.

Pacific Pioneers Library

Of course, opposition to the violence the kids were hearing fell upon deaf ears. For the adults, dramatic programs like *The Man Behind the Gun* entertained, as did variety shows like *The Stage Door Canteen* and *The Army Hour.*

The war also brought censorship by our government on what should and should not be aired on radio. The U.S. Office of Censorship believed that internal spies could gain valuable information from broadcasts. As a result, a wartime code was enforced, asking for "voluntary" censorship of news, foreign language programs, technology reports, war-related reports, casualty reports and even weather.

Although voluntary, these guidelines came with the strong suggestion that broadcasters did not want to test them. Some broadcasters suddenly found themselves cut off during such simple items as weather forecasts.

Additionally, broadcasters were requested to air government propaganda programming, and network executives and personalities were recruited to be a part of special advisory committees to coordinate government propaganda activities. Some prominent personalities like Jack Benny, Kay Kyser, George Burns, Nelson

Known simply as The Incomparable Hildegarde, this singer with the deep gravelly voice was a part of *Nine Men and a Girl* on CBS in 1939, and *Beat the Band* in 1940.

Broadcast Pioneers Library

Ol' Blue Eyes, Frank Sinatra, performing for servicemen at the Hollywood Canteen.

Broadcast Pioneers Library

Eddy and others were a part of these committees.

Radio had a promising future. No time had ever seen the involvement or listenership that radio saw in the '40s. New stars like Bob Hope, Abbott and Costello, Red Skelton and Edgar Bergen and his wooden dummy Charlie McCarthy had emerged as a new generation of entertainers took over the radio, making it stronger than ever.

Situation comedies like *Duffy's Tavern* and *The Adventures of Ozzie and Harriet* became popular, and shows like *Fibber McGee and Molly* remained strong.

As soldiers returned from the war, Americans moved into the

suburbs, a move that radio reflected with *Father Knows Best, My Favorite Husband, Those Websters, Blondie, The Life of Riley, Pepper Young's Family, Ma Perkins, The Aldrich Family, One Man's Family, A Date With Judy* and *The Great Gildersleeve.*

But with the end of the war came the introduction of new technology and new movement in radio, which had been held back during wartime. A new form of radio called Frequency Modulation was introduced to the networks as a possible future technology. This technology offered a cleaner sound and no static.

Although its inventor, Edwin H. Armstrong, had introduced this technology in the 1930s, it had been delayed because of the

During WWII, Americans were unable to purchase radio sets due to the war effort. Following the war, production of new radios set an all-time high. Here, Emerson is producing 3 million sets a year.

Associated Press

war efforts and by RCA's David Sarnoff, who did not want FM to upset the established AM world. Sarnoff was able to keep it at a distance for years, but by 1945 Armstrong managed to get the first experimental FM on the air in Alpine, New Jersey. Soon, other FMs were on the air throughout the United States.

Another technology that had not been embraced by the networks due to the war effort was television; however, once the war was over, it took higher priority. Had WWII not occurred, television would have been launched five years earlier. But television was considered by some to be a flash in the pan, a technology that could not surpass radio, so many continued to ignore it.

The networks' strength was enormous. NBC's Red and Blue Networks continued to generate massive profits. However, in the mid-'40s, the Federal Communications Commission and the U.S. Supreme Court ordered NBC to divest itself of one of its networks

because competition was being stifled.

The Blue Network was sold to the owner of Lifesavers Candy Company, Edward Noble, who named the network the American

During WWII, KDKA became an important part of war effort fund-raising, collecting more than $1 million at this rally and more than $6 million in total.

Broadcast Pioneers Library

Broadcasting Company (ABC). With his $8 million purchase, he acquired 200 affiliates and three owned-and-operated stations.

The mid-'40s also brought another new wave in the radio industry: a lack of direction. Following all the excitement and intensity of the war, listening levels began to drop off. The programs and entertainment that once worked so well to captivate audiences were no longer as effective. Soldiers had returned from the war only to hear programs that were on before they left, with nothing new.

Radio has played an important part in religion since KDKA went on the air. On the program *Hymns of All Churches* in 1943, Dr. Roy Ross reads a citation for 10 years of meritorious service by NBC.

Broadcast Pioneers Library

Radio was willing to try anything to reinvent itself. Programmers searched for fresh ideas and visited old ideas with a new twist. Political talk shows surfaced, due to the awareness generated by the war. *Meet the Press*, *Our Foreign Policy* and *Capitol Cloakroom* became somewhat popular for a while. Quiz shows remained popular. CBS's William Paley saw the need for star power and managed to woo most of the major personalities to his network from NBC and ABC, bringing Jack Benny, Amos and Andy, Red Skelton, Burns and Allen, Edgar Bergen and Charlie McCarthy, Bing Crosby and Groucho Marx.

By 1949, CBS was winning the ratings battle with all but four of the programs in the top 20. NBC, on the other hand, was struggling with an ad revenue loss of $7 million. Advertisers were dropping off the networks for no apparent reason, and the networks responded with a rash of new creativity and new programming.

The big problem was television. Although TV had been announced in April 1930, TV sets weren't available until 1938.

But World War II had stopped what little progress television was making. Research and television manufacturing had come to a stop to concentrate on building military equipment.

The KDKA logo commemorating the 25th anniversary of radio and KDKA.

Broadcast Pioneers Library

Playing the role of a sexy schoolteacher on *Our Miss Brooks*, Eve Arden spent nine years as the star of one of radio's top comedy shows.

Broadcast Pioneers Library

Once the war was over, radio with pictures began to get noticed. Radio personalities saw the value of the medium and recreated their programs on television. By 1948, a majority of the big radio personalities had been on television or had abandoned radio altogether.

The only thing that slowed the movement was the lack of

Together for WGN's *Chicago Theatre of the Air* are Bret Morrison (bottom), Barbara Luddy and Willard Waterman. Each went on to fame in radio, Morrison as *The Shadow*, Waterman as *The Great Gildersleeve* and Luddy on *Lonely Women*.

Pacific Pioneers Library

Barbara Stanwyck and Robert Taylor guest on *The Family Hour of Stars* on CBS.

Pacific Pioneers Library

Dennis Day and Verna Felton, who played his mother on *The Jack Benny Show*.

Pacific Pioneers Library

The war effort and the morale of our boys in uniform became a major part of the lives of radio stars. Eddie Cantor and Dinah Shore took their *Time To Smile* show on the road to broadcast from different Army camps.

Pacific Pioneers Library

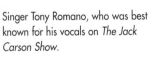

Singer Tony Romano, who was best known for his vocals on *The Jack Carson Show*.

Pacific Pioneers Library

Bill Brennan, producer of *The Jack Smith Show* goes over the script with guest Sue Raney on CBS in 1945.

Pacific Pioneers Library

facilities transmitting television. Most only existed in the big cities like New York and Los Angeles, but that all changed rapidly. In 1948, CBS executive Hubbell Robinson Jr. declared: "Television is about to do to radio what the Sioux did to Custer. There is going to be a massacre."

Radio networks were in a quandary. Were they to put their dollars into saving radio or into providing programming for television?

The answer was obvious, and at the end of the '40s radio began dying a quick, agonizing death. Stations were on their own again, vying for survival without much hope from the networks. Nine out of ten stations were resorting to local talent with deejay programs.

Localism was the only hope for radio, and being in the radio business in 1949 seemed pretty grim. ◼

Alice Reinheart played "Chichi" for eight years on the soap *Life Can Be Beautiful*. She also held major roles in NBC's *The Woman in My House* and *The Abbot Mysteries*.

Pacific Pioneers Library

The king of daytime radio, Tom Breneman and his *Breakfast in Hollywood* became a national phenomenon, heard on more than 220 stations, twice as many as Hope and Benny. The show had 20 million listeners and in 1941 was the most popular daytime show in radio. Needless to say, it was no problem getting stars like young Orson Welles to visit the show.

Pacific Pioneers Library

In spite of more than 800 letters of listener protests, Peg Lynch, author and lead role on *Ethyl and Albert*, kept actor Alan Bunce in the role of Albert when actor Richard Widmark left to pursue film roles. The show started in Minnesota in 1938 and came to ABC in 1944.

Pacific Pioneers Library

Making her national radio debut in 1944 on *The Chase and Sanborn Hour*, 14 year old soprano Jane Powell was often wooed by wooden dummy Charlie McCarthy. Powell went on to be a frequent guest on many musical programs and variety shows, including *The Railroad Hour*.

Pacific Pioneers Library

Leaving on a trip from Los Angeles to New York, Fred Allen carried a gift from Jack Benny.

Pacific Pioneers Library

Campbell's Soup sponsored *The Jack Carson Show* when it first came on the air in June 1943. Carson had previous involvement with *The Sealtest Village Store* and *The Signal Carnival*.

Pacific Pioneers Library

The Great Gildersleeve Hal Peary (left) goes belly to belly with the old goat Judge Horace Hooker, played by Earle Ross.

Pacific Pioneers Library

Tennessee Ernie Ford frequently brought his boyish country charm and Tennessee accent to radio.

Pacific Pioneers Library

Paul Whiteman was getting all the attention at this luncheon, flanked by Dema Harshbarger and Hedda Hopper. Whiteman was one of the leading radio orchestra leaders at the time.

Pacific Pioneers Library

Funnyman Fred Allen reading a script from *Allen's Alley*, a regular feature on his program. Allen would take a stroll down the imaginary street and speak with characters who lived in various tenements, farmhouses and mansions.

Broadcast Pioneers Library

A caricature featuring Fred Allen and the regulars on his program. *The Fred Allen Show.*

Broadcast Pioneers Library

Jack Benny tries his hand at a bigger sound than his violin.

Hearst Newspaper Collection; Special Collections; University of Southern California Library

Radio star Jack Benny hurries past reporters for a court appearance following a charge of smuggling.

Hearst Newspaper Collection; Special Collections; University of Southern California Library

A favorite pastime for millions, a longshoreman passes time with his radio at 42nd Street and Fifth Avenue in New York City (January 29, 1947).

Associated Press

Often called the "man of a thousand sounds," Mel Blanc is shown here during a *Burns and Allen* broadcast. Postman Blanc reads his script as Gracie Allen (left) and George Burns look on (March 1946).

Associated Press

One of the first women to direct radio was NBC's Nancy Osgood, producer of *Consumer Time*. She also played a dramatic role in *Lone Journey* on NBC in the '40s.

Broadcast Pioneers Library

CBS News Correspondent Edward R. Murrow (left) with three of his wartime colleagues in Europe: (l-r) Murrow, Paul Manning, John Daly (who became head of ABC news and moderator of *What's My Line*) and Robert Trout (circa 1945).

Associated Press

It wasn't enough being one of the top radio stars. Freeman Gosden, the Amos of *Amos 'n' Andy*, just couldn't stay away from radio, the medium he loved so much. In his spare time, Gosden was an enthusiastic "ham." He spent hours chatting with other shortwave fans all over the world from his Beverly HIlls, California, home. Gosden is shown here at 49 years old (December 29, 1948).

Associated Press

Mutual's *Meet the Press* often featured controversial figures. This September 1949 broadcast from Washington featured Lycurgis Spinks, Imperial Emperor of the Knights of the Ku Klux Klan. With him are producer Martha Roundtree and moderator (center) Albert Warner (September 2, 1949).

Associated Press

Audience participation was the key to *Kay Kyser's Kollege of Musical Knowledge*. Kyser is shown here with an unidentified participant who croons a tune (January 17, 1949).

Associated Press

Before the show, staff members would have fun with the audience for ABC's *Kay Kyser's Kollege of Musical Knowledge* (January 17, 1949).

Associated Press

Kay Kyser dressed the part of professor for every broadcast of *Kay Kyser's Kollege of Musical Knowledge*.

Pacific Pioneers Library

Announcer Charles Park awaits a cue on Detroit's WJR in 1948.

Broadcast Pioneers Library

Bringing The Power of Positive Thinking to radio, Dr. Norman Vincent Peale was active on the air throughout his life. He was also one of the founders of the National Lone Ranger Council of Honor, which was designed to encourage America's youth to adhere to the principles of good citizenship and clean living.

Broadcast Pioneers Library

This is the "Aldrich Family": (l-r) Jackie Kelk, who played Homer Brown, Ezra Stone (Henry Aldrich); Katherine Raht (Mrs. Aldrich) and House Jameson (Mr. Aldrich) (circa 1947).

Associated Press

Ed and Pegeen Fitzgerald started the trend of husband and wife morning shows in New York on WOR in 1940.
The Fitzgeralds was done on location from their East 36th Street house with no script. They eventually defected to WJZ and the ABC Network.

Broadcast Pioneers Library

BLAST FROM THE PAST: A PICTORIAL HISTORY OF RADIO'S FIRST 75 YEARS

That Brewster Boy was played by Eddie Firestone Jr. on CBS in 1942. He also played a dumb office boy in Mutual-Don Lee's *Let George Do It*, and was one of many who played Pinky on *One Man's Family* Firestone was also in *The Goldbergs*, *Harold Teen*, *The Story of Mary Marlin* and *Woman in White*.

Broadcast Pioneers Library

Exaggerated phrases like "Don't ever doooooo that!" and "Wooooee is me!" had radio audiences in stitches from comedian Joe Penner, whose career ended abruptly in 1940 when he suffered a heart attack at age 36 while on stage in a Philadelphia theater production.

Broadcast Pioneers Library

Laurette Fillbrandt played nurse Pamela Hale in CBS' *Guiding Light* in 1948. She was also heard on *The Adventures of Phillip Marlowe*, *One Man's Family* and *Today's Children* on NBC.

Broadcast Pioneers Library

The First Piano Quartet, heard Sundays on NBC in 1948: (l-r) Frank Mittler, Edward Edson, Adam Garner, Vee Padwa.

Broadcast Pioneers Library

Celebrating the Firestone Tire and Rubber Company's 20 years as an advertiser, on November 29, 1948: Niles Trammell, president of NBC, thanks Harvey S. Firestone Jr.

Broadcast Pioneers Library

One of the most innovative musicians in history, Spike Jones made instruments out of toilet seats and other unusual objects. Born Lindley Armstrong Jones, Spike first played before a radio audience in 1938 as a drummer for Victor Young. His best program was *Spotlight Review*, which aired for two years (1947 and '48) on CBS. Jones died in 1965.

Broadcast Pioneers Library

RUDY: I'm not afraid of you ... I'll stand wherever I like.

JOHN: THEN WHY ARE YOU STANDIN' BEHIND THAT BARN?

RUDY: (COYLY) I like it here! ... Besides, Barrymore, you better

            not shoot me. I got somethin' important to tell you.

JOHN: ALL RIGHT, SON, STEP OUT AND SPEAK UP.

RUDY: Mr. Barrymore, I just found out my mother owns Casper Creek

            and you can't fish there any more.

JOHN: WHAT? I CAN'T FISH AT CASPER CREEK? THEY CAN'T DO THIS

            TO ME ... I'VE BEEN FISHIN' THERE FOR 18 YEARS *(pause)* AND I'M

            EXPECTIN' A BITE ANY DAY NOW.

CLEMENTINE: There's one way out, Pappy ... stop the feudin' and go over

            and make friends with Vallee's ma.

RUDY: Go ahead, Mr. Barrymore. Ma is at home now.

JOHN: IS SHE STILL AROUND? *(pleasanter)* I THOUGHT THE NAVY CALLED IN ALL THE

            OLD BATTLE-WAGONS.

CLEMENTINE: Remember, Pappy -- No go -- no fish.

JOHN: ALL RIGHT ... I'M OFF ON ME ERRAND OF LOVE ... DAUGHTER

            HAND ME ME GUN.

CLEMENTINE: Gosh, I hope it works Rudy.

RUDY: So do I - and while we're waiting, let me express myself in

            song.

CLEMENTINE: I'm a'listenin', Rudy.

Actor John Barrymore often guest-starred on radio programs — and doodled on the scripts while rehearsing.
This is a page from a script he signed and doodled on for *The Rudy Vallee Show* from October 23, 1941.
Pacific Pioneers Library

One of the original matchmaking shows, Arlene Francis (right) hosted *Blind Date* starting July 8, 1943, on NBC.

Pacific Pioneers Library

Comedian "Happy" Felton appeared on many radio programs as a regular, including NBC's *Pot o' Gold* in its 1946 revision, ABC's 1948 *Stop the Music* and his own *Happy Felton Show — Finders Keepers*, which ran Monday through Friday at 11 a.m. on NBC starting on March 28, 1945.

Broadcast Pioneers Library

Originally the announcer for *The Hour of Charm* and its all-girl orchestra, Arlene Francis starred in *What's My Name* Tuesdays on The Mutual-Don Lee Network. The show later became *What's My Line* on television.

Pacific Pioneers Library

Inside the CBS Hollywood studios during a broadcast.

CBS

The voice of Lanny Ross was frequently heard on musical programs such as *Show Boat* and *Your Hit Parade*. He is seen here on an NBC Blue Network bond drive, *For America We Sing*, during WWII (July 28, 1941).

Pacific Pioneers Library

The staff of *The George Burns Show*: (back row) Jimmy Cash, Felix Mills; (front row) Elvia Allman, Mel Blanc, George Burns, Gracie Allen, Hans Conried and Bill Goodman.

Pacific Pioneers Library

Ed Gardner of *Archie's Tavern*.

Pacific Pioneers Library

The American School of the Air was an educational program offered from CBS that ran 18 years starting in 1930. More than 200,000 classes would gather around the radio for daily required lessons.

Broadcast Pioneers Library

CBS featured many programs from auditoriums of schools throughout the country on *The American School of the Air*.

Broadcast Pioneers Library

Starting as one of radio's first concert music shows, *Cities Service Concerts* began in 1927 on NBC. The program mixed concert music and important talk segments from visiting dignitaries and ran through 1956. The Friday night program was eventually housed at the auditorium studio at Radio City in New York.

Broadcast Pioneers Library

NBC News chief William Brooks and Mary Margaret McBride interview Mrs. Omar Bradley in 1945.

Broadcast Pioneers Library

The Quiz Kids visit the Liberty Bell to broadcast their impressions via local affiliate WFIL, Philadelphia.

Broadcast Pioneers Library

Musical act The Three Trumpeteers, heard frequently on NBC musical programs.

Broadcast Pioneers Library

Sponsored by Lucky Strike, *Your Hit Parade* featured the top stars singing the top songs of the week.

Broadcast Pioneers Library

Times have changed since the days when deejay Jack The Rapper would say: "Does you dig my tan?" Rapper started at WJJD in the late '40s and went on to WFEC in Miami in the '50s.

Jack The Rapper

Sergeant Preston and his trusty dog Yukon King came from the mind of WXYZ Detroit's George W. Trendle, creator of *The Lone Ranger* and *The Green Hornet*. Preston was played by Brace Beemer. Audiences in 1947 heard: "Now, as gunshots echo across the windswept, snow-covered reaches of the wild Northwest, Quaker Puffed Wheat (Sfx: gunshot, ricochet) and Quaker Puffed Rice (Sfx: gunshot, ricochet), the breakfast cereal shot from guns (sfx: two gun shots), present *The Challenge of The Yukon!*"

Broadcast Pioneers Library

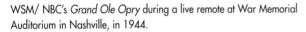

WSM/ NBC's *Grand Ole Opry* during a live remote at War Memorial Auditorium in Nashville, in 1944.

Broadcast Pioneers Library

The family all America knew, as if it was their own. The cast of NBC's *One Man's Family*: Barton Yarborough, Kathleen Wilson, J. Anthony Smythe, Minetta Ellen, Page Gillman, Bernice Berwin and Michael Raffetto.

Broadcast Pioneers Library

In character for this publicity shot for *Ma Perkins* on NBC are Virginia Payne, Murray Forbes and Charles Egelston.

Broadcast Pioneers Library

Norman Brokenshire, one of the great radio announcers on CBS, heard in the '40s on *The Theatre Guild on the Air.*

Broadcast Pioneers Library

Alice Faye with Phil Harris on *The Phil Harris -Alice Faye Show* Sunday nights on NBC. The couple played a happy domestic comedy team and were also married in real life.

Broadcast Pioneers Library

Actor Charles Laughton examines some of the original KDKA microphones and their successors (circa 1940).

Broadcast Pioneers Library

Originating from Chicago's WLS in 1924, *The National Barn Dance* had listeners stompin' to country music for more than 25 years. Hootin' it up are Uncle Ezra (left) and The Hoosier Hotshots from WOWO in Fort Wayne, Indiana (1945).

Broadcast Pioneers Library

Country act Louise Massey and the Westerners backstage before going on NBC's *National Barn Dance*.

Broadcast Pioneers Library

March 29, 1941, at 2:10 a.m., Mr. J.B. Conley and officials of WOWO, Fort Wayne, gathered at the station's transmitter to switch dial positions from 1160 to 1190. WOWO was a 50,000-watt giant that could be heard in more than half of the United States.

Broadcast Pioneers Library

Harry Babbitt, the baritone heard on *Kay Kyser's Kollege of Musical Knowledge.*

Broadcast Pioneers Library

CBS affiliate WBIG's War Bond Commandos, who sold and delivered war bonds.

Broadcast Pioneers Library

Modern Home Forum was celebrating its fifth year on the air (WOWO, Fort Wayne) and invited homemakers into the studio to share in the celebration.

Broadcast Pioneers Library

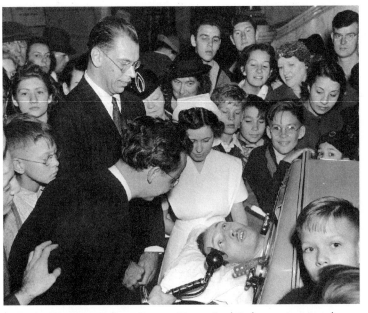

WOWO, Fort Wayne, Indiana, Program Director Frank Tooker was interviewed while inside an iron lung. The stunt was used to raise funds for a local hospital.

Broadcast Pioneers Library

An NBC remote at a talking parrot contest — on a slow day.

Broadcast Pioneers Library

Radio executive in Europe during WWII, known as The Vipers for Armed Forces Radio.

Broadcast Pioneers Library

National personality "Wrong Way" Corrigan wandered the wrong way and ended up being interviewed by a WOWO news commentator in Fort Wayne, Indiana.

Broadcast Pioneers Library

The Army band Flying High from Seymour Johnson Field and WGBR, Goldsboro, North Carolina.

Broadcast Pioneers Library

Comedienne Lucille Ball reads the lead part with Richard Denning in *My Favorite Husband*, her first regular radio program, which started on CBS in July 1948.

Broadcast Pioneers Library

While the men were away fighting WWII, many women took over the controls at local stations like CBS affiliate WBIG. Operators are: (l-r) Margaret Cox and Alice Birkhead.

Broadcast Pioneers Library

An all-soldier production called *On The Beam*.

Broadcast Pioneers Library

WNEW New York's Paula Stone interviews Betty Grable on *Hollywood Digest*.

Broadcast Pioneers Library

Every time this publicity photo was released by one of the networks, we noticed that the mic flag on the microphone to the left was blank. After searching for the original, we found the exact same photo with the missing mic flag intact. Hmmmm.

Broadcast Pioneers Library

Broadcasters cover the christening of the aircraft carrier Hornet at Newport News in 1943.

Broadcast Pioneers Library

Master of Ceremonies Chuck Acree looks at a pair of snowshoes won by a participant on his radio program *Hint Hunt,* which originated from Chicago (September 9, 1948).

Associated Press

After a seven-month layoff, the program *Vic and Sade* returned to the airwaves on June 28, 1945, on the Mutual Broadcasting System. The program, which originated in 1932 on the Blue Network in Chicago, was a comedy built around smalltown life, with actors Bernardine Flynn as Sade Gook; Billy Idelson as Rush Gook, the son, and Art Van Harvey as Vic Gook. The Gooks lived in "a little house halfway up the next block."

Associated Press

Although it never became a network program, *Rambling With Gambling* was the top-rated local program in New York for many decades.

Associated Press

Five-year-old Robin Morgan presided over a 15-minute Mutual network program on Saturday mornings in the '40s.

Associated Press

Radio comedian Bob Hope.

Radio Ink Collection

Radio star Eddie Cantor and Bill "Bojangles" Robinson.

Broadcast Pioneers Library

Jack Benny.

Radio and Records

One of the biggest stars of stage and screen, Groucho Marx never hit it big on radio until *You Bet Your Life*, which premiered on ABC in 1947.

Radio Ink Collection

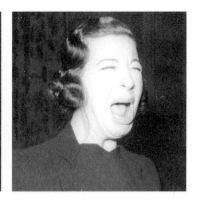

Fanny Brice strikes a usual pose as the spoiled brat Baby Snooks.

Broadcast Pioneers Library

Gathered around the NBC microphone are (l-r) Bob Burns, Tommy Riggs, Charlie McCarthy, Edgar Bergen, Rudy Vallee, Joe Penner.

Broadcast Pioneers Library

The musical entertainment for Joe Penner's (bottom) *The Baker's Broadcast*, Ozzie and Harriet Nelson eventually moved to Hollywood to join *The Red Skelton Show* in 1941. They left three years later when Skelton was drafted, which led to *The Adventures of Ozzie and Harriet*.

Broadcast Pioneers Library

Cliff Arquette and the cast of *Point Sublime*, which ran on NBC in 1940, Mutual-Don Lee in 1942 and ABC in 1947.

Pacific Pioneers Library

Bing Crosby, seen here with his favorite microphone. Although others of the same model existed, Crosby hand-carried the same microphone with him to every broadcast and recording session because of its sweet sound.

CBS

Truth Or Consequences emcee Ralph Edwards is seen here with guest Eddie Cantor.

Pacific Pioneers Library

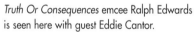

Ralph Edwards, host of *The Quiz Show* on CBS.

Pacific Pioneers Library

A broadcast of *Our Miss Brooks* with Gale Gordon (l) and Eve Arden (r).

CBS

Jack Benny and Eddie "Rochester" Anderson.

CBS

Glamorous Ava Gardner, a frequent radio visitor.

CBS

The King of Swing, Benny Goodman, on CBS.

CBS

Appearing frequently on *The Kraft Music Hall* as a summer replacement, Dorothy Kirsten may have been best known as co-star of NBC's *Light Up Time*.

Pacific Pioneers Library

Once the movie roles began, Groucho Marx sported a moustache, but it wasn't needed on the radio. Groucho, seen hugging Joan Blondell, had four failed radio programs, believed to be caused by his desire to ad lib and not read pre-written material. His biggest success was *You Bet Your Life*.

Pacific Pioneers Library

A director readies the actors for a cue at CBS's KNX Hollywood.

CBS

Radio listeners across America felt sorry for contestant Mrs. Dennis Mullane, who missed a question on radio's *Truth Or Consequences* program. As a result, she received 70,000 letters, earning her more than $11,000.

Pacific Pioneers Library

Actress Mercedes McCambridge on the NBC Red Network.

Pacific Pioneers Library

The Pied Pipers and singer Jo Stafford look through a copy of *Radio Life* to read the latest Hollywood gossip and industry news.

Pacific Pioneers Library

Jim and Marian Jordan spent a lifetime together — both married and on the air together as *Fibber McGee and Molly*.

Associated Press

Stations not only aired drama programming provided by the networks, but many also produced their own local programming. In Schenectady, the staff of WGY creates *The FBI in Action*, a weekly series written from actual FBI files.

Broadcast Pioneers Library

Laughing it up on the NBC Red Network are: (l-r) Judy, Annie and brother Zeke
Canova with Edgar Bergen and Charlie McCarthy on *The Chase and Sanborn Hour*.

Junior Town Meeting was the high school equivalent of *Town Meeting of the Air*, seen here on WSAI in Cincinnati.

Before they hit it big in the movies, Bud Abbott (left) and Lou Costello were a success on radio, starting out on *The Kate Smith Hour* and Edgar Bergen's *The Chase and Sanborn Hour*. They got their own regular show on NBC in October 1942, then switched to ABC from 1947 through 1949, after their NBC contract expired. Their radio popularity with more than 20 million listeners made their films an instant success.

Broadcast Pioneers Library

W.C. Fields (left) curiously wonders what Charlie McCarthy is whispering to Dorothy Lamour as ventriloquist Edgar Bergen controls every word on *The Chase and Sanborn Hour.*

Broadcast Pioneers Library

Perhaps the most well-known radio act of all time, Amos and Andy (Freeman F. Gosden and Charles J. Correll) started in New Orleans in 1920. In 1926, they made their debut on WGN as Sam and Henry. When they switched to CBS' WMAQ two years later, WGN insisted on keeping the name, so they became *Amos and Andy*, remaining on the air until November 1960.

Broadcast Pioneers Library

Once it was decided a female sidekick was needed on Jack Benny's program, auditions were held, but the job ended up going to Benny's wife, Sadie. She became popularized as Mary Livingstone and stayed on the show from 1934 through the early 1950s.

Broadcast Pioneers Library

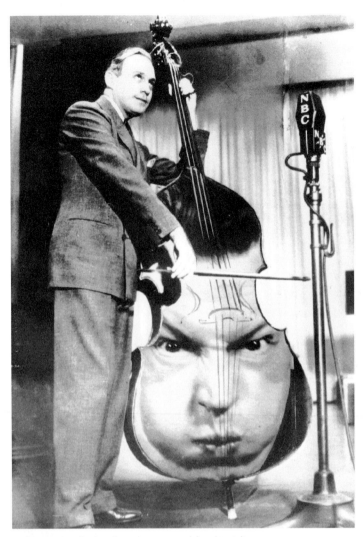

Jack Benny tries his hand at a bigger sound than his violin.

Hearst Newspaper Collection; Special Collections; University of Southern California Library

Spike Jones and Brenda Lee as they appeared on *The Arkansas Traveler* on NBC in the mid-'40s.

Broadcast Pioneers Library

Priding himself as a starmaker, Rudy Vallee (left) is seen here with Eve Arden and Charles Trent (right).

Broadcast Pioneers Library

During an appearance at *Duffy's Tavern*, Archie (Ed Gardner) wears his autographed apron while Cary Grant tries to pull it off.

Pacific Pioneers Library

Ed Gardner played Archie the Manager on *Duffy's Tavern* for 10 years on CBS and then NBC. The Brooklyn-accented bartender would goof with famous guests who stopped in to the bar. Each star signed his bar apron.

Broadcast Pioneers Library

Rehearsing a *Duffy's Tavern* program are: (l-r) Sandra Gould (Miss Duffy), Eddie Green (Eddie the Waiter), Charlie Cantor (Clifton Finnegan) and Ed Gardner (Archie). Duffy himself never appeared on the program.

Broadcast Pioneers Library

Actors William Powell and Sharon Douglas on NBC's *My Mother's Husband.*

Making her national radio debut in 1944 on *The Chase and Sanborn Hour,* 14-year-old soprano Jane Powell was often wooed by wooden dummy Charlie McCarthy. Powell went on to be a frequent guest on many musical programs and variety shows, including *The Railroad Hour.*

Vocalist Lily Pons with noted conductor Andre Kostelanetz as guest on his CBS program *The Pause That Refreshes on the Air.* It was sponsored, of course, by Chesterfield cigarettes. *Pause,* as it was known, first appeared on NBC in 1935. Kostelanetz took the program over on CBS in 1940.

Beating ratings leader Fred Allen on Sunday nights in 1947, Bert Parks' *Stop the Music* would call homes at random for the name of a tune just played on the air. Listeners could win up to $30,000. The program became so popular that Allen's show was discontinued and he was never to return to the air. Eventually, Edgar Bergen and Charlie McCarthy were put against Parks' show, leading to its ratings demise.

Starting a fruitful career in San Francisco in 1928 on *The Spanish Serenader*, Hal Peary became best known as Throckmorton P. Gildersleeve, a character who started as a neighbor on *Fibber McGee and Molly*. He eventually was spun off into *The Great Gildersleeve*, owner of Gildersleeve Girdle Works. Peary is seen with Shirley Mitchell and Louise Erickson.

Broadcast Pioneers Library

The CBS program *Dangerously Yours* was short-lived, leaving actor Victor Jory an opportunity to play many other roles on radio, including *Quick as a Flash* on Mutual in 1944.

Broadcast Pioneers Library

Four radio greats who started out in vaudeville together: (l-r) George Jessel, George Burns, Eddie Cantor and Jack Benny.

Broadcast Pioneers Library

The Danny Kaye Show originated from Hollywood and premiered on CBS in January 1945. It immediately was ranked in fifth place nationally, although it only stayed on for a year. Kaye became known as The Prince of Clowns.

Broadcast Pioneers Library

A caricature of radio clown Danny Kaye.

Broadcast Pioneers Library

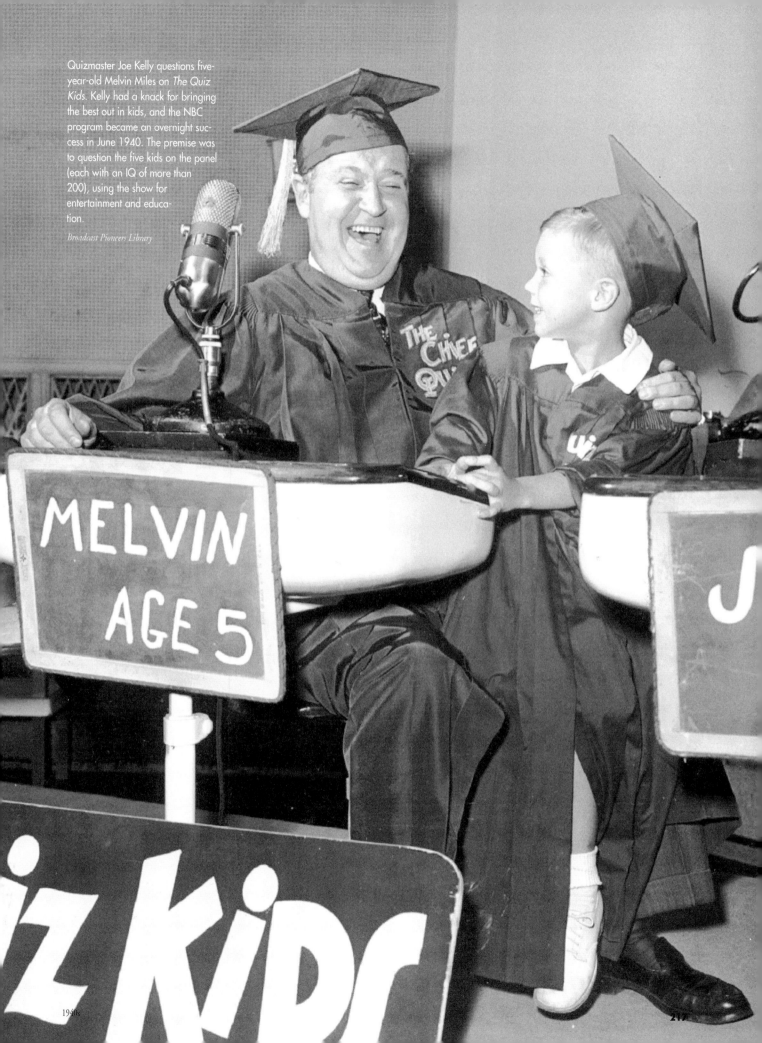

Quizmaster Joe Kelly questions five-year-old Melvin Miles on *The Quiz Kids*. Kelly had a knack for bringing the best out in kids, and the NBC program became an overnight success in June 1940. The premise was to question the five kids on the panel (each with an IQ of more than 200), using the show for entertainment and education.

Broadcast Pioneers Library

Composer-conductor Gordon Jenkins, author of *San Fernando Valley, Indian Giver, Every Time, Homesick* and other hits, also led the 31-piece orchestra on *The Dick Haymes Show* on CBS.

Broadcast Pioneers Library

Jose Morton Gould and pianist Jose Iturbi on *The Cresta Blanca Carnival*, which aired on CBS in 1943.

Broadcast Pioneers Library

Sisters Betty (left) and Marion Hutton were a featured act on many a radio stage.

Broadcast Pioneers Library

Singer Betty Hutton and emcee Win Elliot in *Betty Crocker Magazine on the Air*, which ran daily in the midday in the late '40s on ABC.

Broadcast Pioneers Library

Known for his whiny delivery and gravelly voice, Andy Devine had a healthy career on radio and film. He did comedy on *The Fitch Bandwagon* between 1944 and 1945, and was frequently heard on *The Jack Benny Show* on CBS.

Broadcast Pioneers Library

Parks Johnson and Warren Hull became the voice of the people on CBS' *Vox Pop*, which ran on Monday nights. The interview show started with Johnson (left) in 1932 in Houston and came to NBC from 1935 to 1939, then moved to CBS through 1947, when it jumped to ABC.

Broadcast Pioneers Library

Paul Douglas was one of the most recognized announcers in radio, announcing or acting on *Abie's Irish Rose*; *Buck Rogers in the 25th Century*; *The Chesterfield Supper Club*; *Community Sing*; *The Fred Waring Show*; *The Horn and Hardart Children's Hour*; *Jack Armstrong, the All-American Boy*; *Meyer The Buyer*; *Saturday Night Swing Club* and *The True Story Hour with Mary and Bob*.

Broadcast Pioneers Library

Rex Dale with featured guest Gloria Swanson on WCKY.

Broadcast Pioneers Library

The Cliff Quartet, originating from WRC, Washington.

Broadcast Pioneers Library

NBC's Kathryn Cole conducting auditions for a welcome home program for soldiers after WWII.

Broadcast Pioneers Library

Comedian Jerry Colonna was a regular on *The Bob Hope Show* from 1937 through 1956 on NBC. He started with Hope as a trumpet player but soon evolved into a major sidekick.

Broadcast Pioneers Library

Raymond Walburn on CBS' *That's My Pop*, which ran Sundays at 8 p.m. in August 1945.

Broadcast Pioneers Library

Film actor John Wayne appeared in *Three Sheets to the Wind* on the NBC Red Network every Sunday night.

Broadcast Pioneers Library

Playing Vera Vague, the maid with the high-pitched voice on Bob Hope's *The Pepsodent Show*, Barbara Jo Allen took the character to other programs like *The Jimmy Durante Show* and *The Jack Carson Show*. She also played Beth Holly on *One Man's Family*.

Broadcast Pioneers Library

Actor Robert Taylor reads a dramatic script on *Encore Theater*'s *Men in White* from Hollywood in July 1946.

Broadcast Pioneers Library

Perhaps best known for his work on television's *Tonight Show*, Jack Paar began his career in radio. He is seen here chatting with band-leader Benny Goodman on NBC.

Broadcast Pioneers Library

The many faces of Harry Von Zell as announcer on *Sal Hepatica's Time To Smile* on the NBC Red Network in 1940. Von Zell had the pleasure of first introducing Bing Crosby to a national audience for on CBS in 1931.

Broadcast Pioneers Library

Breakfast Club regular Jack Owens interviews an audience member on NBC's Blue Network. Owens also appeared on NBC's *Tin Pan Alley of the Air*.

Broadcast Pioneers Library

After starting his career in 1931 as an announcer at WMCA, New York, Henry Morgan's first program, *Meet Mr. Morgan*, became a nightly show on WOR, New York. Being known as a bad boy for his irreverent rebel attitude made him even more popular. *The Henry Morgan Show* was only part of his constant radio exposure. He was a frequent guest on many programs and eventually became host on NBC's *Monitor*.

Broadcast Pioneers Library

One Man's Family author Carlton Morse hard at work on a script.

Broadcast Pioneers Library

Radio and Westerns went well together, as evidenced by WOV's cowgirl Dusty Bruce.

Broadcast Pioneers Library

Radio showman Eddie Brandt and his Hollywood Hicks.

Broadcast Pioneers Library

Known as Ish Kabibble on *Kay Kyser's Kollege of Musical Knowledge*, comedian Merwyn A. Bogue became the program's most popular cast member, which resulted in a tenure from 1933 through 1949.

Broadcast Pioneers Library

Known as the first disc jockey, Martin Block created *Make-Believe Ballroom* on WNEW in New York. At a time when most music featured on the radio was live, Block was able to provide any artist on command by using records. Block announced for *The Chesterfield Supper Club* and was also host of ABC's *The Martin Block Show*.

Broadcast Pioneers Library

Dr. Frank Black had one of the more fruitful careers as a conductor, leading more than 10 radio orchestras, including *The Jack Benny Show* and General Motors' *Symphony of the Air*.

Broadcast Pioneers Library

The Chase and Sanborn Hour aired Sundays at 8 p.m. on NBC and starred Edgar Bergen, Charlie McCarthy and many other characters, such as bachelor girl Podine Puffington. Bergen's daughter, Candice, often appeared on her father's later programs.

Broadcast Pioneers Library

Shown acting on CBS' *This Changing World*, Lawson Zerbe played numerous radio roles, such as Pepper on *Pepper Young's Family*, *Murder at Midnight*, *Exploring Tomorrow*, *The Adventures of Frank Merriwell*, *Lora Lawton*, *Road of Life*, *True Detective Mysteries*, *This Is Our Enemy* and *Valiant Lady*.

Broadcast Pioneers Library

Charlie McCarthy (left) and Mortimer Snerd (right) may look like dummies, but by 1945 they made Edgar Bergen (center) about $10,000 a week and $100,000 a year in merchandise royalties.

Broadcast Pioneers Library

Roland Young played the role of Topper in *The Adventures of Topper* in the movies, and on radio in June 1945 as a summer filler program. Young made frequent appearances on *Duffy's Tavern*, and on *Good News of 1938*.

Broadcast Pioneers Library

Although the idea of ventriloquism on the radio seems ridiculous (who cares if the lips are moving?), Edgar Bergen and his wooden dummy Charlie McCarthy became household names. They made their radio debut on *The Rudy Vallee Royal Gelatin Hour* in 1936. Bergen got his own show in May 1937 and remained consistent through 1956.

Broadcast Pioneers Library

CBS correspondents covering the Joint Army-Navy atom bomb tests on surface craft off Bikini Atoll include: (top, l-r) Webley Edwards and Bill Downs; (bottom, l-r) Don Mozley and George Moorad. Downs was aboard the observation plane following the atomic missile.

Broadcast Pioneers Library

Although many voices were associated with the program, Brace Beemer was the voice of *The Lone Ranger* on ABC from 1940 through 1955.

Broadcast Pioneers Library

Showman, commentator, gossip columnist Walter Winchell of *Walter Winchell's Journal* became a giant on radio across America. He always wore his hat while broadcasting and simultaneously tapped a telegraph key for sound impact while talking rapidly. His lead-in became famous: "Good evening, Mr. and Mrs. North and South America and all the ships at sea, let's go to press — Flash!" He was on the radio from 1930 through 1957.

Broadcast Pioneers Library

Orson Welles.

Broadcast Pioneers Library

NBC's Willard Waterman became one of radio's most recognized voices, acting on *The Chicago Theatre of The Air*, *The First Nighter Program*, *Those Websters*, *Tom Mix Ralston Straightshooters* and as the replacement for Harold Peary on *The Great Gildersleeve*.

Broadcast Pioneers Library

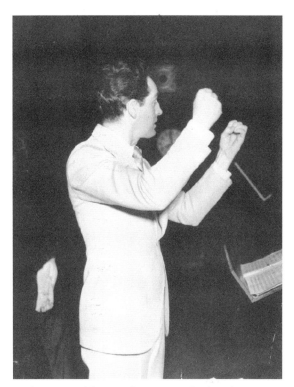

Fred Waring and the Pennsylvanians were first heard in 1932 on CBS and began a 20-year run of radio broadcasting.

Broadcast Pioneers Library

The Voice of Firestone was NBC's premiere musical program, first heard in December 1928. Alfred Wallenstein directed the Firestone Symphony Orchestra for seven years prior to becoming musical director for the Los Angeles Symphony in 1943.

Broadcast Pioneers Library

Two radio legends, Harry Von Zell and Eddie Cantor.

Broadcast Pioneers Library

Raymond Gram Swing, newscaster on NBC Blue, was known for giving his impressions of the fighting fronts in WWII on *The Radio Hall of Fame Broadcasts* (circa 1945).

Broadcast Pioneers Library

Often cast in parts contrary to her surname, Marion Sweet played villainess roles like that of The Dragon Lady in *Terry and the Pirates,* a comic strip-style adventure that started on NBC in 1937 (1944 photo).

Broadcast Pioneers Library

The barn dance became heavily imitated on a local level as stations produced their own. Each market had its stars like "Sunshine Sue" on WRVA, Richmond, on the *Old Dominion Barn Dance.*

Broadcast Pioneers Library

CBS singing sensation Jeri Sullavan, a regular on *The Ray Bolger Show.*

Broadcast Pioneers Library

One of the stars of *The Voice of Firestone*, Eleanor Steber, in 1947.

Broadcast Pioneers Library

Known for his rendition of *The Red, Red Robin*, Whispering Jack Smith started in show business after graduating from Hollywood High School in 1931 and landing a job replacing Bing Crosby at The Coconut Grove Hotel. He often sang on *The Kate Smith Show*, *The Prudential Family Hour* and *Glamor Manor*. *The Jack Smith Show* first aired in 1943 on CBS, running until 1951.

Broadcast Pioneers Library

Baritone Whispering Jack Smith was heard on CBS' *Prudential Family Hour* Sunday evenings in 1941.

Broadcast Pioneers Library

Don McNeill (left) of *The Breakfast Club* and Rudy Vallee (right) try out jokes on a fan.

Broadcast Pioneers Library

Edward R. Murrow is known for his contributions as a CBS newsman during WWII and beyond. However, it is little known that Murrow also played dramatic roles on the radio in *The CBS Mystery Workshop*.

Broadcast Pioneers Library

Comedian Pinky Lee kept audiences in stitches on *The Bickersons* in 1946 on NBC and on *Carefree Carnival* between 1933 and 1935.

Broadcast Pioneers Library

Dale Evans and Bob Hope rehearse a script.

Broadcast Pioneers Library

Helen Forrest, Gordon Jenkins and Dick Haymes (l-r) on CBS. Haymes was featured on *The Chesterfield Supper Club* and had his own show on NBC in 1944. During his heyday, he was considered a rival to Sinatra and Crosby.

Broadcast Pioneers Library

Actress Rita Hayworth reading a message to the boys over there during WWII.

Broadcast Pioneers Library

What do you get when Jimmy Durante joins *The Garry Moore Show*? Answer: *The Durante-Moore Show*. Durante was such a powerful influence on the CBS show that his name was shared with Moore's for four years until Moore's departure in 1947.

Broadcast Pioneers Library

Master storyteller John Nesbitt's *Passing Parade* ran first in 1938 and graced the networks sporadically for years. His stories were of unusual happenings similar to those of *Ripley's Believe It or Not*, but presented without sound effects.

Broadcast Pioneers Library

Maj. George Fielding Eliot, Paul W. White and Quentin Reynolds on CBS in May 1944.

Broadcast Pioneers Library

CBS Special Events director Bill Slocum reads a script during the first broadcast from an Army glider.

Broadcast Pioneers Library

Alfred McCasker, Fulton Lewis Jr., Cecil Brown, Edythe Meserand and Frank Singiser conduct election coverage on Mutal in 1944.

Broadcast Pioneers Library

Presidential election coverage of 1944, with Morgan Beatty of NBC News giving the results as his producer gives a time signal.

Broadcast Pioneers Library

KSL in Salt Lake City broadcasting to the Intermountain Region.

Broadcast Pioneers Library

NBC's Graham McNamee (right) reports as the S.S. Normandie burns in 1942 at Pier 88.

Broadcast Pioneers Library

Presidential candidate Thomas Dewey making a speech from Saginaw, Michigan.

Broadcast Pioneers Library

The newsroom was bustling on D-day as WOW, Omaha, covered the event from a local perspective.

Broadcast Pioneers Library

CBS' Lowell Thomas.

Broadcast Pioneers Library

KGO San Francisco's Berton Bennett, chief announcer; Hayes Hunter (center) and Don Martin, news editor, do West Coast news for the Blue Network.

Broadcast Pioneers Library

Lowell Thomas at home, preparing for a broadcast.

Broadcast Pioneers Library

Lowell Thomas is seen here with CBS chief William Paley on the occasion of Thomas' 20th anniversary at CBS. Thomas spent 30 years at CBS and 16 at NBC, and holds the record for the longest tenure of any news broadcaster.

Associated Press

A CBS News trio: Robert Trout, Linton Wells and Elmer Davis.

Broadcast Pioneers Library

Asa Yoelson, the Russian-born son of a rabbi, became known as The World's Greatest Entertainer under the name Al Jolson. Although he started his career as an actor and was in the first talking motion picture, Jolson was no stranger to radio. His first appearance was in 1928. By November 1932, he had his own series on NBC called *Presenting Al Jolson*.

Associated Press

During World War II, the Supreme Court proved that Marconi was not officially the Father of Radio and that the distinction belonged to Tesla. Some believe that this reversal occurred because the U.S. was at war with Italy. Marconi is seen here leaving the Italian Royal Academy after being elected its president. The ceremony was attended by dictator Mussolini, a friend and confidant of Marconi's.

Associated Press

CBS News anchors prepare for a noon broadcast.

Broadcast Pioneers Library

Doris Day was a singing sensation on NBC's *Your Hit Parade* in the late 1940s.

Broadcast Pioneers Library

Newsman Chet Huntley interviews The King of the Jungle in April 1944.

Pacific Pioneers Library

Radio opera star Jessica Dragonette on November 2, 1946, doing *Hail and Farewell*.

Broadcast Pioneers Library

Arthur Godfrey compares the 12" disc currently used on the radio with Columbia's new 7" record (33$\frac{1}{3}$ speed).

Broadcast Pioneers Library

Radio was king in the 1940s, and NBC was everywhere.

Broadcast Pioneers Library

In 1946, NBC built another elaborate studio facility to accommodate the huge success of the network. Little did they know that radio was only a few years away from disaster.

Broadcast Pioneers Library

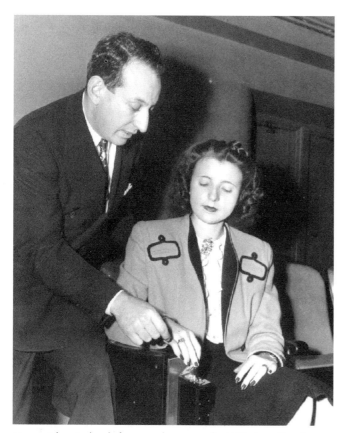

Horace Schwerin, head of a research company for NBC, shows Dorothy Posen how to press a button gauging her reactions to radio programs being tested for listener response (February 9, 1947).

Associated Press

Horace Schwerin, who devised test used by NBC to measure audience reactions, demonstrates his findings to executives.

Associated Press

NBC began taking a scientific route to measure audience response. The biweekly research was conducted by an independent research company, having listeners raise hands as numbers were flashed on a screen while audio was played.

Associated Press

Clerks at NBC tabulate the results of audience tests while Ray Manebal (standing left) and Leonard Kudisch of the Schwerin Research staff look on (circa 1947).

Associated Press

Radio was at its peak for the era of big broadcasts. Along with it came elaborate new studios like Radio City in New York and Radio City in Hollywood at Sunset and Vine.

Broadcast Pioneers Library

Host Ralph Edwards challenges a contestant to *Make Love to a Skunk.*

Pacific Pioneers Library

A WWDC announcer. Note the chimes on the table.

Broadcast Pioneers Library

Anne Ford (standing), Director of Women's Activities, in the studio of WSM-FM, said to be the first commercial FM in the United States. The announcer is Peggy McComas (May 29, 1944).

Broadcast Pioneers Library

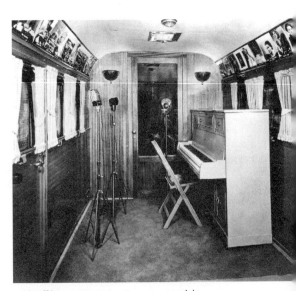

NBC affiliate WIBR, Baton Rouge, created this mobile studio to take the show to the people.

Broadcast Pioneers Library

BLAST FROM THE PAST: A PICTORIAL HISTORY OF RADIO'S FIRST 75 YEARS

Ready, aim, you're on! At the Tennessee State Fair, WSM, Nashville, hostesses Dolly Desrman and Evelyn Carver (l-r) demonstrate the latest in technology — a shotgun mic designed to pick up sounds from long distances.

Broadcast Pioneers Library

The sound effects man was the hero in many a radio drama, making a script come alive. In the '40s, many children wanted to grow up to be sound effects people. This sound effects kit for kids was one of the more popular toys for Christmas, 1948.

Associated Press

This KSL, Salt Lake City, studio was typical for local 1940s radio stations, which included a control console, turntable for transcripts of shows to be played, a studio piano and organ.

Bonneville Collection

Studio A at CBS' new Columbia Square studios in Hollywood.

CBS

Cab Calloway was on network radio in the '30s and hosted *Cab Calloway's Quizzical* on WOR in 1941.

Radio Ink Collection

Big prizes kept America glued to NBC radio's game show *Truth Or Consequences*. Two models pose before $22,500 in prizes, including a new car and a vacation in Hawaii (December 6, 1947).

Associated Press

This device was invented by Morris A. Kay, the man who invented the match. He says it will revolutionize radio listening, giving listeners the option of striking (excuse the pun) radio commercials (circa 1946).

Associated Press

Actress Irene Dunne reviewing a *Lux Radio Theatre* script. Dunne also starred in NBC's *Bright Star* in 1952, and on Mutual's *Family Theatre* in 1947.

Broadcast Pioneers Library

Spike Jones and The City Slickers brought a new meaning to music, adding an element of fun and frolic, incorporating every sound, grunt and noise they could get into a song on the beat. The music satire *Der Fuhrer's Face* brought notoriety to the group and became a regular on *The Bob Burns Show* in 1942.

Broadcast Pioneers Library

Riggers climbed the KDKA tower daily during its construction. The innovative free-standing tower was 718 feet tall and built of 60 tons of metal.

Broadcast Pioneers Library

Jack Benny seen before the mic on January 2, 1949.

Associated Press

An all-night broadcast of a semi-pro baseball tournament in Wichita, Kansas. KGH sports announcers dressed for the occasion.

Broadcast Pioneers Library

As Paul Harvey did his broadcast on WKZO in Kalamazoo, little did he know that he was later to become one of the most-listened-to voices in America on ABC.

Radio Ink Collection

The networks weren't the only ones with elaborate facilities. Many local stations in small-town America were also very prominent, as evidenced by this elaborate lobby at WOWO, Fort Wayne.

Radio Ink Collection

1950s

Radio, it seemed, was washed up. Most of the big stars on the radio were now doing television. As comedian Fred Allen said: "Television is trying to get radio to pucker up for the kiss of death."

Few personalities remained loyal to the medium that made them stars. But their loyalty was to their audiences. Americans were purchasing televisions and wanted to see their favorites on the screen, as opposed to hearing them from a speaker. The radio stars who went to television really had no choice. Television was a fresh, new, powerful medium with pictures and sound, and its impact could not be denied.

Just the same, the radio networks thought there was some hope of maintaining radio listenership, so they gave radio a last chance. NBC's David Sarnoff refused to believe that radio would die, because there were so many radio sets in the market, so NBC created *The Big Show* and pulled out all the stops with massive budgets and the best talent available for a beat-all

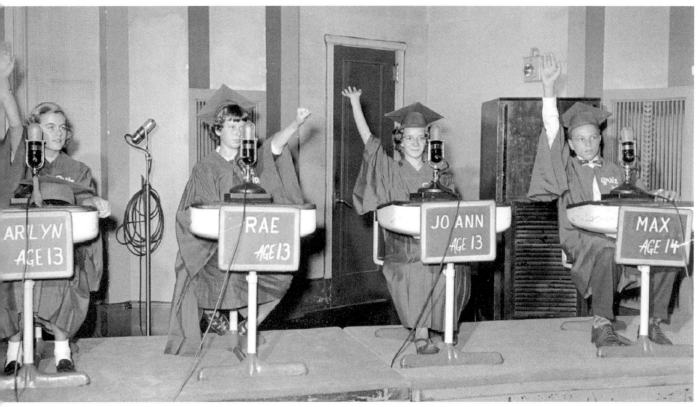

The Quiz Kids became one of America's most popular programs, running from 1940 to 1953.

Broadcast Pioneers Library

variety show from 1951 to 1953.

Some of the best radio ever created came out in the early '50s, including *Gunsmoke, Fort Laramie, Frontier Gentleman, Dimension X, X-Minus One* and *Dragnet*. But despite these creative efforts, the evening programs couldn't even keep radio in the top ten. The highest-rated evening show was *Dragnet* at number 14.

Although more than 46 million households had radios, fewer than a million were listening to the radio.

The good news for radio was that the gradual decline of network listening had given local radio the time to experiment and develop its own programming. Stations across the county experimented with alternatives, mostly in the form of deejay programs, which were much cheaper to produce than live local dramas.

In fact, radio had not fallen out of grace with listeners at all; it had simply failed to reflect society, which had always been its greatest strength. Television was reflecting society, and radio had to

again re-invent itself in order to have a purpose.

Radio's strength came from its localism and its portability. Although it was no longer the focal point of the household, people were familiar with and fond of radio and only had to be shown new ways to use the medium.

Of course, it took radio some time to come to the realization that instant information and instant music were great strengths. With the invention of the transistor, radio became more portable and lightweight and had longer battery life. This made a significant impact.

As the '50s continued, radio began to find a new path to gain listeners; however, the radio industry had suffered a great self-esteem problem. It had been at the top of the world and was no longer able to recapture that position. This was to plague the industry for two decades.

For years, a trend had been brewing that few had noticed.

Deejays played 78s, then 33⅓s and then 45s in the wee hours of the morning, filling non-network time on radio stations. Swing records became the rage with the original disc jockeys, Martin Block and Al Jarvis, who created *Make Believe Ballroom*.

Others, like Mort Lawrence's *Dawn Patrol* on WIP in Philadelphia, Hank The Night Watchman on KFVD, Al Fox on KGFJ and *The Nutty Club* on WBBM Chicago, were starting a new movement by playing jazz records.

Suddenly, the deejays were starting to get noticed. Decca Records was stunned to learn that Kurt Webster, The Midnight Mayor on WBT, Charlotte, was playing a previously released tune called *Heartaches* by Ted Weems. The mere action of the airplay forced a run on the record stores, resulting in the re-release of the record, which became a national hit.

As a spoof, Al Jazzbo Collins played *I'm Looking Over a Four Leaf Clover* for three and a half hours straight in Salt Lake City one night, making the tune a national best seller.

The power of the deejay was being recognized. Variety called the deejay movement "a postwar show business phenomenon as revolutionary as the atomic bomb, and with about the same effect as far as the orthodox form of talent purveyed is concerned."

Suddenly, the airwaves were filled with deejays. Names like Dave Garroway, Jack Paar, Steve Allen, Bob Elliott and Ray Goulding, Dick Martin, Bob Crane and Ernie Kovacs dominated the radio dial.

Deejays became household names in their local markets. People like Jack The Bellboy (Ed McKenzie), Art Hellyer, Wally Phillips, Howard Miller, Bob Severs, Bob Clayton, Bud Weddell, Frank Ward, Alan Courtney, Freddie Robbins, Dick Gilbert, Gene Norman, Jim Hawkins, Pat Henry, Soupy Heinz (later to become Soupy Sales) and William B. Williams played the hit parade.

Late-night deejays like Barry Gray, Steve Allison, Sherm Feller, Mort Sahl, Mike Wallace and his wife, Buff Cobb, carried enormous influence.

Deejays had become entrenched as a part of radio for all kinds of music: swing, jazz, country and western, big band and the hit

Helen Sioussant holds a walkie-talkie for Sen. Austin of Vermont and Michigan's Sen. Vandenberg for a remote CBS interview.

Broadcast Pioneers Library

Amos 'n' Andy were first known as Sam 'n' Henry when they began broadcasting in 1926, shortly after the Cats whisker era ended. They became Amos 'n' Andy on March 19, 1928. The photo on the left is from 1928, and the photo on the right is from the '50s.

Associated Press

Deejay Jo Warner gives "Bedroom Eyes" to the camera as she passes 192 hours awake and on the air. The stunt was designed to raise money for the March of Dimes. She ended up staying awake for 203 hours (February 11, 1959).

Associated Press

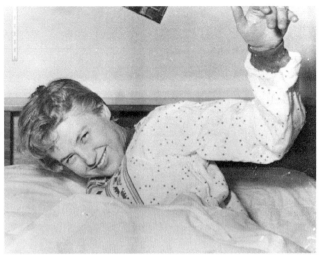

Finally, after a 203-hour "wake-athon" in a Pocatello, Idaho, store window, KYTE deejay Jo Warner waves good night and is about to go to sleep (February 1959).

Associated Press

parade, and a new style called "Negro music," which was only played by Black deejays.

One of the pivotal points ending radio's live music era was when WINS New York's union contract expired and the station said it would no longer air live music and would only use records, employing no musicians. The controversial move created a huge dispute with the union, because playing records was eliminating the jobs of musicians. Stations also began laying off staff announcers because they were no longer needed to introduce the musicians.

Wayne Howell became the first network disc jockey on NBC with a Saturday afternoon half-hour program. This signaled the network realization that the deejay would become a prominent part of programming.

NBC created *Monitor*, hiring deejays Gene Rayburn and Dave Garroway. NBC also converted its flagship, WNBC, to an all-deejay format to compete with WNEW, which was already all-disc jockeys and had a dominant position in New York City. The battle was on, and the war zone was between disc jockeys.

WNEW had Martin Block, and Klavan and Finch, who were

up against deejay shows on WNBC, WHN, WCBS and WINS. Each experimented with mixtures of personality chatter and music, playing recordings from Tony Bennett, Jo Stafford, Rosemary Clooney, Hank Williams and Mitch Miller.

Although radio was gaining some strength after its golden past, this music alone was not enough to bring listening back to previous levels.

Legend has it that a white-owned "Negro music" Memphis radio station, WDIA, had a lot to do with the revitalization of radio when a deejay is said to have played the first rock 'n' roll record. It was the spark that would ignite a generation and incite a movement unlike anything in previous history.

Rock needed radio, and radio needed rock. The marriage of convenience was timed perfectly, and both took off like a rocket. But with the success came controversy. Songs like *Rock Around the Clock* from Bill Haley and the Comets were considered to have too much of a rhythm and blues sound. Many "white" stations feared the "Negro sound" would have a detrimental effect on their listeners, causing advertisers to go elsewhere. Yet that 1954 release became a huge hit, as did *Maybelline* from Chuck Berry.

Following criticism by Sen. Joseph McCarthy of Edward R. Murrow's connection with the Institute of International Education in 1935, Murrow responds on the air (March 12, 1954).

Associated Press

In spite of the outcries that rock 'n' roll would ruin the young generation, only a reluctant few stations held back. Of course, rock 'n' roll skyrocketed to new heights when Memphis deejay George Klein played the first record from Elvis Presley, giving new legs (and hips) to the rock 'n' roll revolution.

At most radio stations, the deejays picked their own music, and their success or failure depended on their ability to "pick the hits." Deejays were playing an Elvis record next to one by Rosemary Clooney, and the eclectic sound was accepted because no one knew better.

But, as fate would have it, a young man by the name of Todd Storz was sitting in a bar near his hometown of Omaha, Nebraska. He noticed that the patrons in the bar would play the same tunes over and over again, and when they left, the bartenders and waitresses would play those same records again and again. He thought it would be wonderful to have a radio station that played all the

KSL Radio often did remote broadcasts like this one from the site of the Utah Salt Flats, where land speed records were often broken (circa 1950).

Bonneville Collection

jukebox hits from the club over and over, all day long.

He believed in his idea so much that he talked his wealthy father, owner of the Storz Brewery, into buying him a local radio station, KOWH. After investing $60,000, the Top 40 format was launched and the station's ratings soared.

Storz then duplicated his success by buying WQAM, Miami; WTIX, New Orleans; WHB, Kansas City, and WDGY, Minneapolis. He took his concept further by creating contests designed to increase the time spent listening to the station.

When broadcasters in Miami heard Storz was coming to town, they filed a complaint with the FCC requiring hearings and delaying the sale. Ultimately, it didn't matter. A few months later, Storz owned a 40 percent share of listening in Miami and made radio history, proving his format would work in a big city.

New York City writers said the Top 40 approach would never work in the Big Apple, but WMCA, WINS and WABC quickly put an end to that theory, taking New York by storm with their Top 40 formats.

Before long, every city in America had two or three Top 40 stations, each with its own variation of the format. In one market, a programmer named Chuck Blore shocked the industry by playing only the Top 40 hits from the past five years, creating the first oldies station.

Top 40, like anything new, wasn't perfect, and it had enormous room for growth. Enter Gordon McClendon, a radio station owner in Dallas who had recently closed down his Liberty network after a few frustrating years of trying to make it fly, not knowing that the network business was about to fold nationwide.

Determined to make his station KLIF the success it once was, McClendon adopted the Todd Storz idea of rotating the hit records frequently. In 1952, McClendon did not allow any of his deejays to repeat any record during their four-hour shift, meaning they could play ten records per hour or 40 per shift. This is where the name Top 40 came from, a phrase which McClendon penned.

McClendon eventually dropped the theory of not repeating records within a shift. Additionally, his deejays played two oldies

Station breaks in the late '40s and early '50s featured three or more announcers — one to give the call letters, one to give the time and one to read announcements. The announcer on the right is KSL Salt Lake City's Joseph A. Kjar.

Bonneville Collection

per hour and a Glen Miller song hourly, because Gordon liked Glen Miller. Eventually, he developed the right formula.

The magic behind McClendon was that he monitored local record store sales and ignored the national charts. McClendon was the first to pay close attention to the listeners' needs, monitoring requests from listeners and designing the format to be listener-friendly. He focused on maintaining a tight, quality sound, incorporated the first radio jingles (singing the call letters) and created

the "Top 40 sound" with his deejays and promotions.

Though Storz discovered or invented Top 40, McClendon perfected it. He, Todd Storz and the Bartell brothers (Jerry, Mel and Lee) were called "the fathers of modern radio" by Sponsor magazine. McClendon was credited with systematizing radio formatics and having more innovations than any other person known to the industry.

The '50s brought the death of radio from the network perspective, but it sprang back to life with the advent of rock 'n' roll music and the idea of Top 40 formats. Top 40 deejays became big personalities in every city in America. Linked closely with the music they were playing, many became big stars in their own rights.

Among the biggest was Moon Dog Alan Freed, who became the consummate deejay with a style and patter all his own. Freed loved rock 'n' roll and, in a way, became its official spokesperson. He piloted some of the first rock 'n' roll concerts in America, called Moon Dog Coronation Balls.

Hundreds of other prominent deejays set the rock 'n' roll tone for an era never to be repeated. It was as compelling and exciting as the golden days of radio, and with it carried huge audience shares and advertiser dollars. Although it couldn't compare to the '30s and '40s and the dominance radio held then, Top 40 radio maintained huge audience shares against its television counterpart.

It became the mood of a generation, just as radio had set the tone for two decades before it.⑩

Singing his theme song, *Ink-a-dink-ado*, Jimmy Durante continued to entertain on radio until there were no more big shows. As a part of NBC's last-ditch effort to keep radio listening alive, *The Big Show* was created in 1950, starring Durante and every other major entertainer. But television had too firm a grip on the audience, which never returned to radio in the same way.

Broadcast Pioneers Library

Although best-known as television anchorman for CBS, Walter Cronkite started out as a war correspondent on radio and is seen here with Sandra Nemser, host of CBS Radio's *Answer Please* (circa 1958).

Associated Press

Jack Roth, Jimmy Durante and Eddie Jackson clowning at the piano.

Pacific Pioneers Library

Edgar Bergen, Charlie McCarthy and Ginger Rogers in 1956, toward the end of the show's long run.

Radio Hall of Fame photo

Jack Benny cracks up during a rehearsal for his radio show in 1954. Benny's radio and TV shows ran continuously for 32 years, until his death in September 1974.

Associated Press

The microphone conveniently placed in Mildred Bailey's kitchen was for her radio program *The Modern Kitchen*.

Broadcast Pioneers Library

One big happy family: (l-r) Mortimer Snerd, Charlie McCarthy, Edgar Bergen and Effie Klinker.

Radio Hall of Fame photo

Gathered together at WNEW, New York, are Louis Prima, Dinah Shore, unidentified woman, Perry Como, Eddie Fisher, Grace Kelly, Ross Martin and Paul Winchell.

Broadcast Pioneers Library

Starting their 30th year as *Amos 'n' Andy*, Freeman Gosden (Amos, left) and Charles Correll (Andy) look serious about the business of making people laugh as the voices in their current CBS Radio series, *The Amos 'n' Andy Music Hall*. Their first *Amos 'n' Andy* broadcast was made in Chicago on March 19, 1928. The two comedians had teamed up eight years earlier on an experimental station in New Orleans. As of 1948, they still had an audience of 30 million listeners on Sunday nights.

Associated Press

Jack Buck, Harry Caray and Joe Garagiola all became nationally known sports broadcasters, seen here as announcers at KMOX, St. Louis, Missouri, in the late 1950s.

R&R Collection

Why did you do it? Each week WLAC, Nashville, went to the State Prison to interview convicts from the warden's office. *Crime Never Pays* was designed to discourage others from a life of crime by talking with those in prison.

Broadcast Pioneers Library

Game shows became the rage on radio as drama programming began to fade. That is, until the government investigated the shows after learning that some were fixed. Contestant Charles Van Doren gives his answer on *The $64,000 Question*.

Pacific Pioneers Library

Actor Douglas Fairbanks during an appearance on *The Hallmark Playhouse* on CBS in 1951.

Broadcast Pioneers Library

Bryon Palme and Joan Weldon from *On A Sunday Afternoon*, which ran Sundays at 5 p.m. from Hollywood on CBS in 1955.

Broadcast Pioneers Library

Most of America listened while Lum and Abner sat around the Jot 'Em Down Store and characters from Pine Ridge dropped in. Starting nationally in Chicago in 1931, the program ran on NBC, CBS and ABC through 1951.

Broadcast Pioneers Library

"Who knows what evil lurks in the hearts of men? The Shadow knows!" Played in later years by Bret Morrison and Grace Matthews, *The Shadow* first aired 1930-1954. Reruns of the program still air on stations to this day.

Broadcast Pioneers Library

Mary Adams (Fanny, Mother Barbour) and J. Anthony Smythe (Father Barbour) giving one another a hug at NBC's 25th anniversary show of Carlton E. Morse's *One Man's Family*. The show, which outlasted all other dramatic shows on radio, began in 1932.

Pacific Pioneers Library

A rare, smiling shot of newsman Edward R. Murrow (circa 1953).

Associated Press

Running for a whopping 23 years, *Let's Pretend* offered some of the finest children's programming. Nila Mack, seen here with the kids, stayed on the show until her death in 1953.

Broadcast Pioneers Library

Nadine Conner and host Gordon MacRae on *The Railroad Hour* on NBC in 1952.

Pacific Pioneers Library

Starting on the NBC Red Network in the Western states in May 1932, *One Man's Family* became the longest-running radio drama in history, ending in May 1959. J. Anthony Smythe (Father Barbour) and Minetta Ellen (Mother Barbour) starred in the show, as generations grew along with them.

Broadcast Pioneers Library

J. Carrol Naish stars as Luigi Basco, an antiques dealer, in CBS's Tuesday night series *Life With Luigi*. He is seen here with his daughter Elaine Naish, who played an occasional role on the program (August 18, 1952).

Associated Press

Anne Seymour (center) as wife Lily serves as a peacemaker between husband Edwin (Monty Woolley) and maid Agnes (Pert Kelton) in the NBC comedy/satire *The Magnificent Montague* (January 18, 1951).

Associated Press

Singers Paula Kelly of the Modernaires and Gisele MacKenzie delighted at the prospect of rejoining head man Bob Crosby on the CBS Radio Network's tuneful *Club 15* when the program returned to the network in 1951.

Broadcast Pioneers Library

Transcription discs were how radio programs were recorded and often played back on the air. This label dated March 28, 1954, is from a Jack Benny program on CBS.

Pacific Pioneers Library

Tony Randall with Nancy Franklin in Mutual's *I Love A Mystery* series, heard weeknights in 1950.

Broadcast Pioneers Library

Actor Gregory Peck acts out a role on ABC's *Screen Guild Theatre*.

Broadcast Pioneers Library

Perhaps the first to regularly broadcast from home, ABC's Mary Margaret McBride conducted her one-hour daily interview program from her Manhattan duplex apartment. When the weather got too hot, she moved the staff and her broadcasts to her Larchmont home on Long Island Sound, where her breezy screened porch studio was 15 degrees cooler than the city (July 1951).

Associated Press

Richard Keith played the editor, John Shuttleworth, of Mutual's *Sunday True Detective Mysteries* dramatizations in 1951.

Broadcast Pioneers Library

Starting as a page boy at NBC, Dave Garroway went though NBC's announcer-training program and graduated at the bottom of the list. Because he lacked the formal NBC style, he took a job at KDKA, Pittsburgh, in the mid-'30s and won an award for best Pittsburgh announcer. Years later, he returned to NBC as host of *Monitor.*

Pacific Pioneers Library

Playing a romantically comic teenager on CBS Radio's Monday evening show *Meet Corliss Archer* was Janet Waldo, with Sam Edwards (who played Dexter, Corliss' boyfriend.) The series was broadcast on CBS and NBC in the '40s and '50s and entered its 12th and final radio year on Mutual in 1954.

Broadcast Pioneers Library

Bill Powell at WIRE, the Indianapolis NBC affiliate.

Broadcast Pioneers Library

One of the more popular "girl singers" of her day, Rosemary Clooney (pictured with John Raitt) was a vocalist on *Songs for Sale* on CBS in 1950.

Broadcast Pioneers Library

Howdy Doody creator "Buffalo" Bob Smith, along with Clarabell the clown, Howdy and friend. The show gained its popularity on television; however, it did spend two years as a radio program.

Broadcast Pioneers Library

Actors Van Johnson and Mary Jane Croft seen playing the title roles in *Old Man's Bride,* on CBS's *General Electric Theatre* in October 1953.

Broadcast Pioneers Library

1950s disc jockey Brook Walters on WSRK.

Broadcast Pioneers Library

One of many pioneers in the '50s deejay era, Pat Byrne on Canada's CFJM.

Broadcast Pioneers Library

Robert Hurleigh and the News could be heard mornings in 1950 on the Mutual Broadcasting Network.

Broadcast Pioneers Library

Running from 1937 to 1956, *Aunt Jenny* was one of the more popular soaps. Agnes Young played the role in the latter years of the program (seen here in 1955). Young also played Aunt Minta on *My Son and I*, a 1939 CBS soap.

Broadcast Pioneers Library

The cry "Whyyyy, daddy, whyyyyy" by Fanny Brice made her one of radio's biggest stars from 1936 through her death in 1951 at the age of 59.

Broadcast Pioneers Library

Ford Nelson ready to tickle the ivories at WDIA.

Broadcast Pioneers Library

Minnie "Hoooowdy" Pearl grew up a star on WSM's *Grand Ole Opry*, seen here in May 1955.

One of the more innovative ways to keep radio alive against the threat of television was to alternate programs between radio and television. NBC's *Dragnet* ran on Sunday nights on NBC radio and Thursday nights on NBC television. Both programs starred Jack Webb.

Broadcast Pioneers Library

CBS news legend Robert Trout in July 1956.

Broadcast Pioneers Library

Wearing white gloves to protect the records, deejay Lavada Durst on KVET holds a "78" record.

Broadcast Pioneers Library

KSAN San Francisco's "Fatso" Berry.

Broadcast Pioneers Library

Rudy Vallee with guest Gwen Verdon in March 1955.

Broadcast Pioneers Library

The comic duo Jack and Jerry were heard early mornings and middays on KWK, St. Louis, in the early '50s.

Broadcast Pioneers Library

This billboard was a sign of the modern times, featuring AM radio, the new FM (Frequency Modulation) radio and the latest fad — television.

Broadcast Pioneers Library

Nationally popularized on television's *Hogan's Heroes*, Bob Crane started his entertainment career as a radio deejay in the 1950s on WLEA.

Broadcast Pioneers Library

Deejay Buddy Deane (reclining) and friends
clowning around during a broadcast.

Broadcast Pioneers Library

Women were a big part of radio during the live drama and music days but became a rarity as
stations hired more and more disc jockeys. Mimi Chandler is shown broadcasting in Miami in
the early '50s.

Broadcast Pioneers Library

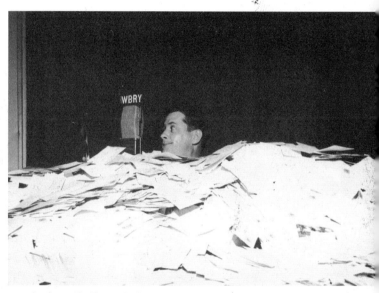

Buried in fan mail, deejay Allan Day of WRBY demonstrated the power of
radio in the early '50s.

Broadcast Pioneers Library

WCKY deejay Don Davis was either a little guy or he had some really big
records.

Broadcast Pioneers Library

Radio remotes have been around since the first days of
broadcasting. This remote trailer is manned by deejay Paul
Drew at WHLS, Port Huron, Michigan, in 1955.

Drew Collection

Elvis Presley had more impact on radio listening than any other single human being. When his music took America by storm, radio became the soul of rock 'n' roll.

Radio and Records

Disc jockey Jim Patterson, a popular local on WBT, Charlotte (circa 1955).

Broadcast Pioneers Library

Broadcasting from the Mutual Don Lee Network in Hollywood was newsman Sam Hayes.

Pacific Pioneers Library

WINS disc jockey Herb Sheldin gets a visit from Sonny the Bunny.

Broadcast Pioneers Library

One of the early and legendary deejays, Peter Potter, worked with KFWB and then jumped ship in 1951 with Al Jarvis to join KLAC (formerly KMTR), the first all-disc jockey station. With call letters sung by The Modernaires, and playing tunes from Peggy Lee, Nat King Cole and Perry Como, the station became the top in Los Angeles in three months.

Broadcast Pioneers Library

Sonny the Bunny makes the rounds, visiting ABC's Jack Lacey.

Broadcast Pioneers Library

Husband and wife team Ronald Colman and Benita Hume took a break from the movies in 1950 to star in *Halls of Ivy*. The ivy league program took place in a small college town where Colman played the president of the school. The show aired on Wednesdays and Friday evenings on NBC until 1952.

Broadcast Pioneers Library

On-air gags were often effective for increasing listenership, but they occasionally failed and got the deejay or the station in trouble. Here deejays picket after suspension for an on-air gag. Bob Power (left) and Hoe Hoppel (right), Lee Whitegead and Miss Sam Barbee of station WCMS, Norfolk.

Associated Press

KECK deejays Greg Gregory and Tom Edwards.

Broadcast Pioneers Library

Bob Van Camp leans on the piano keyboard to talk while discussing a "33" he just played on WSB, Atlanta.

Broadcast Pioneers Library

In the '50s, every deejay had a gimmick designed to make him stand out and gain listenership. Here, KABC, Los Angeles, deejay Don MacKinnon wears his trademark costume (June 30, 1958).

Associated Press

Armed with cigars, a bell, some platters and a bagel, this '50s deejay is ready to rock.

Broadcast Pioneers Library

WPTR, Albany, disc jockey Martin Ross.

Broadcast Pioneers Library

Nifty '50s disc jockey Marc Sorley hailed from KPQ.

Broadcast Pioneers Library

A KWBU disc jockey identified only as "Rosemary."

Broadcast Pioneers Library

You're on! Board operator Bill Howard signals Adrian Munzell at Lexington, Kentucky, station WLAP.

Broadcast Pioneers Library

Ralph Emery at WSM, Nashville, in 1957, where he got his start. Country music's best known DJ later joined The Nashville Network.

Radio Ink Collection

Deejay Robin Seymour on WKMH.

Broadcast Pioneers Library

Up with the chickens: A WKNE announcer's farm report is for the birds.

Broadcast Pioneers Library

WJR Detroit's Bob Barber.

Broadcast Pioneers Library

Won't WAVZ New Haven's Timmy Marcle be surprised when he realizes his arm has been on the turntable arm all this time?

Broadcast Pioneers Library

Legendary New York disc jockey Jack Lacey.

R &R Collection

Bill Weaver of KCBS later became the manager for Gordon McClendon's legendary KLIF in Dallas, where the Top 40 format was perfected.

Broadcast Pioneers Library

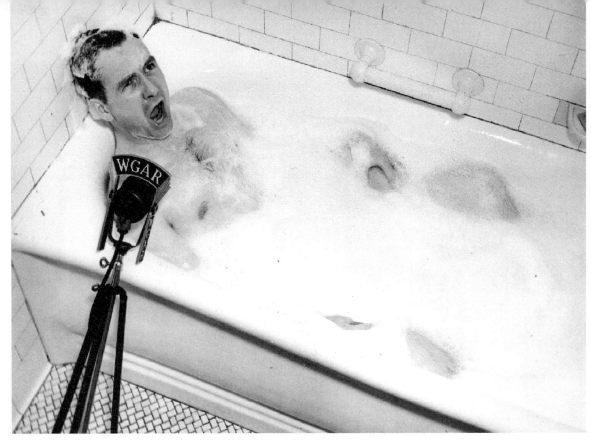

WGAR, Cleveland, takes the unusual remote plunge.

Broadcast Pioneers Library

It's been said that the deejays who played country music were responsible for the success of many country stars. Nelson King was one who played the country hits in the '50s.

Broadcast Pioneers Library

In the '50s, every deejay tried a gimmick to win audiences. Joe Knight's gimmick was "Knight of the Spinning Round Table."

Broadcast Pioneers Library

Deejay Dick Lee.

Broadcast Pioneers Library

In those days, Peggy Lloyd of WOV was referred to as a "girl" deejay, a rarity on the air.

Broadcast Pioneers Library

WFIL disc jockey LeRoy Miller, winner of the first annual Radio and Television Best Disc Jockey Award.

Broadcast Pioneers Library

WSRS Cleveland's cut-up Ray Mullins.

Broadcast Pioneers Library

Milton Q. Ford on WWDC, Washington, D.C., and his pet parrot.

Broadcast Pioneers Library

A pioneer in talk radio, Barry Gray spent years talking on late-night New York radio with *Scout About Town* and *The Barry Gray Show*. Stars would stop by his program after theater appearances.

Broadcast Pioneers Library

The first to simulcast a radio and television show was Art Linkletter's *House Party* on Mutual's Don Lee Network.

Pacific Pioneers Library

Radio stars and their families became well-known because of the many radio magazines that revealed their lifestyles. Dick Powell, June Allyson and their two kids are seen here in 1956.

Pacific Pioneers Library

At a time when anti-segregation movements were starting in Mississippi, "Negro" deejays were influencing music listening on stations across the continent. Hal Jackson, then at WMCA, became one of the most prominent African-Americans in the radio business at the time. Later, at WLIB, Jackson was one of the first to promote shows from the Apollo Theater, bringing black artists into New York City.

Radio Ink Collection

'50s deejay "Doc" Dunlap on WMOB in Mobile, Alabama.

Broadcast Pioneers Library

1950s

Arthur Godfrey became well known for singing tunes while playing his ukulele.

Broadcast Pioneers Library

Probably the most influential radio innovator of the rock 'n' roll era of radio was Gordon McLendon, who was said to have saved radio with the implementation of Top 40. Although the format was invented in part by programmer Todd Storz, it was McClendon who first put jingles on the air and developed wild-sounding, promotionally oriented stations.

R&R Collection

Portland Hoffa and Fred Allen had become one of radio's most popular teams with a reign on the air from 1930 to 1949. In 1952, Allen started a move to television that was halted by a heart attack. He died March 17, 1956, while taking a stroll with his wife, Portland.

Broadcast Pioneers Library

New York DJ Murray the K grabs some attention during the WINS "Sleep in the Subway" promotion.

Radio Ink Collection

Alan Freed was the king of rock 'n' roll radio. He is credited for becoming the voice of rock 'n' roll music and exposing it to America through his radio program and his live concerts.

Radio Ink Collection

The KQV news "cruiser" patrols the waterfront.

KQV

The lineup of disc jockeys who put black artists on the air in 1951 in Nashville: (l-r) John Richbourg, Gene Nobles, Hoss Allen, Herman Grizzard and (standing) Don Whitehead.

Radio Ink Collection

1960s

Radio entered the '60s with several black eyes. In late 1959, the Mutual Broadcasting System's Chairman Hal Roach Jr. and MBS President Alexander Guterma were indicted by a federal grand jury on charges that the network, which had been financially troubled, had accepted advance payment of $750,000 in exchange for "dissemination within the U.S. political propaganda on behalf of and favorable to the Dominican Republic." Guterma was found guilty of fraudulent stock manipulations and got almost five years in the slammer and $160,000 in fines.

Another black eye marred the industry when an investigation of payola began. It was alleged by a Senate subcommittee that radio deejays were taking bribes in exchange for playing records. These bribes of cash, booze, drugs and prostitutes were in exchange for preferential treatment of certain records.

Those offering the bribes — record companies and independent pro-

Zenith's Royal 500-E, an all-transistor "pocket radio," was the world's most powerful radio of its size in 1962. It slipped into pocket or purse for traveling and featured a three-position carrying handle and a non-breakable nylon case.

Radio Ink Collection

moters — had realized that enough air play exposure could sell a lot of records. They also realized that the audience often hung onto the words of a deejay, and that a plug (referred to as plugola) could motivate kids to go out and buy a record.

In 1959, there were almost 2,000 record companies generating as many as 250 new records a week. Not all of them could get their tunes on the air; therefore, payola seemed a logical solution. In Los Angeles, for instance, the disc jockeys were earning

Gordon J. Dinerstein, vice president and general manager of Music Suppliers, Inc., a Boston-based record distribution firm, takes the stand in the hearing room of the House Legislative Oversight Subcommittee as the payola hearings began (February 16, 1960).

Associated Press

WMEX, Boston, disc jockey Arnie "Woo Woo" Ginsberg testifies before the House Administrative Oversight Committee in a payola probe.

Associated Press

Communications Commission began a witch hunt, ordering all radio and television stations to report whenever "things of value" were paid to the station or its employees but not identified on the air.

In the meantime, RCA agreed it would not pay disc jockeys to play records unless the deejays told the audience over the air that they were being paid for air play. At this point, Rep. Oren Harris (D-Ark.), Chairman of the House Legislative Oversight Committee, began an extensive payola investigation. Some felt the investigation was an attempt to stop rock 'n' roll, which was considered by many to be the downfall of America's youth.

Alan Freed, the king of rock 'n' roll disc jockeys, was arrested in May 1960 and charged with commercial bribery for receiving $30,650 from six record companies to plug discs on his show. He pleaded guilty and received a six-month sentence and a $300 fine. After his prison sentence, he was indicted on income tax evasion as a result of unreported income. Freed always maintained that he never accepted advance payola but never turned down a gift after the fact.

Hearings continued, and many popular radio deejays were brought before the House Committee to testify.

Boston jock Stan Richards defended the practice of payola

an extra $300 to $500 a week on top of their $25,000 to $50,000 annual salaries.

In early 1960, the Federal Trade Commission officially charged Cameo Records, London Records, RCA Records and six distributors for bribing disc jockeys. Additionally, the Federal

Federal Communications Commission Chairman Frederick Ford (left) discusses the payola hearings with Chairman Oren Harris (D-Ark.) on April 12, 1960, following the opening of the House hearings aimed at preventing quiz show and payola scandals.
Associated Press

by saying: "This seems to be the American way of life — 'I'll do for you. What will you do for me?' "

According to author Arnold Passman in *The Deejays*: "The Philadelphia-lawyer trappings that surround the legal entanglements of music and radio were put to focus with the investigation of a Philadelphia disc jockey. Clean-cut Dick Clark was the all-American subject, and payola was the temptress."

Although many were investigated, payola was hard to prove. Freed was one of the few to be imprisoned, because a precedent had not existed making payola illegal. Tax evasion was the loophole used for those who had not reported their income. Additionally, all those involved remained tight-lipped, not admitting to any payola activity.

Freed died at the age of 43 in 1965, having taken the fall for the industry.

A third black eye for radio came when Charles Van Doren, a long-running winner on the quiz show *Twenty-One*, admitted that each of his 14 appearances on the show had been rigged. He had been given the answers in advance and walked away with

$130,000. Additional testimony revealed that *The $64,000 Question*, a radio game show, had also been rigged.

Charges were filed and several former quiz-show contestants were charged with perjury. Congress also made amendments to the Communications Act that made the practices of rigging contests and deceiving audiences punishable with revocation of broadcast licenses.

Radio's credibility was in serious question. The newspapers finally had their opportunities to place the final nail in the coffin of the medium they had targeted as their enemy. Not only were

Payola scandals rocked the radio industry in the early '60s. Shown here is WBZ, Boston, announcer Dave Maynard appearing as a witness on February 8, 1960, before the House Subcommittee on Legislative Oversight, which was looking for evidence of payola.
Associated Press

there the Mutual scandal, the payola scandal and the quiz show scandal, but the big network programs were no more, offering more fodder to signal radio's problems. Newspapers in the early '60s were full of unflattering stories about radio.

November 1960 saw the last of the radio soap operas fade

This emotion-filled photo shows the man who invented the term rock 'n' roll, Alan Freed, and his wife, Inga, as they arrive at the District Attorney's office in New York on November 30, 1959. Freed refused to sign a waiver of immunity and testify before a grand jury.

Associated Press

into oblivion. *Ma Perkins, Right to Happiness, Young Dr. Malone, The Second Mrs. Burton, Whispering Streets, Best Seller* and *The Couple Next Door* were pulled off the air due to a lack of audience interest. Actress Virginia Payne, who had played Ma Perkins since that show's start on December 4, 1933, had ended with 7,065 programs under her belt.

In Washington, John F. Kennedy was elected president and Newton Minow became his new chairman of the FCC.

Chairman John C. Doerfer had resigned because of alleged improprieties in his acceptance of vacations on the Storer Broadcasting yacht, and his submission of double and triple billings on his travel expenses.

Minow brought fear into the hearts of broadcasters, demanding that stations embrace the principals of public service, giving indications that he would attempt to circumvent the First Amendment. Broadcasters were concerned that Minow's policies would censor programming, yet he seemed to favor radio more than television.

Minow stated that "while TV is a vast wasteland, radio is America's roommate; radio is America's traveling companion. It travels with us like a welcome shadow. We also know that more people depend on radio for news as it happens, and for news of community affairs, than they do any other means of communication."

The '60s also brought technical improvements that would change the radio business forever, including the approval of stereophonic FM, the invention of radio automation and the launch of satellites. WGFM, Schenectady, New York; WEFM, Chicago, and KMLA, Los Angeles, were the first stereo stations.

But FM stations were nothing more than a burden to most operators, who considered their FM secondary to their AMs. Most FMs aired automated "elevator" music. The words FM became identified with the format of soft, bland, background music.

In 1952, Dick Clark joined Philadelphia's Bob Horn show called *Bandstand* on WFIL. Four years later, Horn was arrested for drunken driving, leaving Clark to run the show alone. A year later, Clark took the program to television. Clark is seen here testifying in the 1961 payola hearings.

Associated Press

WNEW personality Scott Muni looks thrilled to be leaving the District Attorney's office on November 27, 1959, after appearing in payola hearings as VP of the recently formed Disc Jockey Association.

Associated Press

In the early '60s, many stations turned their FMs back to the FCC because they saw no future in FM, and the cost of running an extra station that few listened to was nothing more than a burden. Only a small number of "hi-fi" systems were on the market to take advantages of this new stereo service.

Following the payola scandals, a number of "Eastern" deejays were to head west to restart their careers after facing public embarrassment. Tom "Big Daddy" Donohue and Bobby "The Great" Mitchell left Philadelphia's WIBG, where they had shared the airwaves with other greats like Joe Niagara, Hy Lit and "Humble" Harv Miller.

They began playing many of the black tunes they had played in Philly, and created "Jingle-Free Radio" on KYA in San Francisco. The station, which called itself "The Boss of the Bay," skyrocketed to the top of the ratings. They created audience-

involvement promotions like "The Battle of the New Sounds" under program director Les Crane.

As a result, a new trend in radio began that would again revolutionize radio. In 1961, a young Phil Yarborough, known as Bill Drake, picked up on the trend and created a tightly formatted Top 40 format he called "Boss Radio." The personalities of this format were restricted in the amount of time they could talk and what they could say. This was a huge departure from the earlier stages of Top 40, when personality "chatter" was still allowed.

In the "Boss" format, Drake's disc jockeys would talk over the musical introductions of the records and had to express their personality in very short bursts of energy. Phrases like "more music," "Boss jocks," "Hitbound" and "20/20 news" were the nature of the sound Drake wanted to capture. Be brief, be upbeat and let the music be the star. The music was rotated to play the top songs hourly, in some cases.

Drake, a KYA employee, took his format concept to KYNO in Fresno, which was owned by the visionary Gene Chenault, who had started in the business as a radio actor. The station was up against "K-Make" (KMAK) and was in for a battle to win the ratings KMAK already owned. KMAK's national program director was Ron Jacobs and its program director was Bill Watson, two of the industry's best.

When Drake launched the new KYNO, the famous "battle of Fresno" began. KMAK's air staff consisted of Jacobs, Watson, Frank Terry and Robert W. Morgan. Drake's "Boss" station had Gary Mack, Les Turpin and K.O. Bayley. The stations battled back and forth, each trying to play more music, each trying to out-contest the other.

Ultimately, KYNO, Drake and Chenault were victorious. All the eyes of the radio business were on this legendary Fresno battle, and everyone in radio wanted to duplicate Drake's success. As a result, Drake and Chenault formed a consulting business. Their first success outside of Fresno was at KGB in San Diego, which they took to No. 1.

Drake and Chenault became one of the first radio programming consultancies to duplicate success en masse. Drake's "Boss" sound rapidly found its way to radio stations across the United States. He was one of the most-sought-after consultants in American radio, and also one of the most-imitated. "Boss" radio was in every market in America, either under Drake's direction or as a copycat of his format and jingles.

Drake later returned to San Francisco. He went up against KYA with KFRC, and beat the station that had been "The Boss of the Bay."

1960s

Boss radio became No. 1 in Los Angeles in a heated battle with dominant Top 40 station KFWB/Channel 98. During its heyday, "Boss Radio" KHJ sported names like Robert W. Morgan, The Real Don Steele, Gary Mack, David Diamond, Roger Christian, Johnny Williams, Sam Riddle, Chuck Browning, Scotty Brink, Tom Maule, Humble Harv Miller, Terry Frank, Bobby Tripp, Charlie Tuna, Donn Tyler and Tommy Vance.

Top 40 in its various forms was the predominant radio format in the early '60s. A new breed of deejays came onto the scene, with a faster, tighter way of incorporating their personalities into their very brief "over the record" talk segments. According to programmer Ron Jacobs: "A disc jockey has to have something better to say than the record, which cost thousands of dollars to produce."

About the fast-talking boss jocks, radio personality Steve Allen said: "I am personally put off by the screaming, fast-talking sort of rock 'n' roll deejay. I believe there is an interesting parallel

Radio comedians George Burns (left) and Jack Benny clown around at a charity benefit in May 1961. Benny, who tried to take the place of Gracie Allen, Burns' longtime sidekick and wife, succeeded in proving there is only one Gracie.

Associated Press

Although one does not automatically link Howard Hughes with radio, his push to create satellite communications had a dramatic effect on the radio business. Satellite uplinks eliminated the need for phone lines, thus changing the network business. As satellite technology improved, networks could send "FM" quality audio to stations, eliminating the need for live deejays. Today, "the bird" is affordable for local station uplinks for remotes and other forms of broadcast.

Radio and Records

between the almost mechanical, gibbering, tobacco-auctioneer style in which the modern rock 'n' roll disc jockey speaks and the bulk of the music he presents. It seems to me that what these speakers are selling is not a message, but a sound, a mood, a color. And it is a color consistent with that of the music."

Allen may have been referring to the style of "the fastest in the West," The Real Don Steele. A typical Steele song intro (this one over the 16-second intro of The Beatles' *Day Tripper*): "Three o'clock in Boss Angeles! And HEY, thitz me, The Real Don Steele, a billion-dollar weekend there, and you're looking out of sidewalk call; I got nothing but those groovy golds, we're gonna fit Chuck out here on a fractious Friday boy, got to get a set outside that [unintelligible word resembling blowing bubbles in a glass of water] jumbo city. [Pause] Take a trip. When you chase 'em, daylight."

In Buffalo, New York, WKBW set national trends with radio stars like Joey Reynolds, Danny Neverth, Dick Biondi and

Tommy Shannon. Other jocks around the country revolutionized the Top 40 sound.

In New York, the Top 40 battle was heated between WINS, which had been the No. 1 station, and the newly Top 40-formatted WABC. WINS personalities were Paul Sherman "The Crown Prince of Rock and Roll," Stan Z. Burns, Brad "Battle of the Baritones" Phillips and Murray "The K" Kaufman.

WABC had "the swingin' seven": Herb Oscar Anderson as "The Morning Mayor of New York," Charlie Greer, Jack Carney, Chuck Dunnaway "The round mound of sound," Farrell Smith, Scott Muni and Bill Owen. Carney was later replaced by Dan Ingram, Bruce Morrow came in to replace Dunnaway and Sam Holman was the replacement for Farrell Smith.

The swingin' seven name was later changed to The WABC

Gene Klavan went on to become one of the top New York morning people with Klavan and Finch on WNEW.

Broadcast Pioneers Library

Spike Jones in July 1960.
Broadcast Pioneers Library

Good Guys, but WABC didn't use it much and the phrase was snatched up by competitor WMCA's program director Ruth Meyer. Before long, every time WABC mentioned their good guy name, people thought of the WMCA Good Guys. This began the great Top 40 battle in New York between WINS, WMCA and third-ranked WABC. By 1964, WABC was not only the top station in New York, it was the most-listened-to radio station in North America, thanks to programmer Rick Sklar.

About this time, the FCC ruled that FM stations could no longer be 100 percent simulcast with their sister AMs, and the limit was placed at 50 percent. Stations were faced with decisions about what to do with their programming.

Simultaneously, as America's presence in the Vietnam War escalated, music reflected the change and the mood. America's youth were turning to LSD and demonstrating against the war. Bob Dylan had wedded rock and folk music, and a new breed of artists was being heard on the air: folk rock groups like Simon and Garfunkel, The Byrds, The Turtles and The Mamas and The Papas. The year 1965 was the dawning of the age of Aquarius, which began to be reflected on FM radio.

Starting in San Francisco, Tom Donohue again innovated with a format reflecting the "flower-power" era of the hippie movement. Donohue pioneered what has been referred to as "acid rock," "underground radio" or "progressive" on KMPX, a little-known FM in San Francisco in 1967. Its folk-rock format was referred to as "Black Top 40."

About the same time, KOIT in San Francisco began playing "head rock," hosted by the seductive "KOIT Mother."

Donohue soon left KMPX and headed to KSAN, also in San Francisco. It was there that he perfected the format and its new style of air personalities. Everything about the format was the opposite of Top 40. The personalities were soft-spoken, low-key and sounded stoned (most probably were). Where Top 40 was tight, progressive rock was loose, leaving gaps between records (for those taping the songs) and not talking on top of the music.

Donohue limited the format to eight minutes of commercials per hour, half the amount usually aired on traditional Top 40 stations. The format took off and, again, the concept spread across America.

Local formats were the backbone of radio in the '60s. The role of the networks had been diminished to airing newscasts at the top and bottom of the hour, and providing sports program-

Don McNeill's *Breakfast Club* was a downhome favorite that lasted 34 years. The morning show heavily relied on audience participation, corny jokes and visiting guests. The show ran from June 23, 1933, until December 27, 1968.

Broadcast Pioneers Library

ming and music specials.

In 1967, ABC revolutionized network radio by offering four new services, each provided at times other than the traditional top and bottom of the hour. They launched The American Information Network, The American Personality Network, The American Contemporary Network and the American FM Network. This move signaled the beginning of an era of fragmentation. No longer could the networks provide one product to be picked up by all stations.

As the '60s came to an end, these were the primary music formats on the radio: a much tighter form of Top 40; MOR (middle of the road), which focused on strong personalities and heavy community involvement; Beautiful Music, which was background music primarily aired on unimportant FMs, and progressive rock, which was the new FM format reflecting the anti-war sentiment and the new folk-rock music era. There was also Country and Western and, in some of the bigger cities, soul music.

Radio had captured the mood of the country and developed formats to reflect that mood. In the '60s, radio had buried a president, his brother and a great civil rights leader. Radio had also reported man's first walk on the moon, been the only form of communication for millions in the Northeast during a major blackout and brought reports of a war and eventual withdrawal in Vietnam. Most importantly, radio had become the voice of the young generation, and its constant companion. ⌷

Wow! Nine transistors! This portable AM/FM radio was placed on the market in January 1963. It was said this Westinghouse radio would play 100 hours on four penlight batteries.

Associated Press

Announcer Clifton Fadiman during a broadcast of NBC's *Monitor* in December 1963. Monitor ran most of the day on Saturdays. Fadiman had been the announcer for *Information, Please* in 1938.

Broadcast Pioneers Library

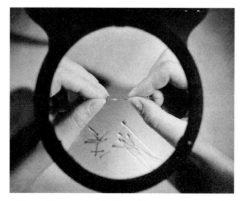

Although invented in the United States, at the time the transistor was not considered significant, and the patent was sold to the Japanese. The transistor became one of the most significant developments in the history of radio, making radios smaller and more portable, with a long battery life.

Associated Press

Miami's WQAM was the center of attention during the rock 'n' roll era. Each week they would hold a talent search at a local amphitheater, always packing the house.

Broadcast Pioneers Library

The WHN Band featuring Hugo Winterhalter in the main ballroom of the Waldorf-Astoria. The WHN Reception and Cocktail Party was held to celebrate the purchase and change of letters from WMOM to WHN (February 28, 1962).

Broadcast Pioneers Library

A WHN, New York, disc jockey keeps his eye on the turntable.

Broadcast Pioneers Library

Beautiful state-of-the-art studios built for WFIL, Philadelphia, in the early '60s.

Broadcast Pioneers Library

Although best-known for his role as sidekick to Johnny Carson on *The Tonight Show*, announcer Ed McMahon started his career in radio. During *The Tonight Show* he also moonlighted as host of a weekend radio show (June 7, 1968).

Associated Press

After 40 years on the air, *Rambling With Gambling* was recognized by New York Mayor Robert Wagner, seen presenting a citation to John B. Gambling (left) and John A. Gambling (right) on March 8, 1968. Gambling's grandson, the third generation, still holds the tradition to this day, meaning the program has been on for more than 67 years as of 1995.

Associated Press

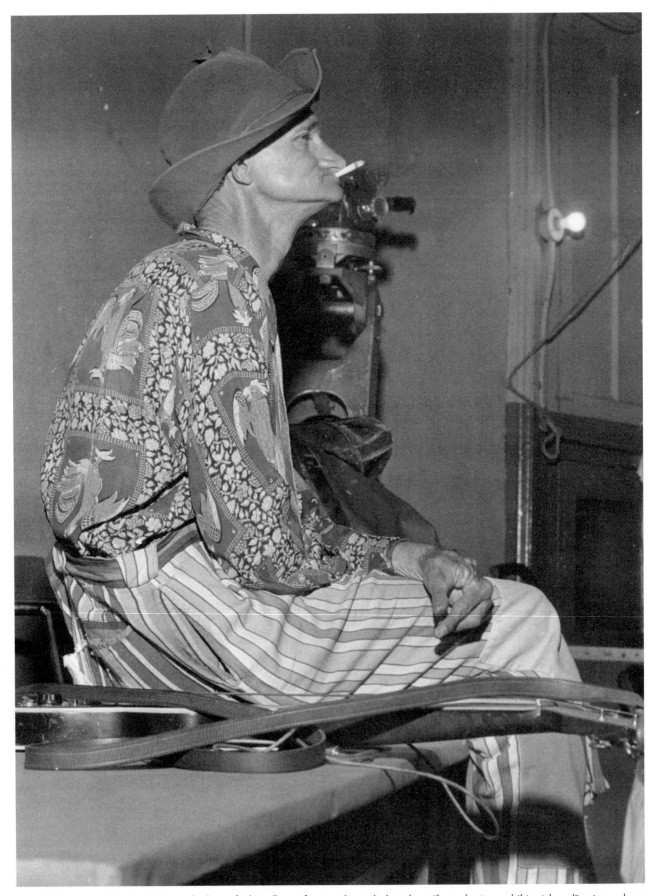

Grand Ole Opry star "Cousin Jody" waits backstage for his call to perform in a live radio broadcast. The steel guitar and "biscuit board" artist was born in Possum Hollow, Tennessee, as James C. Summey.

Associated Press

Generations of radio broadcasters broke into the radio business at a very young age. Here a 16-year-old Tom Daren spins records at a local radio station, only to move on to a career of fame and fortune.

Radio Ink Collection

WABC New York's most-recognized voice was probably Dan Ingram.

R&R Collection

As the rock 'n roll era began to fade, the British invasion rekindled radio listening when The Beatles came on the scene, exposing a whole new generation to a rock revolution, starting with their appearance on *The Ed Sullivan Show*.

Broadcast Pioneers Library

Los Angeles' "Emperor" Bob Hudson, perhaps best known for his Grammy-winning *Ajax Liquor Store* recordings with partner Ron Landry in 1971. In 1966, he was voted Billboard Magazine's top morning personality. He was on the staff of KRLA 1963-65, KFWB in 1967 and '68, KFI in 1974-76 and many others throughout the years.

Radio and Records

Pop sensations Peter, Paul & Mary with CBS Radio's Mike Wallace in December 1965.

Broadcast Pioneers Library

The Joe Pyne Show became a national phenomenon in 1967. Pyne was one of the first to get violently controversial on the air.

Broadcast Pioneers Library

Stan Freberg was a true innovator in radio commercial production. He was the first to develop strong radio creative ideas, and was known for showing that any image can be created in radio commercials with the use of creative writing and sound effects. He offered many syndicated radio programs and is well-known for the commercials he created promoting radio.

Radio Ink Collection

Aside from being the radio announcer seen on television's *Laugh In*, Gary Owens has been a star in Los Angeles radio for 20 years. He was born Gary Altman in 1936 and started on KORN in Mitchell, South Dakota. His first big break came working for Don Burden's KOIL in Omaha.

R&R Collection

The roving eye of CBS News put reporters across the globe to report the news on radio. Foreign correspondent Dallas Townsend was one of CBS' top radio journalists.

CBS

WMCA "Good Guy" Gary Stevens and character Wolley Burger kept teens in New York listening on the edge of their seats to find out what would be said next. Stevens was one of New York's highest-rated deejays in 1967.

Radio Ink Collection

Sporting love beads, underground deejay Chuck Dunnaway receives a visit from Jimi Hendrix (right) and bass player Noel Redding.

Radio Ink Collection

Three generations of Gamblings on WOR-AM, New York: (l-r) John A., John R. and John B.

Radio Ink Collection

Bill Drake and Betty Breneman of Boss Radio KHJ.

Radio Ink Collection

KLIF, Dallas, used spectacular promotions, like this flagpole sitter, to build an audience.

Radio Ink Collection

A promotion piece for the KOGO San Diego news department. The third guy from the right is now seen on the national TV show *Live with Regis & Kathie Lee*. Yes, it's Regis Philbin, circa 1960.

Radio Ink Collection

Boss Jocks above Sunset Strip across from Schwab's Drugstore (now a Virgin Megastore.) These were the original 93 KHJ jocks, except Terry replaced Roger Christian and Mitchell replaced Dave Diamond.

Radio Ink Collection

5 MAVERICKS! 6 WINNERS?

KHJ Maverick-A-Day winners: Guy Zapoleon, Helen Denis, DJ Charlie Tuna, Marsha Clearwater, Ed Brinkley, and Kevin Fahrer.

We just made five of our listeners winners of 1970 Ford Mavericks. They made us a winner too. A winner with the influential 18-49 age group. Our contests are designed to appeal to everyone, especially the 18-49 year olds. The Maverick-A-Day contest is a good example. The five winners, ranged in age from 16-43 . . . from student to housewife.

Be a winner with the 18-49 year olds.

Get with . . .

93/KHJ

This early ad from Boss radio KHJ shows Guy Zapoleon (l) getting bitten by the radio bug as the winner of a car promotion. His first taste of a major market giveaway in 1969 led him to become a major radio programmer.

Radio Ink Collection

Tom Donohue invented Progressive or "Underground" radio. His influence on KSAN, San Francisco, was the first to mirror the artists who were previously receiving no exposure due to their "radical" messages and sound. This sound reflected the hippie movement and the '60s underground movement. At his funeral it was said: "With Tom Donohue went the next great format."

Radio Ink Collection

When the Beatles came to New York in 1965, WABC's Cousin Brucie Morrow and programmer Rick Sklar (foreground) interviewed George Harrison (left) and Ringo Starr. To the right is WABC engineer Jerry Zeller.

Radio Ink Collection

WBZ Boston's staff: (back, l-r) Carl deSuze, Ron Landry, Jay Dunn, Dave Maynard. (front, l-r) Dick Summer, Bob Kennedy, Bruce Bradley.

Radio Ink Collection

Two legendary Top 40 programmers shown in 1961: Paul Drew (left) and Bill Drake (right), seen with recording artist Don Carroll (left center) and Bid Causey (right center).

Drew Collection

Right: The Joy Boys, as advertised in the Washington Daily News on March 26, 1960, were deejays Ed Walker and Willard Scott on WRC.

Radio Ink Collection

A sellout crowd anticipates the arrival of the Beatles for a September 14, 1964, performance in Pittsburgh, sponsored by KQV "Audio 14."

KQV Collection

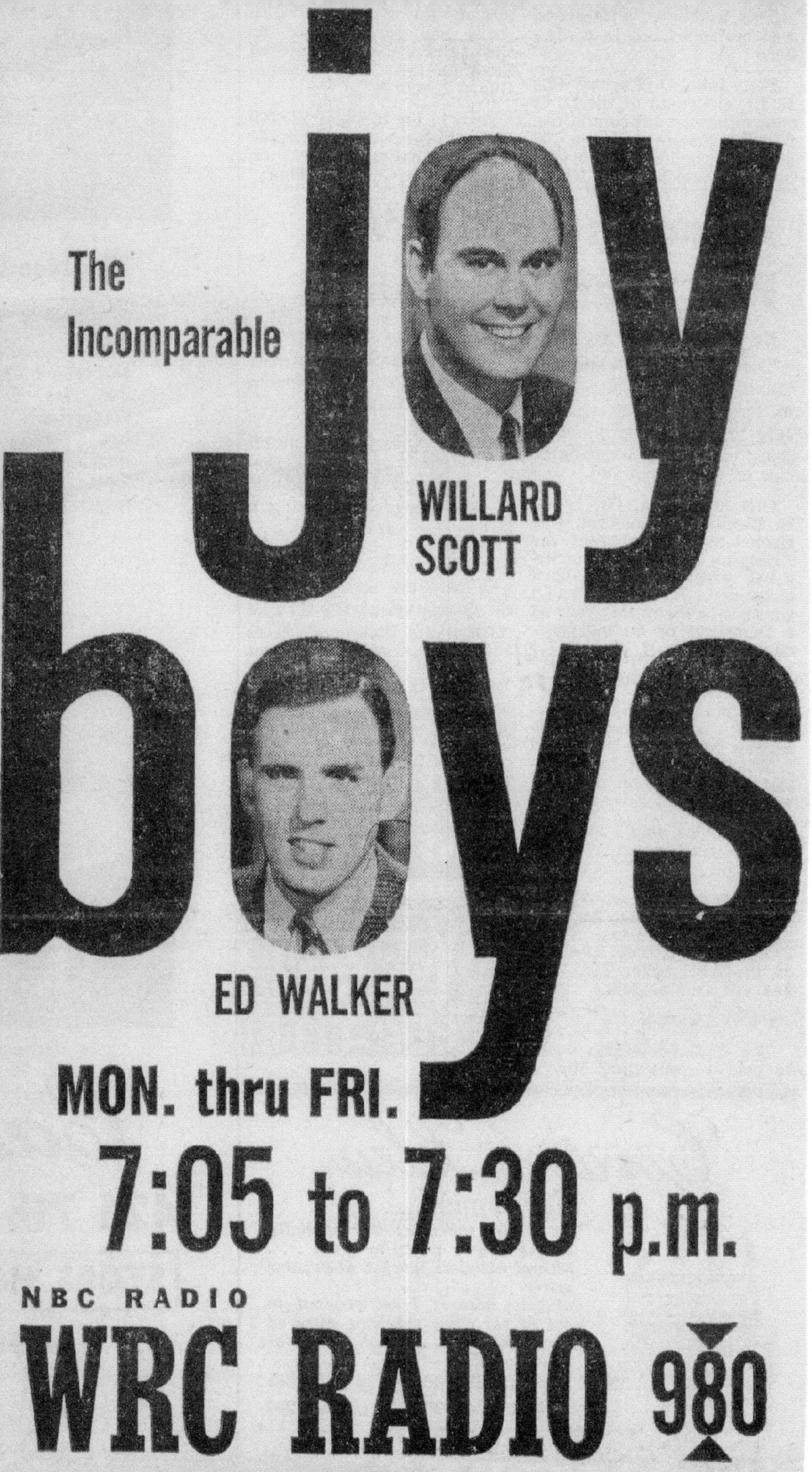

The Incomparable **joy boys**

WILLARD SCOTT

ED WALKER

MON. thru FRI.

7:05 to 7:30 p.m.

NBC RADIO

WRC RADIO 980

1970s

As progressive formats continued to reflect the youth culture of America, Top 40 also reflected the youth. For years, radio programmers had thought everyone within the same age bracket liked the same kinds of music. The separation of a generation by musical tastes had captured their curiosity. With some listeners liking "progressive" music, and some liking Top 40, programmers began to think in terms of listenership by types of music.

Since there were so many stations doing Top 40, and so many doing progressive, programmers started looking for competitive advantages. These competitive moves led to stations being targeted more narrowly. The '70s broke new ground in format development.

Broadcasters were starting to realize that FM radio stations might have some value after all. The progressive or underground FM movement had positioned the FM dial as "cooler" than AM radio, which was filled with static and whistles and had no stereo. A few radio stations began broadcast-

"Doctor" Don Rose became the San Francisco Bay area's most popular radio personality throughout the '70s and '80s, setting the standard for morning radio personalities around the country with his crazy antics, sound effects, comedy and comical abuse of the spoken word.

Radio and Records

ing "mainstream" formats of FM, breaking new ground.

FM Top 40 stations were experimenting in a few cities, and people were putting antennas on their homes to receive FMs from other nearby cities, just to hear the cooler sound, in stereo. Pioneer

FM stations like WNAP, Indianapolis; KSEA, San Diego; WLAC, Lansing, and WMYQ, Miami, to name just a few, were Top 40 on FM. To many listeners, FM was for "elevator music"; to others, FM was for progressive music, but Top 40 belonged on AM. Many broadcasters fought over the idea of putting AM-type formats on FM. A forum of broadcasters was developed with the intention of furthering the future of FM and convincing advertisers that FM was a viable advertising alternative.

Meanwhile, AM radio stations were strong as ever. Great stations like WABC, New York, and WNBC, New York, home of Don Imus, were in heated battles for the ratings.

WLS in Chicago challenged WCFL in one of the great radio battles. The two stations, continually neck-and-neck in the ratings, pumped out some of the top personalities of all time. Programmed by John Gehron, WLS had Larry Lujack and Lyle Dean in the mornings and cranked out legends like John Records Landecker, Fred Winston, Yvonne Daniels, JJ Jefferies and Bob Surat. Across the street, Super 'CFL had Big Ron O'Brien, Dr. Grady Brock and Bob Dearborn.

In Florida, Jim Shulke, a radio programmer, had perfected the FM sound of what was called Beautiful Music. Shulke's tight formatics and strict guidelines for the first time in history created an FM station that had more listeners than AM radio in the market. Once it was proven that FM could dominate listening shares, more and more broadcasters began paying attention to their FMs.

The movement created a whole new breed of radio programmers who perfected new forms of Top 40 stations. The RKO-owned radio stations, led by Dwight Case, and the Bartell-owned station, led by George Wilson, took the lead, creating legendary FM pioneers like WXLO-FM, New York; KRTH-FM, Los Angeles; KCBQ, San Diego, and KSLQ, St. Louis.

The "Q" format was a tighter format than Drake's "Boss" format. Although hard to imagine, the deejays were even more upbeat and had even less time to communicate. Where AM radio had fallen into a trap of running songs of three minutes or less,

Chicago radio legend John "Records truly is my middle name" Landecker initially rocked Chicago on WLS. Lore has it that his middle name is Records because his father was also a disc jockey.
Radio and Records

FM Top 40 stations began airing the long versions of records — five, six, even seven minutes long.

Programmers like Buzz Bennett, Jack McCoy and Jerry Clifton gained reputations as the hot programmers of their day. Their stations did even crazier promotional stunts and brought listeners to the FM dial in droves.

FM radio was taking America hostage, and AM was starting to see erosion in listening. AM wasn't cool anymore. FM stations (and some AMs) were given names to overcome the traditional use of call letters, names that highlighted their FM frequency. The trend lasted well into the '90s. The first known FM to use such a name was "Y-100" in Miami.

With this trend in station names came a new style of contesting. In Miami, the Heftel station was in a heated battle against

One of the biggest stars of *The Grand Ole Opry*, Minnie Pearl has sustained years of success on the radio program she helped pioneer.

Radio and Records

WMYQ, the Bartell station. To win the market, Y-100 debuted on August 3, 1973, with the biggest cash jackpot in radio history. Newspaper ads and radio promos told listeners to answer their phones by saying: "I listen to the new sound of Y-100." Random calls were made, and listeners all over Miami were answering their phone with "the phrase that pays," which, of course, created even higher awareness for the station.

This began a national trend in contesting with big money giveaways at radio stations. Competitors were constantly trying to top one another in the amount they gave away. Jackpots got bigger and bigger. The biggest turned out to be a million-dollar jackpot in Cincinnati. About the only thing ending the trend was the introduction of state lotteries, whose jackpots overshadowed the station jackpots.

While FM gained strength, AM continued to decline. Many looked at the trend as a fad. After all, AM had always been big. But FM was a clean sound, had stereo, and had the perception of bring the hip place to be. For a while, FM was even promoting quadraphonic sound. AM was doomed.

The death of AM came in 1978 when record promoter Robert Stigwood released the musical film *Saturday Night Fever*. Disco became an overnight sensation, and WKTU in New York rose from nowhere to become New York's No. 1 station overnight. The hotter disco became, the more stations became all-disco.

It was a savior, of sorts, for those FM stations unable to succeed otherwise. Stations converted to disco in record numbers and shot up to the top of the ratings in every market. Smart programmers saw the trend as short-lived and mixed some other Top 40

Perhaps the most revered Chicago personality of all time, Wally Phillips spent a lifetime on WGN starting in 1956, where he consistently had the highest ratings, not only in Chicago, but in America. He shares the story of a woman who called the station when it was off the air due to a power outage and said: "I don't hear nothin' [sic] on the radio." Phillips replied: "That's very possible, ma'am. We had a power failure at ten after one." She replied: "Why don't you make an announcement?"

Radio and Records

music into the sound. These stations started doing better than the disco stations.

Disco lasted about a year and died almost as quickly as it was born. Suddenly, WKTU was no longer on top, and the disco stations across the United States started failing. Although disco did not last, it brought so many more listeners to FM that it was the death of AM as a music medium.

Disco also paved the way for the Urban format, which gained huge popularity. It started as a mix of black music, Top 40 music and disco music, with a Top 40 presentation. This became one of the most-listened-to formats, gaining huge success.

One of the premiere programmers was Jerry Clifton, who was one of the pioneers of FM Top 40 in the late '60s and early '70s. Urban Contemporary stations were mainstream stations playing black music, but the format had no race lines. It was popular with whites and blacks alike.

In the '70s, radio saw a shift from AM to FM and the "tightening" of the on-air sound of most stations, meaning a focus more on music and less on personalities. This was the decade that would be the beginning of the FM era in radio.

WQBK, Albany, New York, talk show host Brian Lehrer was credited for saving the life of a listener who was a would-be suicide victim. Lehrer kept the listener on the phone while sending police, who found the man hanging from a rope and rushed him to the hospital, where he survived (November 22, 1976).

Associated Press

Arlene Francis of WOR, New York.

R&R Collection

77 WABC publicity shot of afternoon man Dan Ingram.

R&R Collection

Hal "Aku" Lewis spent years as the top radio personality in Hawaii.

R&R Collection

A slave to the fashion of the day, WNBC's Don Imus emcees an event in April 1976.

Associated Press

WLS, Chicago, morning legend Larry Lujack with singer-composer Billy Joel.

R&R Collection

One of the inventors of Top 40 radio, legendary radio innovator Gordon McLendon is seen here visiting KLIF, Dallas, a station he once owned, which was one of the very first Top 40 stations.

R&R Collection

One of the legendary voices heard on WABC, one of America's most famous Top 40 stations, was Ron Lundy.

R&R Collection

Newsradio has become an integral part of radio listening in America in the '90s. Journalists grace the airwaves in cities across the USA, such as this team from CBS' WBBM Newsradio 78, Chicago: (l-r) anchors Nan Wyatt, Dick Helton and Kris Kridel.

R&R Collection

Leading a format trend in the late 1970s, WWIW (The Way It Was Radio) New Orleans' Ron McArthur reaches for a nostalgic Glen Miller tune. The station made a huge ratings surge by playing music from the '30s, '40s and '50s (1978).

Associated Press

Don Imus went to WNBC from WGAR in Cleveland. He was an instant hit and has been in New York ever since. He is seen here washing his mouth out with soap in 1976. Imus' content often shocked listeners.

Associated Press

Around the country, stations would do elaborate promotions and involve themselves in their communities to boost their popularity and ratings. The raft race was one of the more popular promotions, encouraging listeners to build rafts out of any materials. The concept started at WLYV in Fort Wayne. Seen here are the WLYV "Live Guys": Larry Roberts, Mike Conrad, Chris O'Brien, a listener with Jay Walker, Calvin Richards, Rick Hughes, Gary Lockwood (with beverage), a listener with Bill Anthony.

Radio Ink Collection

Jerry Clifton programmed one of the first FM Top 40 stations, KSEA in San Diego. He was also national program director for Bartell Broadcasting and pioneering stations like WMYQ, Miami; WDRQ, Detroit; KSLQ, St. Louis, and WOKY, Milwaukee.

Radio Ink Collection

In 1976, top rocker 96X (WMJX) tried to bring back the excitement of radio theater in a contemporary way. The station created a radio drama, *A Weekend in X-ville*, that took place between records. Seen recording the special are: (l-r) Gary McKinzie, Jackie Robbins, Frank Reed, Jerry Clifton, "Joanne," Yasarro Hernandez and producer Larry Bessler.

Radio Ink Collection

KOIL, Omaha, Nebraska, disc jockey Gene Shaw plays the last record, *The Sounds of Silence*, as engineer Don Eliason prepares to kill the transmitter at 12:01 a.m.. All the Star Stations were ordered off the air permanently by the FCC for misconduct. KOIL had been on the air for 51 years (September 2, 1976).

Associated Press

Controversial stations and talk hosts always run the risk of upsetting a lunatic, creating a possible danger to those on the air. KWAV deejay Alan Culver points to two of 40 bulletholes left by a gunman who burst into the station shooting. The gunman said the station had poisoned his mind. In this case, no one was injured. Several similar situations at other stations have resulted in deaths of radio personalities.

Associated Press

Answering a last-minute call to fill in as an on-air astrologer, "Jade" became a Miami phenomenon on WMJX and later WIOD/WAIA. Her career blossomed further as she held the top morning slot for many years as "JD" in Jacksonville.

Radio Ink Collection

Dramatic actress Mary Jane Higby actively played roles on radio from 1933 to 1958, and then again when *CBS Mystery Theatre* emerged in the '70s. She was known for *The Romance of Helen Trent, Rosemary, This Is Nora Drake* and *When a Girl Marries.*

Broadcast Pioneers Library/Amundson Collection

After decades on the air, *Our Gal Sunday* and other popular soaps ended in 1959. Vivian Smolen was the second to play the lead, starting in 1946 and continuing through the show's end in 1959. She also played on *Stella Dallas* and other programs, including *CBS Mystery Theatre* in the 1970s.

Broadcast Pioneers Library

A taping is under way at CBS' studio G in New York for a new show, with (from left) Tony Roberts, Lois Nettleton, Norman Rose, Torni Keane and host E.G. Marshall lining up to record one of the *CBS Radio Mystery Theatre* 52-minute programs that aired seven nights a week starting January 6, 1974. After the announcement that CBS would bring radio drama back to the airwaves, The Mutual Broadcasting System launched *Zero Hour,* a 30-minute, five-night-a-week thriller series in November 1973.

Associated Press

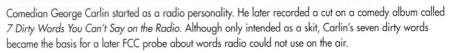

Comedian George Carlin started as a radio personality. He later recorded a cut on a comedy album called *7 Dirty Words You Can't Say on the Radio.* Although only intended as a skit, Carlin's seven dirty words became the basis for a later FCC probe about words radio could not use on the air.

Radio Ink Collection

Programmer Buzz Bennett was first to give stations names like 13Q and Y-100.

Radio Ink Collection

This 1979 photo shows Al Mitchell, air personality and programmer on WBBM-FM, Chicago. Mitchell programmed Group W's WIND as a Top 40 station in the '70s and was the voice of the syndicated program *Rare and Scratchy Rock and Roll* in the mid '80s.

Radio and Records

1980s

B y the time 1980 rolled around, radio was 60 years old and most of the activity was on the FM band. AM listening had dropped to an all-time low, and AM radio stations were going out of business at record speeds. Everyone was trying to develop the next big format for AM, hoping to bring a return to the AM dial. Stations experimented with very narrow formats that provided something listeners could not get elsewhere: specificity.

But no matter what was tried, AM just could not seem to make it. For the most part, radio stations had relied on music formats when their AMs were predominant. When music moved to FM, they took the younger listeners with them. AMs were left with only the older demographics. Only those stations that had built on the strength of their community involvement, their news and their personalities had maintained listeners.

Usually one AM station in a market was doing fine. Stations like WOR in New York, WGN in Chicago, KABC in Los Angeles and WCCO in

Howard Stern awakened a sleeping radio industry with his blatant honesty about anything and anyone. The world was unaccustomed to his controversial humor, direct opinions and explicit descriptions of sexual antics. In 1992, this earned him the highest ratings in radio. It also earned him millions of dollars — and *more* than a million dollars in fines levied by the FCC, most caused by an irate listener, Al Westcott, who felt Stern had gone over the line.

Radio Ink Collection

Minneapolis were not suffering, but the rest were not surviving. One of the big "AM is dead" signals was when legendary music station WABC switched from its music format to an all-talk format. It was a very significant day in radio.

Technology, it was thought, would save AM. Broadcasters thought that if AM could offer improved fidelity and stereo, listeners would return. In 1980, the FCC approved AM stereo, but no single system had been developed as a standard.

Radio legend George Burns went on to television and film and is still active to this day. This 1980 photo shows Burns doing a radio voiceover.

Associated Press

Broadcasters were operating different systems that were not compatible with one another.

As a result, radio manufacturers would not create AM stereo units for a long time. Eventually, some AM stereo units were available; however, the AM broadcasters had misread the market. AM stereo was not appealing, because AM as a music medium was not appealing. They had forgotten to recognize the perceptions that AM had received with the younger audiences: AM just

Live radio and radio drama returned in the 1980s when Garrison Keillor created the program *A Prairie Home Companion*, originating from Minneapolis/St. Paul. The program became an instant nationwide success as it was broadcast on public radio stations every Saturday evening (circa 1987).

Associated Press

"Hello Love" is how Garrison Keillor would open his *A Prairie Home Companion*, a folksy radio program that ran Sunday afternoons on National Public Radio (NPR), chronicling the week's happenings in the fictional small town of Lake Wobegon (April 1986).

Associated Press

wasn't cool. Besides that, AM stereo, with its improved fidelity, wasn't comparable to FM. AM was doomed as a music medium.

In spite of FM being the place for music, many format experiments were tried in an attempt to revive AM. Some markets had "all-Elvis" or "all-Beatles" formats for a while. Others tried "for women only" or "for men only." Few things worked. AM was in crisis. The cost of programming was high, and nothing was working.

One technology that began saving AM stations was the introduction of the satellite music network. Entrepreneur John Tyler was able to provide 24-hour-

Author Garrison Keillor is shown here announcing that he will present a second annual farewell performance of *A Prairie Home Companion* at Radio City Music Hall in June 1988. The weekly program with the same name had originated from Minneapolis/St. Paul for many years before Keillor chose to hang up his microphone to pursue writing books. He eventually returned to radio.

Associated Press

As radios got smaller and more portable, listening increased in the 1980s. GE employee Matt Orioh inspects quality of micro-sized headset stereo at GE warehouse. The AM/FM Action Radio was weather-resistant and designed for outdoor use (circa 1988).

Associated Press

a-day programming via satellite direct to radio stations. He created and offered several formats.

This was a blessing as far as AM was concerned. These formats cost a lot less money than providing local personalities did, yet they had their own personalities between the records. The idea caught on rapidly.

About the same time, Transtar, a second network, was launched (both had been announced the same week). This technology revolutionized radio forever. AMs and FMs were "on the bird," and survival became less difficult.

The '80s were becoming strong. After a ruling from the FCC adopting deregulation and entertainment guidelines, and after a Supreme Court ruling no longer requiring the FCC to approve formats, radio began to blossom like never before.

Another change launched in the '80s was a "continuous mea-

surement" strategy from Arbitron, the major ratings company for radio. In the past, Arbitron had measured twice a year for a few weeks at a time. Radio was able to promote its best during these measurement periods, and not promote the rest of the time.

Advertisers sensed that this short-term promotion created inaccurate measurement of stations due to the extra hype, so they demanded that stations be measured continuously. Arbitron then instituted a quarterly measurement, meaning stations were always being measured. This changed the way stations promoted and forced them to promote year 'round, creating more stability and possibly more regular listening.

Another FCC move made a big difference in the radio industry. According to past FCC rules, a station had to be owned for three years before it could be sold to another buyer. In 1982, the FCC dropped the three-year rule and allowed trading to occur as frequently as broadcasters desired. This created a buying and selling frenzy that was to last most of the '80s. Stations would be sold again, and again, and again, each time for a higher price.

This "trafficking" was profitable for those selling. Eventually, the prices of radio stations skyrocketed to all-time highs and stations had enormous debt. The trick was to buy and sell for a higher price without getting stuck with the station. Eventually, everyone got stuck as the frenzy came to an end in the late '80s. The debt was killing companies and forced many into selling at huge losses, while others struggled to support debt service that was higher than the income of the stations or their marketplaces could justify.

This forced broadcasters to take less risk, because once they stumbled onto something that was generating income, they didn't want to risk losing it.

Before long, radio stations sounded alike all across America. More music, less talk, more variety were the copycat slogans on FM stations nationwide. Radio had become boring, and scientifically programmed. Personalities were squelched even further and told to play the music and shut up.

Radio had become a non-personality medium, and mostly a

Stanford Ungar and Susan Stamberg hosted a national radio news magazine called *All Things Considered* that ran on National Public Radio each afternoon. The show still airs to this day (January 1982).

Associated Press

The bigger the size, the higher the status. As portable stereos hit the streets, radio companies quickly learned that portability wasn't as important as big booming speakers. The Boom Box, often called the "Ghetto Blaster" because of its stereotyped heavy use on the streets of the big-city ghettos, became THE radio of the '80s. Here, a young kid, Kenny Hoff, sits on boom box in New York City.

Associated Press

radio would die because listeners could now watch the bands play as they sang.

But the reverse happened. MTV attracted viewers and exposed them to a whole new type of Top 40 music, creating a new FM format and a need for more stations playing this MTV brand of music. As they watched MTV for the latest releases, they turned their radios on to hear them again and again when they weren't watching the network. MTV had given Top 40 music a rebirth with a new style of artist.

The '80s also brought other new forms of music. The film *Urban Cowboy* began to make country music hip, just as *Saturday Night Fever*, another Robert Stigwood musical starring John Travolta, had done for disco in the '70s. It eliminated the stereotypes the country format had suffered with for years. Country stations began to show up on the FM dial and began to surge with a new form of contemporary country.

But it didn't last long, and as quickly as stations had gone to disco and then abandoned it, country experienced the same thing. It was not until the late '80s that country music began to see a steady resurgence and become a mainstream format contender.

Another new format came out of the '80s. As the "baby boomer" generation began aging, they were not interested in hearing "beautiful music" renditions of their favorite songs. Beautiful music formats that had dominated their markets began to lose listeners.

Almost overnight, the format went from being one of the biggest to one of the least listened-to. Stations were dropping the format and replacing it with soft hit records from the actual artists, not the instrumental versions. This was the beginning of adult contemporary or, as it was first called, "chicken rock."

Adult contemporary opened eyes to new forms of targeted

jukebox. Morning shows were the only programs that had exhibited personality. The rest of the day focused on being less personable. Of course, part of the problem was that good, well-trained personalities were becoming hard to find, due to the "less talk, more music" style of the '70s.

Radio's big fear was that a new entry would take its listeners: cable television. A bright radio programmer from WNBC in New York had left the station to start an all-music cable channel called MTV (music television). The media were filled with reports that

The day the music died was a sad day as Musicradio 77, WABC, dropped its longtime music format for talk radio. It was a familiar scene in radio as AMs across the country gave up music for talk as a means of "saving" the station. WABC deejays Dan Ingram (left) and Ron Lundy commiserate at noon on Monday, May 10, 1982, at the WABC studio as the station changed forever.

Associated Press

programming. Before long, there were many variations of adult contemporary. Some leaned soft, while others were almost Top 40-sounding. Some even mixed country music in with their hits. These hybrids of radio were popping up everywhere. There were variations in country and also in black music.

In the mid-'80s, because of the influence of MTV, television was having a big impact on radio listening. The TV program *Miami Vice* was introducing a hip new style of rock and adult contemporary. Every song played on *Miami Vice* became a national hit the next week. Radio was seeing the outside influences of televi-

sion and film on its programming.

In 1987, the FCC dropped its previous enforcement of the Fairness Doctrine, which had required stations to give equal time to opposing points of view. This move was to result in giving rebirth to AM radio a few years later.

Shortly after the Fairness Doctrine was dropped, Edward McLaughlin, a former ABC executive, saw an opportunity to change radio forever. He knew that AM radio stations needed help, and he knew that nothing else was working, so he introduced a highly opinionated radio talk show host, knowing the Fairness

Lighting up every evening across America, ABC's Tom Snyder became one of the most beloved radio personalities.

R&R Collection

Longtime KNBR, San Francisco, personality Carter B. Smith is showing off his awards in appreciation for help in restoring San Francisco's cable cars (March 1, 1983).

R &R Collection

Doctrine would no longer dilute programming with rebuttals.

His new national talk host was Rush Limbaugh. The radio business, and America, were changed forever.

By the late '80s, FM was still the predominant medium and AM was still struggling. Rush Limbaugh was just getting started and just getting noticed nationally. FM was offering more and more choices in programming.

A generation that had grown up on certain music 20 years earlier was beginning to yearn for a return to its youth, and with it a return to its favorite tunes. Classic Rock was introduced at WRIF, Detroit, by programmer Fred Jacobs in 1986. It was a huge overnight success, especially with males.

Oldies radio was gaining in popularity, too, playing the hits from the baby boomers' high school and college years, mostly appealing to females.

America was loosening up, and the need for good personalities was more evident, but few existed outside of the morning slots. Radio sex therapist Dr. Ruth Westheimer went national after a stint on WNBC in the early '80s. She became one of the most listened-to personalities in America.

Meanwhile, irreverent WNBC personality Don Imus was more popular than ever. It appeared that listeners were craving personality after a serious personality drought from a industry full of "more music" deejays.

In Detroit, then Washington, then New York, Howard Stern was elevated by his listeners as the greatest radio personality of all time. Stern was irreverent, willing to take on anyone and not afraid to say anything on the air. He brought common culture's street language to the airwaves and broke the "forbidden unwritten rules of broadcasting." His audience loved it. Stern stood as

Club deejays became the rage when they took their dance club mixes to the radio in the '80s. Shown here is WJLB, Detroit, mixer The Wizard.

R&R Collection

the hero for their culture as he broke every taboo. He took those markets by storm.

Radio was coming full circle as the '80s came to an end. It had started as a personality medium in the '20s, '30s and '40s, become a music medium with a little less personality in the Top 40 era of the '50s, even more music and less talk in the '70s, reduced further in the '80s.

As any decent personalities emerged, listeners started gravitating to them. It was as if they were telling radio that music alone wasn't enough anymore. ◙

In 1988, WCDU Radio in Washington, D.C., asked Congressman John Conyers (D-Mich.) to guest deejay on *The Felix Grant Show*. Seen with Conyers is General Manager Edith Smith (February 13, 1988).

R&R Collection

Chicago funnyman Fred Winston graced the morning airwaves in the Windy City for many years, including the heyday of WLS.

R&R Collection

WNEW's Ted Brown in 1981.

R&R Collection

WNEW's Jim Lowe in 1981.

R&R Collection

When legendary ABC Top 40 programmer Rick Sklar released his book *Rockin' America*, which told the story of rock 'n' roll on radio, he gathered in June 1984 with the staff of air personalities who helped him make the station great: (l-r) "Cousin" Brucie Morrow, Ron Lundy, Sklar, Chuck Leonard and Harry Harrison. Sklar, a Radio Hall of Fame inductee, met an untimely death following simple foot surgery.

R&R Collection

Radio legend William B. Williams.

R&R Collection

Dick Whittinghill, who held the morning slot at KMPC, Los Angeles, for many years, seen here in the '80s.

R&R Collection

WFYR, Chicago, personality Kevin Malloy (once known as Heavy Keavy) sings a parody song to highlight the problems that plagued the PTL empire. Sung to the tune of *The Monster Mash* was Malloy's *The Ministry Mash* (May 2, 1987).

Associated Press

Wink Martindale, one of the Los Angeles radio personalities who also sidelined as a TV game show host.

R&R Collection

The stories these guys could tell after many years at CBS News! Facing the microphone together for the very last time were Robert Trout and Douglas Edwards, in 1988.

R&R Collection

Host of Mutual's *Line One* radio program and well-known New York personality Scott Muni in May-1987.

R&R Collection

If you've ever driven the open road in the middle of the night, you may have heard T*he Charlie Douglas Road Show*, which was primarily geared to truckers. The program originated from WSM, Nashville, and ran for 20 years (May 1987).

R&R Collection

WLUP's Steve and Gary set Chicago on its ear with the program's crazy antics and open discussions. Steve Dahl and Gary Meyer eventually split up the team, yet both remained a part of the station (July 1984).

R&R Collection

Larry Lujack of WLS, Chicago, was rumored to be the highest-paid air personality in Chicago for many years, and one of the highest-paid in America at the peak of his popularity in the '70s and '80s. He is legendary in Chicago (May 25, 1988).

R&R Collection

Radio legends "Cousin" Brucie and Hoss Allen cut up during a visit in 1988.

R&R Collection

KFRC San Francisco's morning traffic reporter Jane Dornacker.

R&R Collection

Many Los Angeles radio personalities ended up as television game show hosts, while maintaining their radio careers. KMPC/Los Angeles' Jim Lange became well-known as the host of television's *The Dating Game*. He also had a national radio program called *Encore* on the Mutual Broadcasting Network.

R&R Collection

The eerie sound of a squeaking door capped each episode of *The Inner Sanctum*, produced and directed by Himan Brown on the Blue Network starting in 1941. He is seen here in the 1980s receiving an Emerson Radio Award.

R&R Collection

The morning team of Hal and Charley at KHOW, Denver, in 1983.

Radio and Records

San Francisco icon Gene Nelson on KYA Radio.

Radio and Records

WABC Musicradio's Johnny Donovan in 1982.

R&R Collection

The host of Mutual's *Sports Today*, Tony Roberts.

Radio and Records

They said MTV (music television) would kill radio by offering music with video images. Although MTV became a huge success, radio survived. In fact, Mark Goodman (right) one of the early MTV "veejays," returned to radio, seen here with partner Carol Miller in 1982.

Radio and Records

WABC, once the pre-eminent Top 40 station, made a switch to talk in the 1980s. WABC talk host Joanna Langfield interviews actor Hal Linden.

R&R Collection

KFWB, Los Angeles, morning anchor John Leisher.

Radio and Records

Geri Latchford was heard middays on WPIX-FM in New York.

Radio and Records

National Public Radio's Robert Krulwich of *All Things Considered* created an alternative to commercial radio with informative reports on business, economics and the world in general.

Radio and Records

Short-lived as a morning team together were Byron Paul and Phil Reed as *Phil and Byron* on KBIG, Los Angeles, between 1985 and 1987.

Broadcast Pioneers Library

At the time of this photo, New York personality Harry Nelson was heard on WAPP.

Radio and Records

Rick Nelson (left) was best known for his career as a rock star, but he started on the radio in *The Adventures of Ozzie and Harriet* at a very young age. He hadn't learned to read yet, so he would memorize his script, but since it was performed before a live audience, he insisted on having a script in front of him so people wouldn't know he couldn't read. He is seen here with New York radio legend Harry Harrison.

Radio and Records

Three radio legends gathered together at a radio convention: (l-r) Rick Sklar, programmer of WABC and ABC musicradio stations; Cousin Brucie Morrow, WABC personality, and Boston personality Arnie "Woo Woo" Ginsberg.

Radio Ink Collection

Tim Reid (center) star of *WKRP in Cincinnati,* visits KACE in Los Angeles' Cal Shields (left) and Lonzo Miller.

Radio and Records

Dr. Don Rose continued his dominance in San Francisco on KFRC in the '80s.

Radio and Records

NBC Talknet host Bruce Williams.

Along with the new Disney-MGM Studios theme park came this special radio studio housed in the park. The studio has logged thousands of hours from visiting air personalities from around the world.

Shadoe Stevens, the voice of American Top 40 following the departure of Casey Kasem.

Radio Ink Collection

Hired as hostess at a prestigious radio industry awards ceremony, MTV video jock "Downtown" Julie Brown unknowingly motivated most of the audience members to walk out of the event because of what they perceived as a foul mouth and tasteless jokes. She is seen here visiting WZPL in Indianapolis: (l-r) Scott Wheeler, Johnny George, Brown, Tim Foxx and Don Payne.

Radio and Records

After starting as a comedian, Steve Morris began his radio career in Ithaca, New York, working on numerous stations before landing on K-Earth in Los Angeles, where he did the morning show from 1986 to 1990.

Radio and Records

Jack Patterson, the host of Westwood One/Mutual's *Shootin' the Breeze* program (May 1987).

Radio and Records

The first lady of the American theater and longtime radio actress Helen Hayes.

Raido Ink Collection

Air personality Howard Stern (right) speaks out at a rally in New York's Dag Hammarskjold Plaza, where more than 2,000 listeners gathered to show their support after the Federal Communications Commission censured Stern's off-color broadcasts (April 24, 1987).

Associated Press

Sweet little Dr. Ruth Westheimer carried a huge national audience with her program *Sexually Speaking.* Her local WNBC, New York, radio program went national in 1986 on the NBC Radio Network and catapulted her to national stardom.

Radio Ink Collection

WMMS, The Buzzard, became one of the most well-known rock stations in America. Although just a local Cleveland station, under programmer John Goreman (at right, with Tom O'Brien), it exerted tremendous national influence. It singlehandedly pioneered and raised the money for a national Rock and Roll Hall of Fame in Cleveland.

Radio and Records

ABC's National Radio commentator Paul Harvey, shown with wife Lynn Angel Harvey, had become so popular that the street in front of his broadcast studios in Chicago — a one-block stretch of East Wacker — was renamed Paul Harvey Drive (November 1988).

Associated Press

Tanner In The Morning would "get you up and get you off" every weekday for 15 years in the Miami, Florida, area. Bill Tanner held great ratings with his downhome Southern realism and his ability to get people to say almost anything on the phone while on the air.

R&R Collection

Why have breakfast with a bunch of flakes when you can have Howard Stern?

Controversial. Outrageous. Unpredictable. Somehow the same tired adjectives are always used to describe morning personalities. The standard press release cliches are so overworked they've gone out on strike. Now, a disc jockey finally comes along that actually deserves this kind of hype, and all the good words are used up. It's tough to introduce the savior of morning radio when the only words left to describe him are the ones nobody else wanted. Nonetheless, allow us to introduce you to Howard Stern: he's ubiquitous, extemporaneous, historic, epigrammatic, jocose, felicitous, ambidextrous...

Why have breakfast with a bunch of flakes when you can have Howard Stern?

Radio Ink Collection

CBS' Charles Osgood interviews radio legend George Burns.

Radio Ink Collection

Radio has always been good at taking the show on the road and broadcasting in front of the listeners. The Giant Boom Box, created in the late '80s by entrepreneur Eric Rhoads (yes, your author), was a studio on wheels creating a larger-than-life, in-person image for radio stations. These mobile studios that looked like a giant radio are still in use by hundreds of radio stations around the world.

Radio Ink Collection

Singer Chubby Checker drops by the studios of WNBC. Shown: (l-r) Jay "The Jock" Sorenson, Checker, Joey Reynolds and NBC funnyman Al Rosenberg.

Radio Ink Collection

WABC talk personality Dr. Joy Browne was one of the many radio psychologists listeners could call to discuss their problems and seek advice.

Radio Ink Collection

One of the greatest honors in show business is to be given your own star on Hollywood Boulevard in Los Angeles. KIIS-FM radio personality Rick Dees is seen filming a television commercial in 1986 while standing on his star, on which he dropped an ice cream cone.

Radio Ink Collection

WNEW-FM's Dennis Elsas.

Radio Ink Collection

Three generations of *Rambling With Gambling* have been heard by morning audiences on WOR in New York. John A. Gambling (right) is the second generation on the air, and his son John R. Gambling the third generation.

Broadcast Pioneers Library

A cast of characters made up *The Joey Reynolds Show* on WNBC in the early 1980s.

Radio Ink Collection

Morning personality Kid Craddick, known for his stunts, broadcasting live from inside a water tower high above Salt Lake City. Craddick camped out in the tower for three days, broadcasting continuously to raise money for a local charity. He went on to become on of the top-rated morning personalities in Dallas.

Radio Ink Collection

Starting with nothing, entrepreneur Norm Patiz created a small radio network called Westwood One. Eventually, he grew it into one of the biggest radio networks by purchasing the Mutual Network and the NBC radio network. Patiz is seen here onstage at a live Westwood One concert in the '80s.

Radio Ink Collection

In the '80s, Sally Jessy Raphael was one of the few nationally syndicated women on radio. Her evening program ran on hundreds of stations. Simultaneously, Sally did a television program and eventually left radio to do television full time.

Radio Ink Collection

WKRP in Cincinnati, the television show about radio, was too close to the way things all-too-often really are. Each character in the television series was supposedly based on existing radio people. Within the radio industry, it was rumored that the character of "Big Guy" was patterned after WQXI/Atlanta General Manager Gerald S. Blum (February 1977).

R&R Collection

WKRP's "Big Guy" Mr. Calrson, the GM (actor Gordon Jump).

Radio Ink Collection

Winner of the Silver Sow Award, *WKRP* newsman Les Nessman (played by actor Richard Sanders).

Radio Ink Collection

WKRP's slick sales guy Herb Tarlek (actor Frank Bonner).

Radio Ink Collection

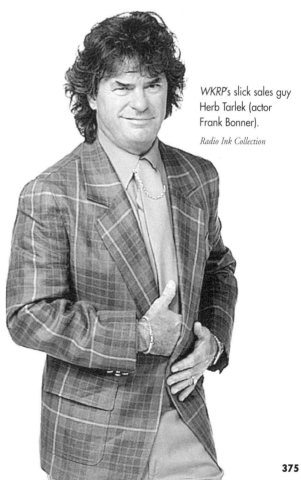

1990s

T he 1990s brought the return of AM radio. Although primary listening still occurs on the FM dial, AM radio has seen a
huge resurgence, primarily as a result of Rush Limbaugh's
popularity. As Limbaugh became more popular in the early 1990s, and as
he gained clout in Washington, his listening levels became enormous.

Most of the radio stations that initially signed with Rush Limbaugh
were struggling AM stations. Today, those stations are having financial success because of the listening audience Limbaugh commands. By 1995,
Limbaugh had more than 20 million daily listeners, more than any other
radio personality since the so-called golden days of radio.

But these stations needed more. Many were up against local AM giants
that had maintained their strength, and once Limbaugh was off the air, they
had nothing. But that changed rapidly. Talk radio was becoming so popular that talk hosts were springing up all around the country.

Talk was nothing new. Local talk hosts like Jerry Williams in Boston

Probably more well-known than any other radio personality on the planet, Casey Kasem became famous with his American Top 40 countdown, which ran in almost every country in the world.

Westwood One Photo

WCBS-FM in New York became the prominent oldies-formatted station over the years. Frequently they would host reunions of top New York rock 'n' roll deejays. Shown: (front, l-r) Dean Anthony, Jack Lacey, Bruce Morrow, Herb Oscar Anderson, Dan Ingram and Ron Lundy; (rear, l-r) CBS VP Rod Calarco, Ed Bear, Harry Harrison, Joe O'Brien, Charlie Greer, Jack Spector, Hal Jackson, Alan Fredericks and Joe McCoy (November 11, 1991).

R&R Collection

have been on the air for many years, but talk was becoming a national phenomena. Historically, talk stations were just someone in the studio talking, but the change came when they began interacting with the audience.

Once the listener became a major part of the programming, talk radio took off. Talk became the conscience of America. It was the town meeting, where every opinion was heard. This made talk radio more interesting and drove the format's success.

Technology also drove the success of talk radio. Satellite technology allowed talk hosts to uplink less expensively, and suddenly the prohibitive costs came down. Previously, only the big networks could bear such expense. Simultaneously, technology for putting phone calls on the air improved, making the sound of callers less irritating.

Radio saw a mass of radio talk hosts and boutique networks enter the national scene. Stations that were already talking locally managed to uplink their personalities to other stations. WOR in New York created national personalities out of locals like The Dolans, who do a financial talk show. The '90s became the era for talk radio.

A new form of talk also emerged. In the past, even the prominent morning hosts on music radio stations were told to do their bits and move back to the music. But it was Howard Stern who broke that pattern. Stern began talking and spent his entire show talking. It was talk in the lifestyle of the listeners, and it was a huge success.

Stern became nationally syndicated and began appearing in markets across the United States. The more popular he became, the more he became a target. Suddenly, his "shock jock" style was no longer just being heard in New York. It was on in Philadelphia, Washington, Miami, Los Angeles and many more cities. Stern was saying things on the air that offended some people, and was often using sexually explicit language.

He was warned to stop or face FCC fines, but Stern contended that there was no specific guideline stating what could and could not be said. His critics said that he should not be censored but that he should not be allowed to use certain language during times when kids were likely to tune in. Stern argued against this, as well.

Enter a listener in Las Vegas, Nevada. Al Westcott felt that Stern was breaking the law and did not appreciate what Stern was saying on the air. Although he was not a stereotypical conservative (Westcott wore long hair and tie-dyed T-shirts), he complained to the FCC on numerous occasions.

Westcott studied the law, taped every Stern broadcast and filed specific FCC complaints. The result was more than a million dollars in fines levied against Stern. One man, using his own money and focusing on Stern, had managed to bring fines against this media giant.

Yet Stern refused to pay the fines and is still in the process of challenging the FCC on their validity. The issue may never be resolved. Westcott's efforts did create a huge awareness of the Stern indecency argument and made stations rethink whether or not they would air the Stern program. Most chose to take the risk, because the financial rewards were so high.

The '90s also brought new legislation that allowed companies to own more than two radio stations in a market. Called "duopoly," this process gave stations new survival capabilities in an over-

These proud radio legends were inducted into the coveted Emerson Radio Hall of Fame in New York on June 6, 1990. Shown: (l-r) Dick Clark, CBS' Charles Osgood, Dr. Frank Stanton and Paul Harvey.

Associated Press

Destined to be the next leading female talk show host in America was Deborah Norville. ABC put all its guns behind Norville as the replacement for Sally Jessy Raphael, who left radio to pursue television full time. Norville had been on about a year when the network decided to close down its talk radio division.

Radio and Records

competitive market.

A radio group was also allowed to own more stations — 20 AMs and 20 FMs. This legislation stimulated the radio economy, and those in the radio industry greatly benefited as the mid-'80s brought the highest billings the industry had seen in its history. At this writing, legislation is in the works to totally deregulate the radio industry, allowing unlimited ownership numbers.

Country became one of the top formats in the '90s because of its push for mainstream acceptance. A new form of Top 40 called "modern rock" is emerging as a new leader.

As radio completes the decade of the '90s, more change will face the industry, and more reaction and resilience will be necessary.

New formats that reflect the culture have always been the strength of radio, and that will not change. New technologies will challenge radio; some will be embraced and others rejected.

Radio in the '90s is faced with many new technologies competing for the time of the listeners: direct satellite television and radio, and cellular telephones that some people use in their cars in place of the radios they used to listen to. Cyber technologies like the internet are also occupying time that may once have gone to radio listening.

But radio always responds and always promotes. It has developed new technologies that will deliver data to car radios and Dick Tracy-style wristwatch radios. New digital delivery systems provide CD-quality sound. And, of course, new formats will always find ways to capture new listeners.

In spite of every challenge throughout the decades, time after time radio responded to the predictions announcing its death, only to re-invent itself with something new. Every decade saw new challenges and technologies that were thought likely to eventually destroy radio. Some did. Yet radio bounced back and always came back stronger than before. It has so many wonderful advantages.

Something magical has always been associated with radio. Some have said that if radio had been invented after television, radio would be a more powerful medium.

After all, the radio can easily travel with you, and you can produce elaborate pictures without much cost or effort. People feel connected to their radio station and radio personalities. They know a lot about them. They share their lives by phoning in, and they know about the radio personalities' lives by listening. It's an ideal relationship for a medium; a relationship that can't be offered with pictures or print.

Radio listening still takes place in the home, the car, at work,

Radio morning team Mc and Jamie became stand up comics using radio as the brunt of their jokes. In May 1990, they gathered video of America's funniest radio personalities for an ABC television show, *Anything For Laughs*.

Radio and Records

After years of no children's programming on the radio, Minneapolis executive Christopher Dahl created The Children's Broadcasting network and *Radio Aahs*, using kid deejays. The crew is seen doing a remote broadcast from Disney World in Florida.

Disney Photo

at play. It accompanies people wherever they go. It doesn't require effort. You don't have to hold it, watch it, read it; you only have to listen. The rest is up to the imagination.

People turn to radio during disasters because it's always there, even when their electricity is off. They rely on radio to entertain and to inform. Radio provides company, and it provides people with a voice that can be heard all the way to Washington, D.C.

Radio has been a part of life for 75 years. Although its face may change, its programming may vary and it may take on new methods of distribution, just as it has in the past, radio will remain a part of life because of the personal connection it offers.

Just as radio's top personalities Jack Benny and Fred Allen eventually went away, their popularity was replaced by other prominent personalities. Someday, Rush Limbaugh, Paul Harvey and Howard Stern will be gone too. But radio will breed new personalities with new ways of communicating.

People will listen. Since radio broadcasting was invented 75 years ago, they always have. ▄

Talk host Larry King gained national popularity doing an all-night talk show on Mutual. After many years, he joined CNN (Cable News Network) for *Larry King Live*, while continuing to do his radio show.

Radio Ink Collection

Country singer Dolly Parton plays a radio talk show host in the movie *Straight Talk*.

Radio Ink Collection

When Larry King left Mutual's all-night talk slot, Jim Bohannon slipped in without skipping a beat. Bohannon is heard by millions every night.

Westwood One Photo

CBS Radio coverage of the 1992 Democratic National Convention with newsman Mitchell Krauss.

Radio Ink Collection

Wearing his trademark bow tie in the CBS newsroom, Charles "See You On The Radio" Osgood.

Radio Ink Collection

CBS sportscaster John Madden is known on both radio and television doing play-by-play football. In spite of his hectic schedule, Madden refuses to fly on airplanes and does all of his travel in his own bus, the Madden Cruiser.

Radio Ink Collection

Talknet host Bruce Williams stops in at Disney World for a broadcast during the celebration of Mickey Mouse's 50th birthday.

Radio Ink Collection

Conservative talk show host Rush Limbaugh became one of the most powerful men in America when his national talk show reached 20 million people daily, and his political stance influenced voters. He is shown here in September 1992 interviewing President George Bush at the WABC studios in New York.

Associated Press

Dave Polston of Orlando leaves Blackie's House of Beef in Washington, D.C., past a sign advertising Rush Limbaugh's radio program. The restaurant is one of hundreds of "Rush Rooms" that played Limbaugh's broadcast during lunchtime so faithful listeners wouldn't have to miss a word of the program (October 1993).

Associated Press

Talk host Lee Mirabell rises to the challenge of any caller or guest on her national program, *The Lee Mirabell Show*.

Radio Ink Collection

Political analyst and talk host Michael Reagan, son of former President Ronald Reagan.

Radio Ink Collection

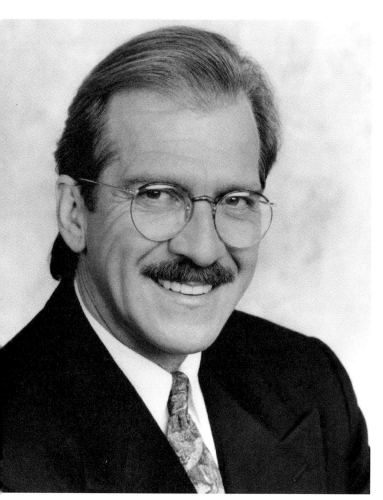

CBS Sports' Pat O'Brien, frequently heard on the CBS Radio Networks.

Radio Ink Collection

The man with more inside scoop than anyone else is The National Enquirer's Mike Walker. His radio debut came on WJNO in West Palm Beach and led to national syndication on the Westwood One Radio Network.

Radio Ink Collection

CBS News anchor Christopher Glenn.

CBS Photo

As much a legend as the sports stars he covers, Vin Scully toils in the broadcast booth as a part of the CBS Sports team.

Radio Ink Collection

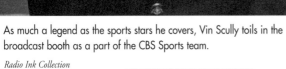

What do politicians do when they leave office? In 1995, the fad was to become a radio talk show host, as evidenced by former Virginia Gov. Doug Wilder, now a host on WRVA.

Radio Ink Collection

In Chicago, The Museum of Broadcast Communications held a black tie event honoring television's Hugh Downs for his contributions to broadcasting. Downs started as a radio deejay just after WWII in Lima, Ohio. By age 18, he moved to WWJ in Detroit, and to WMAQ Radio in Chicago by age 20. Pictured: (l-r) Museum founder, president and national talk show host Bruce DuMont, Illinois Gov. Jim Edgar and Downs.

Museum of Broadcast Communications Photo

Sports fans all know radio play-by-play guys Hank Stram (left) and Jack Buck, an integral part of the CBS Radio Sports team.

Radio Ink Collection

Financial wizard Don McDonald, the one on the right, does his nightly call-in talk show from the Disney MGM Radio studios in Orlando.

Disney Photo

Known locally in Houston as "The Radio Gawds," Stevens and Pruett continually gain high shares at KLOL.

Radio Ink Collection

The team of "Don and Mike" became so popular in their native Washington, D.C., that they were syndicated on stations across the United States.

Westwood One Photo

CBS Radio and television sportscaster Bob Costas.

CBS Photo

CBS Radio Network news anchor Dave Ross.

CBS Photo

WLS, Chicago, personality Chuck Britton.

Radio Ink Collection

Westwood One Radio Network's Bob Grant, known for his financial programs.

Radio Ink Collection

CBS Radio Network newsman Bill Lynch.

CBS Photo

Controversial talk show host Alan Colmes, heard daily on Major Networks.

Major Networks Photo

Holding down the "morning drive" slot on WCBS Newsradio 88 in New York City are Robert Vaught (left) and Jim Donnelly. All-news radio became an important and widespread format in the 1980s and 1990s.

R&R Collection

Chuck Leonard, morning drive personality of WKYS, Washington, had one of the eight largest cumulative audiences in America. Leonard was a part of the original WABC team during its Top 40 days in New York.

Radio and Records

Nationally syndicated talk host Barry Farber has a long legacy of radio broadcasts after years on late nights in New York.

Radio Ink Collection

A familiar voice in Los Angeles, Mucho Morales first hit Los Angeles on KHJ Radio in 1977. He then moved to KRLA, KGFJ and eventually to the original staff of KPWR (known as Power 106). He eventually returned to KRLA.

Radio and Records

Chicago personality Gary Meyer went solo after years on the team of "Steve and Gary" on "The Loop," WLUP, in Chicago.

Radio and Records

Television star Ed McMahon (left) returns to radio for a visit with KROQ, Los Angeles, morning team Kevin and Bean, who were broadcasting "live" from the Disney/MGM Studios.

Radio and Records

National Public Radio's president, Frank Mankiewicz.

R&R Collection

Singer Tony Bennett visits with Johnathon Schwartz of WNEW, New York, in 1991.

Radio and Records

Commentator Charles Osgood may have been radio's biggest fan. The CBS radio commentator would rhyme each of his commentaries on radio and television, ending both with: "I'll see you on the radio." He often played his banjo at personal appearances.

Radio and Records

Playing rock 'n' roll's greatest hits was ABC's Dick Bartley, whose Saturday night oldies broadcasts were heard nationwide (May 1991).

R &R Collection

NATIONAL ASSOCIATION of RADIO TALK SHOW HOSTS

Talk host Larry King speaks to the National Association of Radio Talk Show Hosts after receiving their 1993 Host of the Year award. King was simultaneously doing national talk shows on radio's Mutual Network and television's Cable News Network (CNN).

Associated Press

Dr. Judy Kuriansky reacts to a caller's response on her radio talk show *Love Phones*, which began on WHTZ (Z100) in New York in November 1992. Kuriansky, a clinical psychologist, addressed relationships, sexuality and lifestyle trends. The love phones trend became popular throughout the United States.

Associated Press

In the 90s, radio discovered that if you want the people to listen, air personalities should reflect what they're thinking about. Talk station WABC, New York, airs the words of Curtis and Lisa Sliwa of the Guardian Angels, a New York vigilante group.

R&R Collection

Commanding attention in New York City at any station he joined, Scott Shannon, seen here with Todd Pettengill, spent years as one of the top morning "jocks" in New York on Z-100 and later on WPLJ (1994 photo).

Radio and Records

New York deejays Jimmy Buff (right) and Curt Chaplin run over the news during a morning broadcast of *Radio Free New York* at their tiny studio in Manhattan. The renegade "jocks" were forgoing sleep, paychecks and common sense to broadcast the kind of music "nobody else will play" (March 14, 1993).

Associated Press

For years, the legendary Imus In The Morning was heard by local New York audiences, but in 1995 Don Imus became a national celebrity, with his program running on more than 50 stations.

Radio Ink Collection

With the talk show world leaning to the conservative right, talk host Tom Leykis saw an open window for his primarily liberal opinions. The show went into national syndication and is heard on hundreds of stations via the Westwood One Radio Network.

Radio Ink Collection

Mike Harvey's oldies show *Solid Gold Saturday Night* is heard coast-to-coast as he stimulates musical memories on the Westwood One Radio Network.

Radio Ink Collection

CBS talk show host Gil Gross has one of the most-listened-to radio programs in late night America. Prior to his talk career, he was a newsman on CBS and ABC.

Radio Ink Collection

You know you've "made it" in Los Angeles when your picture gets on the wall of The Palm restaurant. Los Angeles radio star The Real Don Steele points to his likeness, presented in May 1992 honoring his years in Los Angeles radio.

R&R Collection

Talknet's Bruce Williams celebrated 25 years on the air in 1995. Williams is considered a pioneer in talk radio and was among the first national talk personalities in America. His national show reaches more than 10 million people each week.

Radio and Records

In spite of his controversial nature, talk show host G. Gordon Liddy was awarded The Freedom of Speech Award by the National Association of Radio Talk Show Hosts in 1995. The controversy surrounded comments Liddy made on the air which gave some the impression he was suggesting attacking government agents.

Radio Ink Collection

Positioned as "Two Fat Mexicans," the Baka Boyz (yes, boyz) wildly awaken listeners in the Los Angeles area, hailing from Power 106, KPWR. Nick and Eric Vidal took over the morning slot in their early 20s in 1994. Their street sound is non-traditional and a breath of fresh air.

R&R Collection

Ready to extinguish anything he might have said, Houston personality Locke Siebenhausen lights up the airwaves at KLOL.

R&R Collection

Wolfman Jack, aka Bob Smith, hosted many national radio programs throughout his career, including one launched a few months before his death in July 1995. He was the original "border" jock on XERB, the big gun, high-power station from Mexico that could be heard in New York. He was popularized nationally by the film *American Graffiti*.

R&R Collection

Jay Thomas first gained notoriety on WAYS in Charlotte. His show became so popular that he moved from Charlotte to New York City, which was an almost unheard-of leap. While doing mornings in New York, he secured television acting parts on *Mork And Mindy*. He later moved to Power 106 in Los Angeles and ended up with numerous prominent acting roles.

Radio Ink Collection

When Tom Snyder made the switch to CBS in 1995 to do the *Late Late Show* following David Letterman, he insisted on bringing his first love (radio) along. Snyder simulcasts his TV show "live" on the CBS Radio Networks, and then teams up with Elliott Forrest for a second hour together on just the radio.

Radio Ink Collection

Television personality David Letterman's *Late Show* Top Ten Countdown is so popular that stations began paying CBS for its use on their morning shows. Letterman started his career in radio working for WERK in Muncie, Indiana.

Radio Ink Collection

Television hosts Tom Snyder (left) and David Letterman (right) at a press conference to announce that *The Tom Snyder Show* will follow the *Late Show With David Letterman* on CBS. Snyder's television show was simulcast on the CBS radio network. Letterman and Snyder both started their careers as radio personalities. Snyder hosted a nationally syndicated talk show for many years on ABC's Talknet (August 1994).

Associated Press

Putting the fun back in funerals, Howard Stern and Robin Quivers traditionally held a local funeral for other morning personalities they beat in the ratings, or planned to beat, with their nationally syndicated morning show. They are seen here at a funeral for Los Angeles morning team Mark and Brien (November 1992).

R&R Collection

When Al Westcott first filed claims with the FCC about Howard Stern's alleged indecency, it was thought that Al Westcott was a staunch conservative. He was found to be anything but that.

Radio Ink Collection

"Shock Jock" Howard Stern announced his plans to run for governor of New York on March 23, 1994. He planned to run under the Libertarian Party banner. Many politicians believed he could win if all of his listeners voted. He is seen here with on-air sidekick Robin Quivers.

Associated Press

Howard Stern is seen here at a press conference where he announced he was dropping out of the New York gubernatorial race because he did not want to disclose his financial records. With FCC rules relating to candidates, Stern would also have been required to leave the airwaves during his candidacy (August 4, 1994).

Associated Press

Comedian David Brenner decided he had more to share with the world than just jokes, so he joined the Westwood One Radio Network and created *The David Brenner Show*, a national talk format featuring Brenner and guests.

Westwood One Photo

KISS 100 90 Philadelphia morning personality Kris Chandler.

Radio Ink Collection

WABC talk personality Art Rust Jr.

Radio Ink Collection

WCBS' Bill Brown has been heard on the station for more than 25 years.

Radio Ink Collection

CBS' Bill Lynch provides expanded election night coverage during the Clinton/Bush battle in 1990.

Radio Ink Collection

CBS sports personality Bob Costas airs a report from his home station, KMOX, in St. Louis.

Radio Ink Collection

WTIC-AM's Bob Steele is a legend in Hartford, Connecticut, after being on the air for 51 consecutive years.

Radio Ink Collection

Comedian David Brenner became a radio talk host in 1994, bringing with him the ability to attract such big-name entertainers as Ed McMahon (left) and Richard Lewis (right).

Radio Ink Collection

Brian McCann, host of *The Sunday Funnies* on Chicago's Loop FM.

Radio Ink Collection

Child star Danny Bonaduce, from the television show *The Partridge Family*, grew up to become one of Chicago's top radio personalities. Characters from his program are: (l-r) Bonaduce, "Shemp," Kelly Mohr, Neil "Hajee" Sant and Joy Masada. The crew is heard afternoons on The Loop FM.

Radio Ink Collection

If you were looking for controversy, you could always hear it on national talk host Chuck Harder's program.

Radio Ink Collection

For years, Charlie Tuna has graced the airwaves of Los Angeles morning radio. Tuna began as one of the original "Boss Jocks" on KHJ in the 1960s.

Radio Ink Collection

Detroit funnyman Dick Purtan is seen wearing a bulletproof vest while visiting with a representative of the Detroit police. Purtan has dodged a few ratings bullets in his day and has always remained a leader in Detroit morning radio.

Radio Ink Collection

You may not recognize the face, but Dick Orkin's voice is instantly recognizable as one of the top voices in advertising. Orkin's radio spots have always been considered the best on the air. Newsweek called him "The established master of the Advertising Theatre of the Absurd." Orkin was also the voice behind the 1970s series *The Adventures of Chickenman*.

Radio Ink Collection

Former New York City Mayor Ed Koch turned to radio for a daily talk show following his political career.

Radio Ink Collection

WBLS New York's Frankie Crocker "owned" the African-American ratings in New York for decades.

Radio Ink Collection

The '90s was the age of talk radio, and many former politicians became talk hosts. Former California governor and presidential candidate Jerry Brown was one with a national talk show.

Radio Ink Collection

WHDH Boston personality Jess Cain changes a street sign to "Sinatra Street" to celebrate a Sinatra benefit concert.

Radio Ink Collection

In Chicago, being known as a "Kev Head" means you listen to Kevin Matthews on The Loop FM.

Radio Ink Collection

The crew from "Live 105" in San Francisco broadcast *The Alex Bennett Show* from the ABC Radio Network studios in New York. Guests included Howard Cosell, Wendy O Williams, David Brenner, The B-52s and others. Seated: (l-r) Lori Thompson, Christy Fraser and Alex Bennett. Standing: (l-r) Susan O'Connell, Ed Krampf, Sue Lee and Barry Brady.

Radio Ink Collection

Although talk radio gained huge popularity in the '90s, WRKO Boston's Jerry Williams was one of the first high-profile talk personalities.

Radio Ink Collection

The "Nastyman" aboard KIIS-FM in Los Angeles with singing group Jade.

Radio Ink Collection

The WNEW New York Breakfast Club: (l-r) Lisa Glasberg, Marc McEwen and Richard Neer.

Radio Ink Collection

In Salt Lake City, the name Marc Van Wagner was a household word. Van Wagner was one of the top personalities on KSL radio, seen here at a remote broadcast from Disney/MGM Studios in Orlando, Florida.

Radio Ink Collection

Buried in baseball cards, sports broadcaster "Papa Joe" lets his call-in audience try to settle the 1994 baseball strike on the One-On-One sports radio network.

Radio Ink Collection

Q-107 in Washington, D.C., is seen doing a live remote from the metro train station: (l-r) Steve Sreelany, David Page, Scott Woodside and Jim Eliott.

Radio Ink Collection

Radio psychologist Dr. Laura Schlessinger grabbed some of the highest ratings in the national syndication business. Her local Los Angeles program was the highest-rated in her time slot and second only to Rush Limbaugh, fueling her growth on to hundreds of stations and national popularity.

Radio Ink Collection

Dallas' top country radio personality, Terry Dorsey, on KSCS.

Radio Ink Collection

National Public Radio's Susan Stamberg from the program *All Things Considered.*

Photo: Max Hirshfeld/Radio Ink Collection

The Dallas morning team of Steve Johnson (left) and John Walton.

Radio Ink Collection

WCBS-FM's Cousin Brucie featured in an Archie cartoon.

Radio Ink Collection

Cousin Brucie Morrow became a radio legend at "77 WABC" in the 1960s and stayed on the air well into the '90s on WCBS-FM in New York.

Radio Ink Collection

After decades of popularity, Casey Kasem still hosted *Casey's Top 40* and *Casey's Biggest*, two programs on Westwood One's radio network.

Radio Ink Collection

WBZ morning personality Dave Maynard.

Radio Ink Collection

A second generation of the hits from coast to coast: Westwood One introduced Mike Kasem, son of Casey Kasem, in his own program, *Inside Track*, in 1995.

Radio Ink Collection

On-air lunatic John DeBella was Philadelphia's top morning personality in the 1990s.

Radio Ink Collection

Jim Bohannan, talk show host, when he first got into radio.

Radio Ink Collection

If you turn your radio on in the middle of the night, you're likely to hear Jim Bohannon on the Mutual Network. Bohannon's discussions and guests focus on topical issues of the '90s.

Radio Ink Collection

As oldies radio regained popularity, K-Earth in Los Angeles found legendary programmer Bill Drake and asked him to re-create the sound that made the music popular when it was first played. The station became one of the best-sounding oldies stations in America.

Radio Ink Collection

In Detroit, everyone knew the name of J.P. McCarthy of WJR. McCarthy spent decades doing mornings on the AM giant.

Radio Ink Collection

One of the top country radio disc jockeys is WSIX/Nashville's Gerry House. Not only was he one of the funniest entertainers on the radio in Nashville, House was also nationally syndicated, and was a successful country music songwriter.

Radio Ink Collection

Sixteen-year-old Jennifer Hawkins started on WBZT, West Palm Beach, Florida, at age 14 and is known as the youngest radio talk show host in America.

Radio Ink Collection

Former VH1 video jockey and longtime air personality J.J. Jackson starred in Westwood One's program *The Beatle Years*.

Radio Ink Collection

WHO, Des Moines, has a reputation for being visited by presidents. President Bill Clinton visits with WHO-AM's News Director Bob Quinn in May 1993.

Radio Ink Collection

Showing off his legs, Rick Dees prepares to "Walk a Mile in Women's Shoes" down the Hollywood Walk of Fame. Dees is known for his crazy promotional gimmicks.

Radio Ink Collection

Television personality Leeza Gibbons also starred in her own syndicated radio show.

Radio Ink Collection

Hailing from KIIS, Hollywood Hamilton became one of the top "night guys" in Los Angeles. He was also nationally syndicated on the Unistar Radio Network.

Radio Ink Collection

Kid deejays make up the Radio Aahs national network just for kids: (l-r) Stephanie Watson, Jimmy Freeman and Danielle DeMarsh.

Radio Ink Collection

Simply known as Moby, this crazyman entertained audiences across the country, reigning from the ABC Radio Network studios in Dallas.

Radio Ink Collection

Radio personality, historian and professor Michael Keith has probably trained more young radio professionals than any other single person. Keith has written several books that are international best sellers in the radio broadcast education field.

Radio Ink Collection

Referred to as "the Flyjock," Tom Joyner flew between his home in Dallas and the city of Chicago every day, five days a week, for several years. Joyner did a radio show in each city live every weekday and accumulated more frequent flyer miles than anyone else in history. Once satellite technology came into play, Joyner was able to send his show from Dallas via satellite, not only to Chicago, but to cities across the United States. He is one of the biggest stars on the ABC Radio Network.

Radio Ink Collection

President Bill Clinton on his weekly broadcast to the nation.

The White House

ABC's Tom Joyner received the ultimate upgrade when invited to travel onboard Air Force One with President Bill Clinton in March 1994.

Radio Ink Collection

Westwood One Radio Network personality and AOR pioneer, Mary Turner-Pattiz.

Radio Ink Collection

Controversial talk host G. Gordon Liddy interviews entertainer and former radio personality Steve Allen in 1994.

Radio Ink Collection

Enduring for generations of popularity, Paul Harvey is one of America's most-listened-to journalists. Harvey is heard mornings and at noon on the ABC Radio Network.

Radio Ink Collection

During the 1990 presidential campaign, Vice President Dan Quayle makes an appearances with Rush Limbaugh.

Radio Ink Collection

Talk host Raleigh James was one of the innovators in the revamping of talk radio in the 1990s.

Radio Ink Collection

If Rush Limbaugh seems happy, it could have to do with him being one of the most successful radio personalities of all time — and one of the highest-paid. Limbaugh's program saved AM radio, and led the radio industry into success with talk radio.

Radio Ink Collection

Miami, Florida, shock jock Neil Rogers on WIOD.

Radio Ink Collection

In Los Angeles, the name Fred Gallagher gets the attention of anyone involved or interested in sports. Gallagher is sports editor on KNX.

Radio Ink Collection

Tom Leykis in a live broadcast outside of OJ Simpson's house following OJ's arrest.

Radio Ink Collection

Doug Tracht was better known to audiences as The Greeseman. Tracht's act was heard in Jacksonville, Florida, and Washington, D.C., and in 1995 became nationally syndicated. The Greeseman is considered one of the zaniest personalities ever on the air.

Radio Ink Collection

Finally, some recognition for Rush Limbaugh. After lots of criticism for saying what he feels on the radio, which is often unpopular with liberals, Rush Limbaugh receives The Radio Hall of Fame Network Personality induction. Limbaugh was introduced by TV talk host Sally Jessy Raphael, who blasted Rush and his opinions as she introduced him.

Radio Ink Collection

ABC programmer, Rick Sklar.

ABC

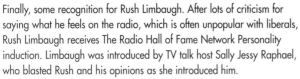

Doug Stephan's Good Day USA is heard nationally on more than 100 stations. Stephan's morning talk show is one of the few that broadcasts on location from wherever international affairs are taking place. Stephan's call-in program is filled with energy, opinion and some hilarious moments.

Radio Ink Collection

Nationally syndicated talk show host Doug Stephan interviews George Shultz in Madrid in 1994.

Radio Ink Collection

In New York, oldies station WCBS became known for its rock 'n' roll reunions. Radio greats Ed Bear, Dean Anthony and Dan Ingram are shown during a 1995 reunion.

Radio Ink Collection

During the '90s, Tom Bodet's radio commercials for Motel 6 made him a radio celebrity. Bodet's folksy commercials increased the chain's business overnight, using only radio.

Radio Ink Collection

No stranger to a radio microphone, comedian Bob Hope paid a visit to Larry King's program on The Mutual Broadcasting System. Hope was in Los Angeles with Gary Landis, while King was in Washington.

Wolfman Jack howled for the last time in July 1995 as he returned home from an exhaustive book tour. Born Bob Smith, the Wolfman became a radio legend in the early '50s as he was heard nationwide from a high-powered "border" station across the Rio Grande in Mexico. Smith is seen here presenting a Marconi Award at a radio broadcasters convention.

Radio Ink Collection

Funnyman Jim Zippo was one of the first deejays to go national with ABC's Satellite Music network, to be heard on hundreds of radio stations nationwide.

Radio Ink Collection

Working mothers in America became a big issue in the 1990s. Here, Debbie Nigro hosts her program *Working Mom On The Run*, originating from New York on 100 stations nationwide. Nigro called her show "standup comedy sitting down, a family show geared toward working mothers" (August 20, 1994).

Associated Press

Former First Lady Barbara Bush had her own national radio show called *Mrs. Bush's Storytime*. The program was targeted to children.

ABC Photo

Presidential candidate Pat Buchanan's national talk show is heard across the United States on the Mutual Broadcasting System.

Radio Ink Collection

WGCI Chicago's Doug Banks became so popular that his program went national on ABC.

Radio Ink Collection

Former New York governor turned radio talk host Mario Cuomo airs nationally on the SW network.

Radio Ink Collection

Known as one of America's finest attorneys, Alan Dershowitz also has his own national radio talk show on the SW network.

Radio Ink Collection

America's oldest teenager, Dick Clark, with Nick Verbitski, president of United Stations Radio Network, syndicator of Clark's *National Countdown*.

Radio Ink Collection

Nationally broadcast on the WOR radio network, Ken and Daria Dolan have been giving Americans financial advice for years.

Radio Ink Collection

Bob Kingsley, host of ABC's American Country Countdown.

Radio Ink Collection

Nancy Donnellan, the female first national sports talk host, affectionately known as "The Fabulous Sports Babe."

ABC Photo

Love-Lines host Dr. Judy Kuriansky.

Radio Ink Collection

Chicago funnyman Jonathon Brandmeier.

Radio Ink Collection

Conservative radio/television talk show host Mary Matalin.

Radio Ink Collection

One of the highest-paid personalities in America, Rick Dees signs one of the largest financial deals in radio history with ABC Radio Networks for his national countdown show *Weekly Top 40*. Dees (left) is with ABC Network mogul David Kantor.

Radio Ink Collection

Actors Phil Hartman (left) and Dave Foley (right) on NBC's hit TV series *News Radio*, about a news/talk radio station. In 1995, talk radio became a popular subject for television audiences.

NBC Photo

"This is Frasier Crane. I'm listening ....," became familiar words on one of television's highest-rated shows, *Frasier*. Kelsey Grammer played a psychologist turned radio talk show host.

NBC Photo

The Radio
Hall of Fame

by Michael C. Keith

When the first radio practitioners plied their fledgling skills under the drab tarpaulin of KDKA's rooftop studio during the early part of this century, they could little imagine the future existence of a hall of fame honoring their medium. An indoor facility was the stuff of their dreams at the time.

As the all-too-familiar cloud of black soot from surrounding smokestacks and passing locomotives deposited a gritty patina on the primitive equipment and its stalwart operators at the modest broadcast site, the future of the infant medium seemed uncertain indeed. That it would one day have a profound impact on the lives of nearly every man, woman and child seemed a remote possibility except to a handful of visionaries, such as David Sarnoff, Lee De Forest and Edwin Armstrong, who believed that radio was destined to become an integral part of the American household and lifestyle.

Located in the Museum of Broadcast Communications and created to pay due homage to the titans of the airwaves, whose glorious emanations have long filled what Orson Welles called (in his infamous Martian broad-

The Chicago Cultural Center, home of The Museum of Broadcast Communications and The Radio Hall of Fame.

Radio Hall of Fame Group: (l-r) Gary Owens, Paul Harvey, Garrison Keillor, Rich Little, Leonard Maltin.

The Museum of Broadcast Communications newscenter.

Edgar Bergen's original "partners," one of the many displays at The Radio Hall of Fame.

cast) the "vast ethereal plain," the Radio Hall of Fame recognizes and showcases contemporary talent from today's diverse programming formats, as well as the pioneers who shaped the medium during its infancy.

Founded by the Emerson Radio Corporation in 1988, the administration of The Hall of Fame was assumed by The Museum of Broadcast Communications in Chicago in September 1991. Existing radio organizations and professionals throughout the United States share in the process of nominating future inductees.

Throughout the year, the Radio Hall of Fame presents special events commemorating significant moments in radio history, as well as public forums showcasing inductees. An annual celebration for the induction of new members takes place each fall in Chicago. It is a lavish, black-tie affair and is broadcast live across the country via the Radio Hall off Fame Network.

The Museum's president and founder, Bruce DuMont, extends a cordial invitation to the public to attend this auspicious event. "The Radio Hall of Fame and the Museum of Broadcast Communications exist for all. I wholeheartedly invite the world to take pleasure in what we have assembled here."

In the past, the ceremony has been hosted by prominent radio figures, such as Larry King, Paul Harvey, Charles Osgood and Tom Snyder. The roster of current Radio Hall of Fame inductees includes Jack Benny, Dick Clark, Arthur Godfrey, Bob Hope, Groucho Marx, Paul Harvey, William Paley, Norman Corwin, Red Skelton, Lowell Thomas, Rush Limbaugh and Frank Stanton, among others.

The medium's most popular and distinguished programs have also been honored. Among the inductees in this category are *All Things Considered, Burns and Allen, The Goldbergs, Grand Ole Opry, Mercury Theatre On the Air, You Bet Your Life* and many more. The Radio Hall of Fame houses the world's finest radio archives, including memorabilia of radio greats such as Charlie McCarthy and friends, Jack Benny's vault, Fibber McGee's closet and more than 50,000 hours of radio broadcasts. It also features the Lynne "Angel" Harvey Radio Center, a state-of-the-art studio available to stations throughout the country for remote broadcasts.

The Radio Hall of Fame is located in Chicago's magnificent Cultural Center on Michigan Avenue at Washington Street. It is open to the public seven days a week and admission is free.

This important archive has become a true national treasure as it strives to preserve and share with everyone a unique part of our cultural heritage.

Information pertaining to exhibitions and programs may be obtained by calling The Museum of Broadcast Communications at 312-629-6000. ▣

The Broadcast Pioneers Library

The Broadcast Pioneers Library (BPL) is a wide-ranging collection of audio/video recordings, books, pamphlets, periodicals, personal paper collections, photographs, scripts and vertical files devoted exclusively to the history of radio and television. Located at the University of Maryland at College Park since October 1994, the Library is housed alongside their National Public Broadcasting Archives, making the two collections an exciting resource for both commercial and non-commercial broadcasting research.

BPL is a rich and nuanced tapestry of both textual and non-print materials, most of which are unavailable elsewhere. Since its founding in 1971, the Library has hosted thousands of researchers, answered innumerable reference requests and established itself as an indispensable repository of broadcast history. BPL serves both academia and the broadcasting industry; its patrons represent a variety of interests and disciplines. The components of the Broadcast Pioneers Library include:

AUDIO/VIDEO RECORDINGS:

BPL contains nearly 900 oral histories, interviews and speeches (most of which are transcribed) by such notables as Norman Corwin, Edgar Bergen, Niles Trammell, Frank E. Mullen, Rosel H. Hyde and Leonard H. Goldenson. The Library also maintains the Westinghouse News Collection (1958-1982), consisting of raw feeds from their Washington bureau. The Library houses 3,300 transcription discs, including more than 1,000 commercials in the Radio Advertising Bureau Collection, V-Discs and news reports. A selection of radio programming is also available, including substantial runs of *Columbia Workshop* (1941-1946), *Can You Top This?* (1942-1948) and the 1930s-era children's program *Secret Agent K-7 Returns*.

BOOKS:

There are more than 3,000 volumes that run the gamut from programming histories to engineering manuals. Of particular interest are books published in the 1920s and 1930s that trace the evolution of broadcasting from its earliest days.

PAMPHLETS:

The pamphlet holdings are quite extensive, with more than 3,000 titles, ranging from 1920s vintage Bell Laboratories radio engineering bulletins to promotional materials and internal studies generated by the broadcast networks. The Library also has an impressive array of government documents, including the Navigation Bureau List of Radio Stations (1913-1943), FRC/FCC decisions and Congressional reports and hearings.

PERIODICALS:

More than 250 periodical titles, including many that are difficult to find, are available at the Library. Among these are runs of *Broadcast Weekly* (1930-1936), the *Heinl Radio Business Letter* (1930-1950), *Radio and Television News* (1919-1958), *Radio Guide* (1931-1943), *Ross Reports/Television Index* (1949-present), *Sponsor* (1946-1964) and *Wireless Age* (1913-1925).

PERSONAL COLLECTIONS:

Many prominent broadcasters have donated material to the Library, including:

William S. Hedges: Mr. Hedges, former NBC executive and president of the NAB, arranged some 13,000 items in 540 subject categories for the Broadcast Pioneers History Project (1964-1971) that formed the core collection of the Library.

Carl Haverlin: The first president of Broadcast Music, Inc., Mr. Haverlin donated tapes from BMI Program Clinics (1951-1957) along with photos and documents that chronicle the founding of BMI.

Alois Havrilla: The Havrilla collection chronicles the life of this longtime radio announcer whose career began in 1924. He worked on more than 100 programs with such notables as Jack Benny, Al Jolson and Paul Whiteman.

Elmo N. Pickerill: Mr. Pickerill was an engineer who worked with RCA and Lee De Forest. His materials include correspondence with Guglielmo Marconi, David B. Sarnoff and De Forest, scrapbooks and early publications on wireless telegraphy.

Edythe J. Meserand: Ms. Meserand donated items from her tenure as first president of the American Women in Radio and Television, her career as a documentary producer and other material relating to women in broadcasting.

PHOTOGRAPHS:

The photograph collection of the Broadcast Pioneers Library contains more than 25,000 photos, slides and negatives, dating from the 1920s to the present, offering the researcher a pictorial history of the evolution of broadcasting in the United States. The images illustrate a wide variety of subjects, including the people involved in broadcasting; radio and television programs; the studios, facilities and community activities of local radio stations; and the activities of organizations related to broadcasting. The collection is arranged in several categories, including Advertising, Associations, Audience, Awards, Biography, Buildings, Genre, Sound Effects, Stations, Studios, Technology and Women in Broadcasting. This component is quite popular with researchers; many of the Library's photographs have been published in numerous books and articles, including *Blast From the Past.*

SCRIPTS:

The Library maintains more than 1,300 scripts from various radio and television programs, including *The Stebbins Boys* (1931-1932), *Sky King* (1947-1950), *Cab Calloway's Quizzicale* (1941-1942) and complete runs of *Your Show of Shows* (1950-1954) and *Wisdom* (1952-1959).

VERTICAL FILES:

BPL has extensive vertical files on *Your Show of Shows* (1950-1954) and *Wisdom* (1952-1959).

Of particular interest are materials from individual stations around the United States. There are more than one million items in this component.

The Broadcast Pioneers Library actively seeks donations in all aspects of broadcast history. If you have any material you would like to see preserved for future generations, we urge you to contact the BPL staff.

The Broadcast Pioneers Library is open 9 a.m. to 5 p.m., Monday-Friday. Telephone and E-mail research requests are welcomed.

Broadcast Pioneers Library

Hornbake Library

University of Maryland

College Park, Maryland 20742

phone: (301) 405-9160

e-mail: bp50@umail.umd.edu

World WideWeb:http://www.itd.umd.edu/UMCPLibraries/
BPL/hbplintro.ht

Radio Fan Directory

W hile researching this book, we found that many people wanted to know more about how they could get involved with collecting old radios, radio memorabilia and old radio programs. We thought it might be helpful to list the organizations, publications and museums we've encountered.

Museums and Archives:

American Radio Relay League, 225 Main St, Newington, CT 06111. 203-666-1541. The ARRL collection includes early Amateur Radio gear, vacuum tubes, keys, microphones and ARRL/QST items going back to the 'teens.

Antique Wireless Association Electronic Communication Museum, 59 Main St, Village Green, Routes 5 & 20, Bloomfield, NY 14469. 716-657-6260.

Atwater Kent Museum, 15 S. 7th St, Philadelphia. 215-922-3031. Although the museum was founded by radio giant Atwater Kent, early radio gear makes up only a small part of the items displayed.

Baltimore Historical Electronics Museum, 920 Elkridge Landing Rd, Baltimore, MD. 410-765-2345. Originally funded by Westinghouse, the museum displays primarily military electronic items manufactured that company. The display includes a Marconi magnetic detector.

Bellingham Antique Radio Museum, 1315 Railroad Ave, Bellingham, WA 98225. 206-734-4168. The collection includes more than a thousand radios (and related items), most of which are pre-1930.

Bighorn Museum, 301 Main St, Genoa, CO 80818. 719-763-2220. A large collection of Amateur Radio equipment.

Broadcast Pioneers Archives (by appointment only), Hornbake Library, University of Maryland, College Park, MD 20742. Contact: Tom Connors/Mike Mashon, (301) 405-9160.

Jaspers's Antique Radio Museum, 2022 Cherokee, St Louis, MO. 314-421-8313. The col-lection includes more than 6000 broadcast and ham radios housed in two large buildings. The staff also rapairs and sells vintage radio equipment.

Marconi State Historical Park, 18500 State Rt 1, Marshall, CA 94940. 415-663-9020. Several turn-of-the-century Marconi Company buildings can be seen here, and pictures of early Marconi Company operations are on display.

Muchow's Historical Radio Museum, 107 Center St, Elgin, IL 60120. 708-742-0183. This facility, which houses thousands of vintage radios and related items, is only open to the public one day each year! Vintage radio buffs from all over the world can be found in attendance. A large swapmeet is held in conjunction with Muchow's open house.

Museum of Broadcast Communications/Radio Hall of Fame, Chicago Cultural Center, 78 East Washington, Chicago, IL 60602-3407. (312) 629-6000.

Museum of Radio and Technology (Antique Radio Club of America), 1640 Florence Ave, Huntington, WV. 304-525-8890. This collec-tion has a dynamic inventory and is housed in an old schoolhouse.

Museum of Radio and Television, 25 West 52nd St., New York, NY 10019. (212) 621-6600, Fax (212) 621-6715.

New England Museum of Wireless and Steam, Inc., Tillinghast Rd., East Greenwich, RI 02818. (401) 884-1710, Fax (401) 884-0683. This collec-tion, housed in two buildings, features items from 1890 through the 1940s.

Nikola Tesla Museum, 2220 E Bijou, Colorado Springs, CO 80909. 719-475-0918. This is a small exhibit of Tesla-related historic items (and a Tesla-oriented bookstore).

Pacific Pioneers Museum (by appointment only),.Home Savings Building, Sunset and Vine, Hollywood, CA. Contact: Ron Wolf, (213) 462-9606.

Paquette's Microphone Museum, 107 E National Ave, Milwaukee, WI 53204. 414-645-1600. The collection contains more than 1000 vintage microphones and pre-1940 radios.

Pavek Museum, 3515 Raleigh Ave., St.Louis Park, MN 55416. Contact: Steve Raymer, (612) 926-9199. This huge collection features thousands of radios and related items from hundreds of early manufacturers.

US Army Communications-Electronics Museum, exit 105 on the Garden State Parkway, Bldg 275, Kaplan Hall, Fort Monmouth, Ft Monmouth, NJ 07703. 908-532-9000. This collection includes radios, radar and related items from the early 1900s through the 1980s.

Van Dyke Broadcasting Museum, 2 Squires Ave., East Quogue, NY 11942. (516) 728-9835.

Western Heritage Museum of Omaha, 801 S 10th St, Omaha, NE 68108. 402-444-5071. This 2500-square-foot display of Amateur Radio items was founded by Leo Meyerson, W0GFQ, who many consider the last living member of the"giants of radio." Leo started the historic World Radio Laboratories (WRL) with its popular Globe series of transmitters. The museum is housed in the nation's first restored Art Deco train station.

Western Union Collection, Division of Electricity and Modern Physics, National Museum of American History, Smithsonian Institution, 14th and Constitution Ave, Washington, DC. 202-357-3270.

Ye Olde Transmitting Tube Museum, 150 Tanbark Ln, Crescent City, CA 95531. 707-464-6470. The collection includes more than 4000 tubes, and they make duplicates available to other collectors/restorers free of charge!

Publications and Organizations:

Daily Sentinel, Robert Brunet, 21 W 74 St., New York, NY 10023. bimonthly $9/yr.

Hello Again, Jay Hickerson, Box 4321, Hamden CT 06513. bimonthly $12/yr.

Nara News, Janis DeMoss, 134 Vincewood Dr., Nicholasville, KY 40356. quarterly $15/yr.

Nostalgia Digest, Chuck Schaden, Box 421, Morton Grove, IL 60053. bimonthly $12/yr.

Old Time Radio Digest, Bob Burchett and George Wagner, 4114 Montgomery Rd., Cincinnati OH 45212. bimonthly $12.50/yr.

Old Time Radio Gazette, Tom Miller, 2004 E 6th St., Superior, WI 54880. monthly $8.50/yr.

Thrilling Days of Yesteryear, John Rayburn, Box 36106, Denver CO 80236. bimonthly $15.

TUNE IN, Rob Imes, 1844 E Longmeadow, Trenton, MI 48183. bimonthly $6.

Vintage Radio Logue, Ron Statley, 5632 Van Nuys Blvd., Ste 368, Van Nuys CA 91401. quarterly $35.

Old Radios and Phonographs:

Horn Speaker, Jim Cranshaw, Rt. 3 Box 79, Dallas, TX 75103. 10 times/yr $10/yr.

Mid-Atlantic Antique Radio Club, Joe Koester, 249 Spring Gap South, Laurel, MD 20810. $12.50/yr.

Old Timers' Bulletin, Bruce Kelley, Main St., Holcomb, NY 14469. quarterly $5/yr, Journal of the Antique Wireless Association

Antique Radio Classifieds, John Terry, Publisher, One River Rd., P.O. Box 2, Carlisle, MA 01741. (508) 371-0512, (508) 371-7129. Monthly $34.95.

Antique Wireless Association Old Timers' Bulletin, Box E, Breesport, NY 14816. $12/yr.

Antique Electronic Supply, P.O. Box 27468, Tempe, AZ 85283. (602) 820-5411, Fax (800) 706-6789. Available catalog of tubes, parts, books and supplies.

Waves, 32 East 13th St., New York, NY 10003. (212) 989-9284. Contact: Bruce Mager. Retail store selling old radios and phonographs.

Rainy Day Books, P.O. Box 775, Fitzwilliam, NH 03447. (603) 585-3448.

Vintage Radio Videos, WBW Entertainment, 970 E. Lake Dr., Bartow, FL 33830-5917.

Ozark Vintage Radio, 3923 East Latoka St., Springfield, MO 65809. Books, collectors' guides, manuals, restoration videos.

E.H. Scott Historical Society, 3712 N. Broadway, #4450, Chicago, IL 60613.

Antique Radio Store, 8376 La Mesa Blvd., La Mesa, CA 91941. (619) 668-5653.
Radiomania, 2109 Carterdale Rd., Baltimore, MD 21209.

Playthings of the Past, 9511 Sunrise Blvd., #J23, Cleveland, OH 44133. (216) 251-3714.

Puett Electronics, P.O. Box 28572, Dallas, TX 75228. Books, schematics, literature, manuals, old-time radio programs, tubes, parts and more.

Nostalgia and Miscellaneous:

Laugh, Peter Tatchell, 40 Bambra Rd., Caulfield, Victoria, Australia 3161. $4 an issue, comedy magazine; has many radio logs and discographies.

Movie-Entertainment Book Club, 15 Oakland Ave., Harrison, NY 10528. monthly offering of books on all areas of entertainment and nostalgia.

Past Times, Jordan Young and Randy Skretvedt, 73008 Fillmore Dr., Buena Park, CA 90620. $9/4 issues; articles on movies, music OTR, popular culture, TV, theater.

Radio Active, Dennis Burns, 10248 Lola Ct., Concord Twp., OH 44077. 3 times/yr Top 40 survey collectors.

Clubs:

Abbott and Costello Fan Club, Chris Costello, Box 2084, Toluca Lake, CA 91610. (Abbott and Costello Quarterly)

Al Jolson Society, Jim Brockson, 933 Fifth Ave., Prospect Park, PA 19076. (Jolson Journal)

Broadcast Pioneers (New York), 212-586-2000. Branches also exist in several other cities.

Cinnamon Bear Fan Club, Carolyn Breen Kolibaban 19419 N.E. Knot, Portland OR 97220. $2/yr.

Eddie Cantor Appreciation Society, Sheila Riddle, Box 312, Mount Gay, WV 25637.

Golden Radio Buffs, Owens Pomeroy, 3613 Chestnut Dr., Baltimore, MD 21211. $20/yr. (On the Air)

Illinois OTR Society, 10 South 540 County Line Rd., Hinsdale, IL 60521.

Indiana Recording Club, William Davis, 1729 E. 77th, Indianapolis, IN 46240. (Tape Squeal)

Jack Benny Fan Club, Laura Lee, 3910 Oak Rd., #03, Walnut, CA 94596.

Kate Smith Foundation, Box 3575, Cranston, RI 02910.

Lum and Abner Fan Club, Tim Holllis, 81 Sharon Blvd, Dora, AL 35062.

Manhattan Radio Club, Paul Mellos, 331 E. 81st St., New York, NY 10028.

Metropolitan Washington OTR Club, James Burnette, 6704 Bodensee Lane, Manassas, VA 22111. $15/yr. (Radio Recall)

Milwaukee Area Radio Enthusiasts, Ken Pabst, 4442 N. 77th St., Milwaukee, WI 53218.

National OTR Enthusiasts, Steve Hiss, Rt. 1 Box 253, Alacha, FL 32615.

North American Radio Archives NARA, See NARA News; also publishes Through the Horn.

Old Time Radio Club, 100 Harvey Dr., Lancaster, NY 14806. $17.50/yr. (Illustrated Press) (Memories)

Old Time Radio Show Collectors' Association of England (ORCA), Barry Hill: write to Tom Monroe, 2055 Elmwood Ave., Lakewood, OH 44107. $15/yr.

Old Time Radio Show Collectors' Association (ORCA Canadian counterpart), Reg Hubert, 45 Barry St., Sudbury, Ontario,

Canada P3B 3H6. $6/yr.

Radio Collectors of America, Bob Levin, 8 Ardsley Cir., Brockton, MA 02402. (RCA Newsletter)

Radio Historical Association of Colorado, Vicki Blake, Box 1908, Englewood, CO 80150. $20/yr (Return With Us Now)

Radio Listener's Lyceum, Robert Newman, 11509 Islandale Dr., Forest Park, OH 45240. (RLL on the Air)

Revival of Creative Radio, Tim Coco, Box 1585, Haverhill, MA 01831. $12/yr. (Wavelengths)

Straight Arrow PowWow, Bill Harper, 301 East Buena Vista Ave., North Augusta, GA 29841.

Yesterday USA, Bill Bragg, 2001 Plymouth Rock, Richardson, TX 75081. (Airwaves)

Vic and Sade Society, Barbara Schwarz, 7232 Keystone Ave., Lincolnwood, IL 60646.

Sources for circulating shows/sources who trade, sell or lend programs (Many of the clubs listed separately have lending libraries):

AVPRO Distributors (Conaston; Terry Salomonson), Box 1392, Lake Elsinore, CA 92531.

Bob Flatter, 3126 N. 12 St., Wausau, WI 54401. (Big Band)

RBC Productions (Bob Burnham), Box 2645, Livonia, MI 48151.

Carl Froelich Jr., 2 Heritage Farm Dr., New Freedom, PA 17349.

Dave Siegel, 419 Granite Springs Rd., Yorktown Heights, NY 10598. (Trades only)

Ed Carr, 216 Shaner St.,

Boyertown, PA 19512.

Erstwhile Radio, P.O. Box 2284, Peabody, MA 01960.

Golden Age Radio (Rex Bills), Box 252515, Portland, OR 97225.

Golden Era Records, Box 126, Reseda, CA 91335

Hall Closet (Chuck Schaden), Box 421, Morton Grove, IL 60053.

Hello Again Radio (Bob Burchett), Box 6176, Cincinnati, OH 45206.

Heritage Radio Classics (Tom Heathwood), Box 16, Chestnut Hill, MA 02167.

James Albert, 2732 Queensboro Ave., Pittsburgh, PA 15226.

John Barber, Box 70711, New Orleans, LA 70172.

Ken Mills, 907 Maple Ave., Ridgefield, NJ 07657.

Laval Archives (Lawrence Rao), 1009 Autumn Woods Lane, #106, Virginia Beach, VA 23454.

McCoy's Recordings (Pat McCoy), Box 1069, Richland, WA 99352.

Memories of Radio (Dick Judge), 362 Browncroft, Rochester, NY 14609.

Metacom (Adventures in Cassettes), 5353 Nathan Ln. North, Plymouth, MN 55442.

Mind's Eye (Bob Lewis), Box 1060, Petaluma, CA 94953.

Nostalgia Central (Gary Kramer), Box 528, Mt. Morris, MI 48458.

Nostalgia Company (David Kiner), Box 82, Redmond, WA 98073.

Nostalgia Radio Company (Jerry

and Jean Gibbs), Box 519137, St. Louis, MO 63151.

Radio Showcase (Steve Kelez), Box 4357, Santa Rosa, CA 95402.

Radio Spirits (Carl Amari), P.O. Box 2141, Schiller Park, IL 60176.

Radio Vault (Roger Massel), Box 9032, Wyoming, MI 49509.

RJR Enterprises (Rusty Wolfe), Box 21428, Chattanooga, TN 37421.

SPERDVAC, Box 1587 Hollywood, CA 90078. (Club Lending Library: Thom Salome, 492 4th St., Brooklyn, NY 11215)

Vintage Broadcasts (Andy Blatt), 42 Bowling Green, Staten Island, NY 10314.

James Albert, 2732 Queensboro Ave., Pittsburgh, PA 15226.

AudioFile Tapes, 209-25 18 Ave., Bayside, NY 11360.

AVPRO, P. O. Box 1392, Lake Elsinore, CA 92331-1392.

Barnes & Noble, 126 Fifth Ave, New York, NY 10010.

L. Bilyou Sr., Box 864, Norwalk, CT 06856.

Bowie and Weatherford, Box 5, Southworth, WA 98386.

The Can Corner, Box DC 1173, Linwood, PA 19061.

Detectives on Tape, Box 455 Dept S-91521, Joppa, MD 21085.

Echoes of the Past, Box 9593, Alexandria, VA 22304.

Folk Arts Records, 3611 Adams Ave., San Diego, CA 92116.

John Ford, 411 Truitt St., Salisbury, MD 21801.

Galore, Box 1321, Ellicott City, MD 21043.

Charlie Garant, P.O. Box 331, Greeneville, TN 37744.

Adriana Vargas, The Great American Audio Collection, 33 Portman Rd., New Rochelle, NY 10801.

Highbridge, 274 Fillmore Ave. E., St. Paul, MN 55107.

Bob Burchett, Hello Again Radio, Box 6176, Cincinnati, OH 45206.

Keelan's Music Shoppe, Sutter Place Mall, 5221 S. 48th St., Lincoln, NE 68516.

Metro Golden Memories, 5425 W Addison, Chicago. IL 60641.

Mind Imagery, 6135 Olson Memorial Highway, Golden Valley, MN 55422.

Mr. Nostalgia, Box 414201, Miami Beach, FL 33141.

National Recording Company, Box 395, Glenview, IL 60025.

Okay, Box 441, Whitestone, NY 11357.

Postings, P.O. Box 8001, Hilliard, OH 43026-8001.

Radio Classics, 1105 N. Main St., Suite 9-E, Gainesville, FL 32601.

The Radio Store, Box 203, Oradell, NJ 07649.

Radio Hall of Fame, 412 Redbud Lane, Oxford, MS 38655.

Radio Time Productions, 1513 Loring Run, Bakersfield, CA 93309.

Radio Yesteryear, (aka Radiola /Sandy Hook Records), Box C, Sandy Hook, CT 06482.

Lawrence Rao, 700 Cherokee Rd #E, Portsmouth, VA 23701.

RJR Enterprises, Box 21428, Chattanooga, TN 37421.

Thom Salome, 196 Lawrence Ave, Brooklyn, NY 11230.

Anthony Tollin, The Shadow Log, 47 Riveredge Dr., Fairfield, NJ 70006.
The Shadow's Sanctum, 630 East Harry, Wichita, KS 67211.

Signals,274 Fillmore Ave., E. St. Paul, MN 51072.

Stoneground Features, P.O. Box 7585, Urbandale, PA 50322.

Barbara Davies, Treasure Hunters, Box 463, Mansfield Center, CT 06250.

Time Warner Sound Exchange, 45 N. Industry Ct., Deer Park, NY 11729-4614.

Andy Blatt, Vintage Broadcasts, 42 Bowling Green, Staten Island, NY 10314.

Voyager Company, 1351 Pacific Coast Hwy, Santa Monica, CA 90401.

Stuart Jay Weiss, 33 Von Braun Ave., Staten Island, NY 10312.

Wireless, Box 64422, St. Paul, MN 55164-0422.

Radio Logs and Books:
Gordon Kelley, 8600 University Blvd., Evansville, IN 47712 Sherlock Holmes (95% complete) $10.

Richard Hayes, 59 Myrtle Ave., Cranston, RI 02910.
Kate Smith R20 (Radio and TV).

Terry Salomonson (ABPRO), Box 1392, Lake Elsinore, CA 92531.
Lone Ranger (103pp) $22.50.
Challenge of the Yukon $6.50.
Dragnet $7.50.
Escape $17.50.
Yours Truly, Johnny Dollar $12.50.
Green Hornet $7.50.

John Gassman, Box 1163, Whittier, CA 90604.
Jack Benny $15.

Randy Eidemiller, 7700 Lampson, #37, Garden Grove, CA 92641.
Dragnet $13.
Suspense $23.

Jerry Austin, 4312 Pearl Ct., Cypress, CA 90630.
Life of Riley $8.
Family Theater cost unknown.

David Kiner, Box 82 Redmond, WA 98073.
Bing Crosby, Cremo Singer (1931-32) cost unknown.

Peter Tatchell, 40 Bambra Rd., Caulfield, Victoria, Australia 3161.
Al Jolson Career Guide (complete) $6.

Thomas Heathwood, Box 16, Chestnut Hill, MA 02167.
The Adventures of Ozzie and Harriet (Third season) cost unknown.

Re-creations (Some people and groups who perform re-creations of older radio shows on a fairly regular basis):
Gary Yoggy, 72 Bissell Ave., Corning, NY 14830.

Bob Bowers, 127 Melville Ave., Dorchester, MA 02124.

SPERDVAC, Box 7177, Van Nuys, CA 91409.

Friends of Old-time Radio (Jay Hickerson), Box 4321, Hamden CT 06517.

Bob Burchett, 10280 Gunpowder Rd., Florence, KY 41042.

Gene Ewan, 202 Church St., Atco, NJ 08004.

Radio Historical Association of Colorado, Box 1908, Englewood, CO 80150.

Radio Enthusiasts of Puget Sound, 9936 Northeast 197th St.,

Bothell, WA 98011.
New Orleans Radio Theater (John Barber), Box 70711, New Orleans, LA, 70172.

The Mighty Simpson Art Players (Bob Simpson), 4565 S.E. 57th Ln., Ocala, FL 32671.
Golden Radio Buffs (Owens Pomeroy), 3613 Chestnut Ave., Baltimore, MD 21211.

Shubert Radio Theater (Bert Garskof), 439 Ellsworth Ave., New Haven, CT 06511.
Groups who perform new radio drama:

Radio Works (Sue Zizza), c/o WRHU, Hofstra Univ., Hempstead, NY 11550.

Bank Street College Radio (Irwin Gonshak), 610 W. 112th St., New York, NY 10025.

Blue Ridge Players, Box 933, Hendersonville, NC 28793.

Bay Area Players (Eric Bauersfeld), Box 5615, Berkeley, CA 94705.

Other World Media (David Osman), Box 566, Freeland, WA 98249.

ZPPR Productions (Sarah Montague), 34 Gansvoort St., New York, NY 10014.

Voices International (Everett Frost), 2 Washington Square Village, New York, NY 10007.

Radio Arts Production (Charles Potter), 838 West End Ave., New York, NY 10025.

Midwest Radio Theater Workshop, KOPN-FM (Diane Huneke), 915 E Broadway, Columbia, MO 65201.

New Radio and Performing Arts (Helen Thornington), 284 Eastern Parkway, Brooklyn, NY 11225.
Pacifica Program Service, Box 8092, Universal City, CA 91607.

California Artist Radio Theater (Peggy Webber), 6612 Whitley Ter., Hollywood, CA 90028.

30 Minutes to Curtain (KCSN), 1811 Nordoff St., Northridge, CA 91330.

Oasis Theater (Brian Jennings), 230 E. 9th St., New York, NY 10003.

WBAI Radio, 505 8th Ave., New York, NY 10008.

Jim French (KVI), 7th Ave. and Olive Way, Seattle, WA 98101.

American Radio Theater (J. Steven Coleman), 3035 23rd St., San Francisco, CA 94110.

Scripts:

Frank Bequaert, Box 775, Fitzwilliam NH 03447.

NARA (Scott Jones), 47478 E. Grant St., Fresno, CA 93700. (Members Only).

Current Radio Resources:

Radio Advertising Bureau, 1320 Greenway Drive, Suite 500, Irving, TX 75038. (214) 753-6750, Fax (214) 753-6727. Contact: Gary Fries.

National Association of Broadcasters, 1771 N Street NW, Washington, DC 20036. (202) 429-5420, Fax (202) 775-3523. Contact: Edward O. Fritts.

Radio Ink Magazine, 224 Datura Street, Suite 701, West Palm Beach, FL 33401. (407) 655-8778, Fax (407) 655-8498. Contact: Eric Rhoads.

Country Radio Broadcasters, 50 Music Square West, Suite 702, Nashville, TN 37203. (615) 327-4487, Fax (615) 327-4492. Contact: Dave Nichols.

The following listing of old radio collecting organizations is provided by Antique Radio Classified, a monthly magazine for collectors, P.O. Box 2-V94, Carlisle, MA 01741.

Antique Wireless Association (AWA). Box "E", Breesport, NY 14816. Pub: The Old Timer's Bulletin, quarterly. Dues: $12. National annual conference and regional meets. Museum.

Alabama Historical Radio Society (ALHRS). 2413 Old Briar Trail, Birmingham, AL 35226. Newsletter, monthly. Dues: $20. Meetings 4th Mon. evening each month but Dec.; annual show/swap meet. Don Kresge Radio Museum, Fairfield Civic Center, 6509 E.J. Oliver Blvd., Fairfield, AL.

Antique Radio Club of Illinois (ARCI). Carolyn Knipfel, RR 3, 200 Langham, Morton, IL 61550. Pub: ARCI News, quarterly. Dues: $12. Annual August Radiofest and additional meets each year.

Antique Radio Collectors Club of Ft. Smith, Arkansas (ARCCF-SA). Wanda Conatser, 7917 Hermitage Dr., Ft. Smith, AR 72903. Dues: $10. Monthly meetings, annual show.

Antique Radio Collectors & Historians (ARCH) of Greater St. Louis. Derek Cohn, 23 Topton Way, Apt. 1 East, Clayton, MO 63105. Dues: $10. Monthly newsletter and meetings, annual picnic and swap meet.

Antique Radio Collectors of Ohio (ARCO). PO Box 292292, Kettering, OH 45429. Pub: The ARCO Code, quarterly. Dues: $10. Monthly meetings, August show and auction.

Arkansas Chapter/AWA. Arkansas Antique Radio Club (AARC). Tom Burgess, P.O. Box 191117, Little Rock, AR 72219. Dues: $5. Monthly meets.

Arizona Antique Radio Club (AARC). Art Heikkila, 4002 W. Beryl Ln., Phoenix, AZ 85051. Pub: The Arizona Antique Radio Club News, quarterly. Dues: $15. Meetings, swap meets.

Belleville Area Antique Radio Club (BAARC). Charles Haynes, 219 W. Spring, Marissa, IL 62257. Monthly newsletter. Dues: $10. Monthly meetings.

Buckeye Antique Radio and Phonograph Club (BARPC). Steve Dando, 4572 Mark Trail, Copley, OH 44321. Pub: News From: BARPC, bimonthly. Dues: $7. Monthly meetings, two mall shows, March swap meet with PARS.

California Historical Radio Society (CHRS). P.O. Box 31659, San Francisco, CA 94131. 24-hour newsline: (415) 978-9100. Dale Sanford, 107 St. Thomas Way, Tiburon, CA 94920. Pubs: The Journal, biannual; newsletter, 3-4/year. Biannual audio tape. Dues: $15. Quarterly swap meets.

North Valley Chapter, CHRS (NVC-CHRS). Chris Galantine, 15853 Ontario Pl., Redding, CA 96001-9785. Bimonthly newsletter. Dues: $5 (+ $15 CHRS). Bimonthly meetings.

Cincinnati Antique Radio Collectors (CARC). Tom Ducro, 6805 Palmetto, Cincinnati, OH 45227. Informal organization. Write to be put on mailing list. Two meets per year.

Colorado Radio Collectors (CRC). Larry Weide, 5270 E. Nassau Circle, Englewood, CO 80110. Pub: The Flash!!, bimonthly. Dues: $12. Bimonthly meetings/swap

meets. April Show & Swap Meet, July Family Picnic and September Auction.

Delaware Valley Historic Radio Club (DVHRC). P.O. Box 41031, Philadelphia, PA 19127-0031. Mike Koste: (215) 646-6488. Pub: The Oscillator, monthly. Dues: $10. Monthly meetings with swap meets, quarterly flea market.

Florida Antique Wireless Group (FAWG). Paul Currie, Box 738, Chuluota, FL 32766. Pub: FAWGhorn News, quarterly. Monthly tailgate swap meets, fall auction and quarterly flea markets.

Greater Boston Antique Radio Collectors (GBARC). Richard Foster, 12 Shawmut Ave., Cochituate, MA 01778. Informal organization. Write to be put on mailing list. One winter and one spring meet each year.

Greater New York Vintage Wireless Association (GNYVWA). Bob Scheps, 12 Garrity Ave., Ronkonkoma, NY 11779. Pub: Meeting notices. Dues: $4. Six meets/year and monthly meetings.

Houston Vintage Radio Association (HVRA). HVRA, P.O. Box 31276, Houston, TX 77231-1276. Membership info: David Moore, 3213 Regal Oaks, Pearland, TX 77581. Pub: The Grid Leak, monthly. Dues: $15. Monthly meetings and special regional events.

Hudson Valley Antique Radio and Phonograph Society-AWA (HARPS). John Gramm, P.O. Box 1, Rt. 207, Campbell Hall, NY 10916. Pub: HARPS Newsletter, quarterly. Dues: $15. Monthly meetings, annual Old Time Radio & Phono Show.

Hudson Valley Vintage Radio Club. Al Weiner, 507 Violet Ave., Hyde Park, NY 12538. Dues: None. Meets, 2 a year.

Indiana Historical Radio Society (IHRS). 245 N. Oakland Ave., Indianapolis, IN 46201. Pub: IHRS Bulletin, quarterly. Dues: $10. Quarterly swap meets in various areas of state.

Iowa Antique Radio Club and Historical Society (IARCHS). New club forming. Gerald Lange, 2191 Graham Cir., Dubuque, IA 52002. Pub: IARCHS Newsletter, quarterly. Dues: $12. Annual Radiofest.

Michigan Antique Radio Club (MARC). Bruce Eddy, 2590 W. Needmore Hwy., Charlotte, MI 48813. Pub: The Michigan Antique Radio Chronicle, quarterly. Dues: $12. Annual Extravaganza and other quarterly meets.

Mid-America Antique Radio Club (MAARC). Monty Greenstreet, 220 Bayview, Lee's Summit, MO 64064. Pub: The Broadcaster, quarterly. Dues: $10. Semi-annual auctions, swap meets.

Mid-Atlantic Antique Radio Club (MAARC). Jay Kiessling, P.O. Box 67, Upperco, MD 21155. Pub: Radio Age, monthly. Dues: $20. Monthly meetings.

Mid-South Antique Radio Collectors (MSARC). Linda Ramirez, 811 Maple St., Providence, KY 42450-1857. Pub: Old Radio Times, quarterly. Dues: $10. Two meets per year.

Mississippi Historical Radio and Broadcasting Society (MHR&BS). Pub: MHR&BS newsletter, monthly. Dues: $10. Randy Guttery, 2412 C St., Meridian, MS 39301. Monthly meetings and workshops.

Mountains 'N' Plains Radio

Collectors' Association (MPRCA). New club forming. MPRCA, 1249 Solstice Ln., Fort Collins, CO 80525-1239. Pub: Newsletter, six a year. Dues: $12. Meetings.

Music City Vintage Radio & Phonograph Society. P.O. Box 22291, Nashville, TN 37202. Pub: Newsletter, bimonthly. Dues: $10. Bimonthly meetings, bimonthly "Chat 'N' Chew," fall swap meet.

Nebraska Antique Radio Collectors Club (NARCC). Steve Morton, 905 West First, North Platte, NE 69101. Pub: Mountains 'N Plains newsletter, six a year. Dues: $13. Monthly meetings Apr. to Oct. in West Nebraska, annual auction in Kearney.

New England Antique Radio Club (NEARC). NEARC Internet address: nearc@aol.com. NEARC info line: (617) 923-2665. Judy Gauthier, 113 Barretts Hill Rd., Hudson, NH 03051. Pub: Escutcheon Newsletter, quarterly. Dues: $10. Quarterly meets and auctions.

New Jersey Antique Radio Club (NJARC). Kathleen Flanagan, 92 Joysan Ter., Freehold, NJ 07728. Pub: New Jersey Antique Radio Club News, quarterly. Dues: $15. Monthly meetings, three swap meets a year.

New Mexico Radio Collectors Club (NMRCC). New club forming. Bill Schultz, 11605 Versailles Ave. NE, Albuquerque, NM 87111. Pub: Newsletter, monthly. Dues: $5. Annual Sale & Show and monthly meetings.

Niagara Frontier Wireless Association (NFWA). Gary Parzy, 135 Autumnwood, Cheektowaga, NY 14227. Pub: NFWA Chronicle, quarterly. Dues: $9. Regional meets. Permanent antique radio display and research

center at the Amherst Museum, Amherst, NY.

Northland Antique Radio Club (NARC). P.O. Box 18362, Minneapolis, MN 55418. Pub: The NARC Newsletter, six/year. Dues: $10. About six meets and two swap meets per year.

Northwest Vintage Radio Society (NWVRS). P.O. Box 82379, Portland, OR 97282-0379. Pub: The Call Letter, monthly. Dues: $15. Monthly meetings.

Oklahoma Vintage Radio Collectors Club (OKVRC). P.O. Box 332, Wheatland, OK 73097. Mike Lapuzza, 2015 E. Willow Creek Ter., Mustang, OK 73064-6146. Pub: OKVRC Broadcast News, monthly. Dues: $12. Monthly meetings, spring and fall swap meets.

Pittsburgh Antique Radio Society, Inc. (PARS). Richard J. Harris Jr., Secretary, 407 Woodside Rd., Pittsburgh, PA 15221. Pub: The Pittsburgh Oscillator, quarterly. Dues: $10. Quarterly meetings, Spring Fever event and annual March meet.

Puget Sound Antique Radio Association (PSARA). P.O. Box 125, Snohomish, WA 98291-0125. Pub: The Horn of Plenty, monthly. Dues: $20, $15 for out-of-state. Monthly meetings and swap meets, November show and August swap meet.

Radio Enthusiasts of Puget Sound. (REPS). Dick Zornes, 12837 109th NE, Kirkland, WA 98034. Pub: Air Check, quarterly newsletter. Dues: $18 ($22 first year). Monthly meetings, annual REPS Radio Showcase, special OTR guests biannually, annual script writing contest, cassette and printed libraries.

Radio History Society, Inc. (RHS). New museum and library forming. Steve Snyderman,

4147 Lenox Dr., Fairfax, VA 22032. Dues: $15 and up (various membership levels).

Sacramento Historical Radio Society (SHRS). P.O. Box 162612, Sacramento, CA 95816-9998. Pub: The Announcer, quarterly. Dues: $10. Special meets, monthly meetings.

E.H. Scott Historical Society Inc. (EHSHS). New club forming. John T. Meredith, P.O. Box 1070, Niceville, FL 32588-1070. Pub: Scott News, quarterly. Dues: $20. Displays, presentations, registry, publications.

Society for the Preservation of Antique Radio Knowledge (SPARK). Harold Parshall, 915 East Central Ave., West Carrollton, OH 45449. Pubs: The Electronic Collector (TEC), quarterly; SPARK Notes, monthly. Dues: $12. Monthly meetings, quarterly swap meets.

Society of Wireless Pioneers Inc. (SOWP). Paul N. Dane, W6WOW, 146 Coleen St., Livermore, CA 94550. Pub: The World Wireless Beacon, quarterly. Dues: $10.

Southeastern Antique Radio Society (SARS). Charles Milton, president, SARS, P.O. Box 500025, Atlanta, GA 31150. Dues: $10. Spring and fall swap meets. Mini-meet before monthly meetings.

Southern California Antique Radio Society (SCARS). Clarence Hill, 6934 Orion Ave., Van Nuys, CA 91406. Pub: California Antique Radio Gazette, quarterly. Dues: $15. Quarterly meets in L.A. area and mini meets, two-day November meeting, annual auction.

Southern Vintage Wireless Association (SVWA). Bill Moore, 3049 Box Canyon

Rd., Huntsville, AL 35803. Pub: SVWA Newsletter, 3/year. Dues: $5. Three swap meets/meetings per year.

Vintage Audio Listeners and Valve Enthusiasts (VALVE). Dan Schmalle, 1127 N.W. Bright Star Ln., Poulsbo, WA 98370. Monthly swap meets.

Vintage Radio & Phonograph Society (VRPS). Larry Lamia, P.O. Box 165345, Irving, TX 75016. Pubs: The Reproducer, quarterly. Soundwaves, monthly between the quarterly. Dues: $13.50. Monthly meetings, spring auction, annual convention.

Vintage Radio Unique Society (VRUS). Jerryl W. Sears, 312 Auburndale St., Winston-Salem, NC 27104.

Western Wisconsin Antique Radio Collectors Club (WWAR-CC). Dave Wiggert, 1611 Redfield St., La Crosse, WI 54601. Pub: Radio Recollections, 5 per year. Dues: $12. Bi-monthly meetings, annual June Nostalgic Radio swap meet, early Sept. Hobby Electronics swap meet, two mall display shows, and display and Hands-on Day at local museum.

W. Va. Chapter, ARCA (AWA-WVC). Geoff Bourne, 405 8th Ave., St. Albans, WV 25177. (304) 722-4690. Newsletter, monthly. Dues: $25 (includes museum membership). Quarterly meets, monthly meetings.

Xtal Set Society (XSS). Phil Anderson, 789 N. 1500 Rd., Lawrence, KS 66049-9194. Pub: Xtal Set Society Newsletter, bimonthly. Dues: $9.95. Bimonthly meeting.

Foreign clubs:

Australia: Historical Radio Society of Australia (HRSA). J.R. Wales, P.O. Box 283, Mt. Waverley, Victoria 3149, Australia. Pub: HRSA Newsletter, quarterly. Dues:

$15. Monthly meetings.

Australia: North East Vintage Radio Club. Monthly meetings at Wangaratta T.A.F.E. electronic unit. Info: Noel Meagher, 62 3149; Ian Milne, 62 5153; Rodney Champness, 62 1454 (all Benalla numbers).

Canada: Canadian Vintage Radio Society (CVRS). CVRS, P.O. Box 43012, Standard Life Building P.O., Edmonton, Alberta, Canada T5J 4M8. Nap Pepin, 144 Calico Dr., Sherwood Park, Alberta, Canada T8A 5P9. Pub: Radio Waves, bimonthly. Dues: $17 U.S. ($21 Canadian). Bimonthly meetings. Chapters in provinces, i.e. in B.C., Manitoba and others.

Canada, Ontario: London Vintage Radio Club (LVRC). Dave Noon, 19 Honeysuckle Cres., London, Ontario, Canada N5Y 4P3. Pub: LVRC Newsletter. Dues: $15 Canadian. Six meetings yearly.

Canada, Ontario: Ottawa Vintage Radio Club (OVRC). Box 84084, Pinecrest P.O., Ottawa, Ontario K2C 3Z2. Pub: OVRC, quarterly newsletter. Dues: $10. Monthly meetings.

England: British Vintage Wireless Society (BVWS). Gerald Wells, Vintage Wireless Museum, 23, Rosendale Rd., West Dulwich, London, SE21 8DS, England. Pub: Vintage Wireless, monthly. Dues: £20. Meetings and swap meets.

England: Eddystone User Group (EUG). C/o Eddystone Radio Ltd., Alvechurch Rd., Birmingham B31 3PP, England. Pub. EUG Newsletter, 6 per year. Dues: £10 UK, £11 Europe.

France: Club Histoire et Collection Radio (CHCR). Jean Le Galudec, 26 Rue de l'Oratoire, 54000 Nancy,

France. Pub: Telegraphie et Telephonie Sans Fil Electricite Ancienne, quarterly. Dues: 185 francs for U.S., 170 francs France. Library of old books and schematics library. Annual May event in Riquewihr, Sept. Bar Le Duc event, local meetings.

France: French Antique Radio Association (Association des Amis du Musee de l'Electro-Acoustique). M. Kopito, Eric Tresorier A.E.A., 135, av. du President Wilson, 93100 Montreuil, France. Pub: Journal Officiel de L'Association. Dues: 250 F.

Germany: German Society of Wireless History. Prof. Otto Künzel, Belm Tannenhof 55, 7900 Ulm 10, West Germany. Pub: Funkgeschichte, bimonthly. Dues: DM 50 + DM 6 first registration.

Holland: N.V.H.R. Hed. Ver. voor Hist. Radio, Paulus Pofferstr. 19, 6814 K.T. Arnhem, Holland.

Ireland: Irish Vintage Radio & Sound Society. Vincent Farrell, 39A Lower Drumcondra Rd., Dublin 9, Ireland. Quarterly newsletter. Dues: $16. Winter meetings weekly, summer meetings monthly.

Israel: Antique Radio and Broadcasting Museum. Museum forming in Tel-Aviv. Bruno Pinto, 24 Remez St., #7, Tel-Aviv, Israel 62192.

Italy: Associazione Italiana Radio d'Epoca (AIRE). Fausto Casi, President. Via di Pellicceria, 23-52100 Arezzo, Italy. Pub: Bollettino-Notiziario, bimonthly. Dues: 60 Lire (±$55).

Japan: Antique Wireless Club (AWC). Noriyoshi Tezuka, JA1NTF, Secretary AWC, 1-11-2-403 Hiroo, Shibuyaku, Tokyo 150, Japan. Monthly

meetings and newsletter.

New Zealand: New Zealand Vintage Radio Society (NZVRS). Bryan Marsh, Treasurer, 20 Rimu Rd., Mangere Bridge, Auckland, New Zealand 1701. NZVRS Bulletin, quarterly.

Norway: Norsk Radiohistorisk Forening (NRHF). P.O. Box 465 Sentrum, N-0105 Oslo 1, Norway. Bimonthly journal. Dues: $22. Regular Tues. open house at Soria Moria, Oslo. Antique net on ham radio.

Spain, Barcelona (Granollers): Friends of Radio Cultural Association. New club forming. Associacio Cultural Amicos de la Radio, c/o Rei Jaume, 55, 08840 Cardedeu, Spain.

Sweden: The Radio-Historical Society in West-Sweden. Anders Carlssons, Gata 2, 417 55 Guteborg, Sweden. Pub: Audionen. Amateur radio station: SK6RM. Museum.

Inactive/New/Forming Organizations:

Antique Radio Club of Schenectady (ARCS). Jack Nelson, W2FW, 915 Sherman St. Schenectady, NY 12303. (lately inactive, formerly monthly meetings except summer.)

Carolina Chapter/AWA. New club forming. Kenny Mullis, 1236 Autumn Oaks Dr., Lancaster, SC 29720.

Central New York/Northern Pa. Antique Radio Club (CNY/NPAARC). New club forming. Mark Gilbert, 711 Elm St., Groton, NY 13073.

Central Pa. Radio Collectors Club. New club forming. Frank Hagenbuch, 1440 Lafayette Parkway, Williamsport, PA 17701, or Mike Heffner, 501 S. Market St., Muncy, PA 17756.

Connecticut Vintage Radio Club (CVRC). New club forming. Ray Lamont, 70 Litchfield Rd., Unionville, CT 06085.

Connecticut Area Antique Radio Collectors. Walt Buffinton, 500 Tobacco St., Lebanon, CT 06249. Informal organization. No newsletter, no dues. Meets.

East Carolina Antique Radio Club. New club forming. Bill Engstrom, 218 Bent Creek Dr., Greenville, NC 27834.

Hawaii Chapter/AWA. New club forming. Leonard Chung, 95-2044 Waikalani Pl. C-401, Mililani, HI 96789. Workshops, children's classes, Window on the World program.

Hawaii Historical Radio Club (HHRC). New club forming. Kevin Dooley, 45 Ala Kimo Dr., Honolulu, HI 96817-5221.

International Antique Radio Club, World-Wide. New club forming. Richard G. Brill, P.O. Box 5261, Old Bridge, NJ 08857. Membership free.

Kentucky Chapter/AWA. New club forming. John Caperton, 3114 Boxhill Ct., Louisville, KY 40222. Meetings, meets, future museum.

Louisiana Gulf Coast Club. New club forming in Baton Rouge and New Orleans, La., area. Phil Boydston, 102 Concorde Pl., Mandeville, AL 70471.

Midwest Radio Club. New club forming. P.O. Box 6291, Lincoln, NE 68516-0291.

Rhode Island Antique Radio Enthusiasts (RARE). New club forming. Len Arzoomanian, 61 Columbus Ave., N. Providence, RI 02911. Informal monthly meetings.

SPARK Chapters. New clubs forming:
Cincinnati Chapter of SPARK. Tim Kaiser, P.O. Box 81, Newport, KY 41071. Monthly meetings.

Columbus Chapter of SPARK. Sharon or Kenny Fullerton, 2327 E. Livingston Ave., Columbus, OH 43209. Monthly meetings.

South Florida Antique Radio Collectors. Thomas Valenti, Suite 315, 172 West Flagler St., Miami, FL 33130.

Tidewater Antique Radio Association (TARA).

New club forming. Phil Stroud, 2328 Springfield Ave., Norfolk, VA 23523.

Internet:

There are a number of radio forums on The Internet. Simply search radio, radio + antique, Radio + programs or old-time radio. There are also forums on Compuserve for radio professionals (BP Forum) and antique radio and program collectors. These are also available on America On-Line. AOL also offers NPR and ABC forums. There are hundreds of forums on The World Wide Web. If you have a web-browsing program, search the word "Radio."

Bibliography

Banning, William Peck. *Commercial Broadcasting Pioneer: The WEAF Experiment 1922-1926.* Harvard Press, Cambridge, MA, 1946.

Barnouw, Erik. *A Tower In Babel: A History of Broadcasting in the United States; volume I to 1933.* Oxford University Press, New York, 1966.

Barnouw, Erik. *The Golden Web: A History of Broadcasting in the United States; volume II 1933 to 1953.* Oxford University Press, New York, 1968.

Buxton, Frank and Owen, Bill. *Radio's Golden Age: The Programs & The Personalities.* Easton Valley Press, New York, 1966

Buxton, Frank and Owen, Bill. *The Big Broadcast: 1920-1950.* Viking Press, New York, 1966, 1972.

Crews, Albert R. *Radio Production Directing.* Riverside Press, Cambridge, MA, 1944.

Cain, John. *The BBC: 70 Years of Broadcasting.* British Broadcasting Company, London, 1992.

Dixon, Peter. *Radio Writing.* The Century Co., New York, 1931.

Dumont, Bruce. Museum of Broadcast Communications. Chicago.

Cheney, Margaret. *Tesla: A Man Out Of Time.* Dell Publishing, New York, 1981.

Pease, Edward C. and Dennis, Everette E. *Radio The Forgotten Medium.* New

Brunswick, NJ, Transaction Publishers, 1995, originally published in the Media Studies Journal, Summer, 1993.

Metz, Robert. *CBS Reflections in a Bloodshot Eye.* Playboy Press, Chicago, 1975.

Shaden, Chuck. *Nostalgia Digest.* (708) 965-7763.

Sklar, Rick. *Rocking America How the All-Hit Radio Stations Took Over.* St. Martin's Press, New York, 1984.

Passman, Arnold. *The Deejays.* The Macmillan Company, New York, 1971.

Wylie, Max. *Radio Writing.* Farrar & Rinehart, New York, 1939.

Thomas, Lowell. *So Long Until Tomorrow.* William Morrow and Company, Inc., New York.

Seehafer, Gene F. and Laemmar, Jack W. *Successful Television and Radio Advertising.* McGraw-Hill Book Co., Inc., New York, 1959.

Lyons, Eugene. *David Sarnoff.* Harper & Row Publishers, New York, 1966.

Skues, Keith. *Pop Went The Pirates.* Black Bear Press Ltd. Cambridge, England, 1994.

Slide, Anthony. *Great Radio Personalities.* The Vestal Press, Ltd., New York, 1982.

Gross, Lynne S. *See/Hear An Introduction to Broadcasting.* Wm. C. Brown Company Publishers, Dubuque, Iowa, 1979.

McNeill, Don. *Breakfast Club Family Album.* Chicago, 1942.

Wilson, Bob. *R & R The First Fifteen Years.* Radio & Records. Radio & Records, Inc., Los Angeles, 1988.

Wilson, Bob. *R & R Twenty Years of Excellence.* Radio & Records. Radio & Records, Inc., Los Angeles, 1993.

Robertson-Cataract Electric Company. *Radio Equipment & Supplies.* Buffalo, New York, 1922.

Gernsback, Hugo. *Radio-Craft.* Mount Morris, Illinois. Continental Publications, Inc., 1936.

Racina, Thom. *-FM-.* Harcourt Brace Jovanovich, New York, 1978.

Hall, Claude. *This Business of Radio Programming.* Billboard Publications, New York, 1977.

Hall, Monty and Libby, Bill. *Emcee Monty Hall.* Grosset & Dunlap, New York, 1973.

Lord Inman. *BBC Year Book 1947.* The Hollen Street Press, Ltd. London, England, 1947.

Linkletter, with Bishop, George. *Hobo on the Way to Heaven.* David C. Cook Publishing Company, Elgin, IL 1980.

Wertheim, Arthur Frank. *Radio Comedy.* Oxford University Press, New York, 1979.

Toll, C. Robert. *The Entertainment Machine.* Oxford University Press, New York, 1982.

Crabb, Richard. *Radio's Beautiful Day.* North Plains Press of Aberdeen, South Dakota, 1983.

Perry, Dick. *Not Just a Sound The Story of WLW.* Prentice-Hall, Inc., Englewood Cliffs, NJ, 1971.

Emery, Ralph with Carter, Tom. *Memories The Autobiography of Ralph Emery.* McMillan Publishing Company, New York, 1991.

McMahon, Morgan, E. *Vintage Radio.* Second Edition. Vintage Radio, Palos Verdes Peninsula, CA, 1973.

McMahon, Morgan, E. A *Flick of the Switch: 1930-1950.* Vintage Radio, Palos Verdes Peninsula, CA, 1975.

Kaltenborn, H.V. *Fifty Fabulous Years.* G.P. Putnam's Sons, New York, 1950.

St. John, Robert. *Encyclopedia of Radio and Television Broadcasting.* Cathedral Square Publishing Company, Milwaukee, WI., 1967.

Waller, Judith, C. *Radio The Fifth Estate.* Houghton Mifflin Company, Boston, 1946.

Raby, Ormond. *Radio's First Voice.* The Macmillan Company of Canada Limited, Toronto, 1970.

Lerch, John H. *Careers in Broadcasting.* Meredith Publishing Company, New York, 1962.

Schechter, A.A. with Anthony, Edward. *I Live on Air.* Frederick A. Stokes Company, New York, 1941.

Blanc, Mel and Bashe, Philip. *That's Not All, Folks.* Warner Books, Inc., New York, 1988.

Hyde, Stuart, W. *Television and Radio Announcing.* Second Edition. Houghton Mifflin Company, Boston, 1971.

Sperber, A.M. *Murrow: His Life and Times.* Freundlich Books, New York, 1986.

Hamilton, Bob, D. *Operating Manual for Starship Radio '73.* Vance A. Briggs, Lithographer. Los Angeles, 1973.

Bannerman, R. LeRoy. *Norman Corwin and Radio: The Golden Years.* The University of Alabama Press, Alabama, 1986.

Douglas, Alan. *Radio Manufacturers of the 1920s. Vol. 1.* The Vestal Press, Ltd., Vestal, New York, 1943.

Breed, Robert F. *Collecting Transistor Novelty Radios a Value Guide.* L-W Book Sales, Gas City, IN, 1990.

Editors of *Broadcasting Magazine. The First 50 Years of Broadcasting.* Broadcasting Publications, Inc. Washington, D.C., 1982.

Sideli, John. *Classic Plastic Radios of the 1930s and 1940s.* E.P. Dutton, New York, 1990.

Bittner, John R. *Broadcasting an Introduction.* Prentice-Hall, Inc. Englewood Cliffs, New Jersey, 1980.

Salowitz, Stew. *Chicago's Personality Radio.* Bloomington Offset Process, Incorporated, Bloomington, IL, 1993.

McBride, Mary Margaret. *Out of the Air.* Doubleday & Company, Inc. New York, 1960.

Abbott, Waldo. *Handbook of Broadcasting.* Second Edition. McGraw-Hill Book Company, Inc., New York, 1941.

Wing, Willis Kingsley. *Radio Broadcast.* Doubleday, Doran & Company, Inc., New York, 1928.

Read, Oliver. *Radio & Television News.* Ziff-Davis Publishing Company, Chicago, Il, October 1949.

Earl, Bill. *When Radio was Boss.* Research Archives, Montebello, CA, 1989.

Schaden, Chuck. *WBBM Radio Yesterday & Today.* WBBM Newsradio 78, Chicago, IL, 1988.

Smulyan, Susan. *Selling Radio.* Smithsonian Institution Press, Washington, D.C., 1994.

Christman, Trent. *Brass Button Broadcasters.* Turner Publishing Company, Paducah, KY, 1992.

Keith, Michael C and Krause, Joseph M. *The Radio Station.* Second Edition. Focal Press an imprint of Butterworth-Heinemann, Stoneham, MA, 1989.

Schiffer, Michael Brian. *The Portable Radio in American Life.* The University of Arizona Press, Tucson, 1991.

Vaughn, Gene and Staff of The WFBM Stations. *From Crystal to Color WFBM.* The WFBM Stations, Indianapolis, IN, 1964.

MacDonald, J. Fred. *Don't Touch That Dial: Radio Programming in American Life, 1920-1960.* Nelson-Hall, Chicago, 1979.

Dunning, John. *Tune In Yesterday: The Ultimate Encyclopedia of Old Time Radio, 1925-1976.* Prentice-Hall, Inc., Englewood Cliffs, NJ, 1976.

Garay, Ronald. *Gordon McLendon, The Maverick of Radio.* Greenwood Press, New York, 1992.

Poteet, G. Howard. *Radio!* Pflaum Publishing, Dayton, OH, 1975.

Barrett, Don. *Los Angeles Radio People: a booktory of Los Angeles Disc Jockeys 1957-1994.* DB Marketing, 1995.

Henderson, Amy. *On The Air: Pioneers of American Broadcasting.* Smithsonian Institution Press/National Portrait Gallery, Washington, 1988.

Index

X

Y

Z

About The Author

Eric Rhoads was in love with radio even before his on-air debut at the age of 14 as a DJ for a college station in Fort Wayne, Indiana.

By age 17 he was spinning Top 40 at Y–100 in Miami and had become the youngest full-time major market radio talent in America. Eric worked almost every radio job imaginable — program director, programming consultant, station general manager and radio group owner. By the age of 32, he had created the Giant Boom Box, the now famous mobile home-size radio that houses remote radio stations.

What started out 25 years ago as the simple hobby of a radio buff has developed into an almost obsessive search for rare photographs and items depicting radio's rich, diverse 75-year history. Besides augmenting his now substantial collection of radio memorabilia, Eric — through archival research and personal interviews with some of radio's most famous and infamous personalities — has accumulated scores of anecdotes, myths and trivia tidbits about this medium's most provocative personalities.

When not roaming the country in search of additions to his collection, Eric publishes the trade magazine *Radio Ink* and participates in the ongoing preservation of radio history as a steering committee member of the Radio Hall of Fame in Chicago.

Eric has written extensively on the history of radio for communications and media studies journals. He decided to write *Blast From The Past* not only as a tribute to radio's past on- and off-air talents, but also to honor the men and women who have succeeded in reviving and renewing this ever-popular medium.

Eric resides with his wife, Laurie, and his collection of more than 100 antique radios and microphones, in Palm Beach County, Florida. ▣

THE *WLS* CREED

"TO ME RADIO IS FAR MORE THAN A MERE MEDIUM OF ENTERTAINMENT. IT IS A GOD-GIVEN INSTRUMENT WHICH MAKES POSSIBLE VITAL ECONOMIC, EDUCATIONAL AND INSPIRATIONAL SERVICE TO THE HOME-LOVING MEN, WOMEN, AND CHILDREN OF AMERICA. AS LONG AS IT IS OUR PRIVILEGE TO DIRECT THE DESTINIES OF *WLS*, WE WILL HOLD SACRED THIS TRUST THAT HAS BEEN PLACED IN OUR HANDS. NO MEDIUM DEVELOPED BY MANKIND IS DOING MORE TO BROADEN THE LIVES OF RICH AND POOR ALIKE THAN RADIO.

"WHEN YOU STEP UP TO THE MICROPHONE NEVER FORGET THIS RESPONSIBILITY AND THAT YOU ARE WALKING AS A GUEST INTO ALL THOSE HOMES BEYOND THE MICROPHONE."

NOVEMBER 12, 1938   *Burridge D. Butler*